GENTLE VENGEANCE

also by Charles LeBaron
THE DIAMOND SKY, *a novel*

GENTLE VENGEANCE

*An Account of the First Year at
Harvard Medical School*

by Charles LeBaron

Richard Marek Publishers   New York

B
LeBaron

Grateful acknowledgment is made for permission
to use the following copyright material:
  Excerpt from *Energy Flow in Biology* by Harold J. Morowitz, copyright ©
1968 by Harold J. Morowitz, reprinted by permission of Academic Press,
Inc., and the author.
  Excerpt from *Human Physiology* by A. J. Vander, J. H. Sherman and D. S.
Luciano, copyright © 1975 by McGraw-Hill, Inc., reprinted by permission
of McGraw-Hill, Inc.

Library of Congress Cataloging in Publication Data

LeBaron, Charles, date.
  Gentle vengeance.

  1. LeBaron, Charles, date–   2. Medical
students—Massachusetts—Biography.   3. Harvard
University. Medical School.   I. Title.
R154.L34A33   610'.92'4   [B]   80-25228
ISBN 0-399-90112-4

PRINTED IN THE UNITED STATES OF AMERICA

For
James Wade LeBaron
and
Doris Davison LeBaron,
who will never read this book.

Contents

Part Three
GENTLE VENGEANCE

GENTLE VENGEANCE

Part One

CITGO OR BUST

You're always angry for all you're interested in is intelligence.

—Fyodor Dostoevsky, *The Brothers Karamazov*

Chapter 1

Revolution Already?

I arrived at Harvard in the middle of the night with all my worldly possessions, from an apartment in the Lower East Side, jammed into a rented station wagon. Vanderbilt Hall, the medical school's sole dormitory, was an ivy-covered effort at an Italian palazzo with odd touches of Spanish hacienda and Ruskin Gothic decorations. A small, stone rotunda served as lobby, its curved ceiling painted in elaborate designs of gold and green and red. Sculpted into that dome was a coat of arms whose charges incorporated twined serpents and retorts and apothecary's vials. Around the lintel was an inscription in French: "In the field of observation, chance favors only the prepared mind."

Off the lobby were side chambers with Persian rugs, dark wood paneling, leather armchairs, a grand piano, and paintings of nineteenth-century physicians with pork chop whiskers and impressive scowls. I picked up the keys to my room from a security guard behind a desk and went upstairs. After the Versailles of the lobby, the living quarters seemed like barracks—cement staircases, low ceilings, plain white paint, long sets of identical doors. Inside my room there was a desk, dresser, and a narrow, hard bed. A pamphlet of rules on the desk informed me that animals, birds, and reptiles were forbidden, along with waterbeds and stolen goods. I had to carry an official identification at all times, I might be relocated without notice to another room, and a false alarm might result in my "imprisonment in a jail or house of correction for not more than one year." Nevertheless, after the mice and cockroaches and lack of heat in the tenement where I'd stayed in New York, this was quite livable.

After moving my cardboard boxes upstairs, I took a midnight stroll around the campus in the warm September night. The medical school was on the other side of the city from Cambridge and the rest of Harvard, sequestered among museums and parks, surrounded by private hospitals. But a block away, across Huntington Avenue, was the all-black ghetto of Roxbury: squat projects, broken glass, gutted cars. Harvard maintained a private police force to patrol its possessions and protect its students.

In contrast to the undergraduate campus, whose tree-lined squares of colonial buildings created an air of genteel, courteous traditions, even intimacy, the medical school was designed around the turn of the century as one great quadrangle of Roman temples facing a massive, empty lawn. The temples, with their five-story marble columns and giant capitals, seemed to shine of their own in the night, without need of nature's superfluous moonlight.

At thirty-four, I was the oldest student in the first-year class, perhaps in the whole school. And one of the least prepared as well. While nine-tenths of my classmates had been science majors, some even having completed advanced degrees and doctorates, I'd never been exposed to anything but literature and history years ago as an undergraduate at Princeton. Over the decade since then, I'd worked in semimenial capacities in various hospitals and institutions, and it was only by going to night school for the past two years that I'd gained the bare minimum of credits in chemistry and physics and biology. With that kind of scanty and eccentric background, could I survive?

And what I'd be studying, the human body, was, from that tiny bit I knew about it, such a dazzlingly complex biological organization—our tissues will respond to concentrations of hormones more dilute than a teaspoon of sugar in an Olympic swimming pool; each ounce of skeletal muscle is latticed with forty miles of blood vessels; we can detect sounds so faint that the vibrations they set up in our eardrums have amplitudes no greater than the diameter of a hydrogen atom. Unfortunately, it was anomalous facts such as these, rather than the required information, that I tended to retain. The most painful experience known to man was said to be the passage of kidney stones. But did I remember that last tidbit from introductory biology or from Montaigne, who'd devoted some essays to the philosophical import of that experience? And the kidney itself—now what was that? I tended to get it mixed up with the liver. One had to do with urine, and the other . . . ? It was two in the morning; I'd ask someone at registration tomorrow.

But upstairs in bed a phrase kept returning to me from that one introductory biology text I'd studied. Like the inscription in the lobby, it was in French, but by a nineteenth-century physiologist, Claude Bernard, who had reflected on the ability of different organisms to survive under conditions of desiccation and imbalance. The phrase seemed to hold wider implications, so I'd written it out and made a bookmark of the scrap of paper. "The stability of the internal environment," said Bernard, "is the condition of the free life."

The next morning, all one hundred and sixty-five of us from the first-year class were crowded into an amphitheater in one of the Roman temples, filling out forms. Off to one side, up front, was a ten-foot-wide model of a skull sectioned in half, a giant plaster pelvis on rollers, and a skeleton hung by the head on a movable stand, its hollow eyes seeming to regard us with a permanently shocked expression. On a wall was a larger-than-life portrait of a bulky man in a gray lab coat whose strained-forward posture indicated either myopia or an irresistible desire to vault out of the frame and start lecturing on the spot. Walter Bradford Cannon, it said, 1871– . Apparently someone Harvard didn't want to acknowledge was off the rolls.

Before I could look around further, a young woman next to me shyly introduced herself as Robin Danwood. With brownish-blond hair the color of New England autumn and round blue eyes, she was so pretty I started gulping. She'd gone to Radcliffe, and she dressed with the casual understatement that bespoke old wealth. Later in the year, I was searching for a book in the library and happened upon an old leather-bound medical tome by a Cornelius Danwood who had been professor of neurology at Harvard at the end of the last century. I asked Robin if he were a relative. Blushing a little in embarrassment, Robin explained that he was her great-grandfather.

"And your father went here, too?"

"Yes, but—"

"So you're a fourth generation—"

"No, no—my grandfather didn't. He didn't go here. He didn't at all. He managed the family business. So I'm not fourth generation at all."

Robin introduced me to another Radcliffe graduate, Michelle Levy, who was from Shaker Heights, and whose rounded face had an intent, searching expression.

"What do you think of these Saturday morning classes?" Michelle asked me.

"Awful," I said. "Nine till noon. Messes up the whole weekend."

"It's hard to understand why they have them," said Robin, blinking. "None of the other medical schools around here do. And Tuesdays and Thursdays we have nothing scheduled at all from nine-thirty on. I'd like to get away from here once in a while on weekends."

"Last spring I spoke to someone in the second-year class," said Michelle. "She said it took them a while to get organized, but when they did they got rid of them for the second semester."

"I hope our class gets organized faster," I said. "I wouldn't mind having a weekend to myself, once in a while."

Before we went further, a young Puerto Rican fellow with a black goatee had stood up in front of the class with a microphone, introduced himself as Felipe Santiago and begun a welcoming speech. Leaning against the lab bench under the portrait of Walter Bradford Cannon, Felipe had the fluent demeanor of someone accustomed to speaking to groups and having them quiet instantly at his approach. Over the course of the first year, I'd see him occasionally bopping in and out of lectures and labs in a sleeveless sweatshirt, wide-brimmed hat, and dark sunglasses. And later that month I read in the student newspaper his impressions of his own first year:

> After a while, it became a question of knowing when to go and when not to go to class. Having the choice of resting for an hour or hearing a poorly delivered lecture was no real choice at all. It was an example of how this place wasn't all that it was supposed to be. Sure, it's an amazing place when one considers the resources that are concentrated in this medical monstrosity. But what a shame that so many hospitals and services are restricted to so small an area The new Affiliated Hospitals Center appears to be needed here as much as Henry VIII needed another meal. In a way, it is gluttony. And it's perpetuated by hierarchy and conservatism.

But for greeting us, Felipe had donned a three-piece, pinstripe suit and made no references to the drawbacks of Harvard. Afterwards, the question kept recurring to me: knowing his point of view, why had Harvard made him the master of ceremonies in its orientation session for incoming medical students?

Then the director of alumni relations was at the microphone. We were the Bicentennial Class, he said, the two-hundredth class ever to graduate from Harvard Medical School! And our graduation four years hence would be the occasion of massive festivities. A little stir went through the class: I didn't know that, did you?

We were also "the best and the brightest" of all the medical students in the nation, perhaps the world, he went on.

Whatever the difficulties of the upcoming year, we should always remember that we would all make it.

"You will *all* be graduated from this school," he said. "It is more difficult to get out of Harvard Medical School without a degree than to get in."

Who else had told me the same thing: "They don't let you leave"? What did it mean? Were they just being reassuring, or was it something else?

Before I could figure that out, a psychiatrist from Beth Israel Hospital, who was chairman of the Council of Faculty Advisors, stood up. All our advisors, he assured us, were only too ready to help us; that's why they'd volunteered. But we shouldn't ask too much of the system. For any kind of crisis we should see Dean Marita Feinstein who, as a psychiatrist and medical school ombudsman, would try to help us herself or refer us to outside professionals.

The psychiatrist was succeeded by Dr. Myron Chanesohn, the dean of students and alumni, a tall man in his late forties whose bow tie, bald head, and chubby face conspired to swell his face into an improbably large oval. With a pixieish grin, he seemed like a teenager who'd never grown up, something I'd noticed in less attractive variations in many doctors. Was it that they'd been isolated from the normal course of life at some critical period, wrenched from adolescence directly to middle age, with no interval of maturation? In Chanesohn's case, there was a deft, quick, light intelligence, frisking about with an almost childish sense of humor. He also urged us to see Dean Marita Feinstein if we encountered any problems, practical or emotional, then launched into a ten-minute paean of the next speaker, Dr. Nathaniel Hastings, the newly appointed dean of the entire medical school with its six hundred and fifty students and three thousand faculty. Already renowned for his brilliant performance as an administrator, Dean Hastings continued to capture awards for his fundamental biophysical research. And, to boot, he ran five miles a day and swam hundreds of laps a week.

By that time, we were expecting Louis Pasteur in track shoes. And as we applauded loudly, a small, thin, energetic man in a three-piece suit, with close-cropped brown hair moved swiftly to the front and unfolded a neat stack of papers. He wanted to talk to us about strategies for our medical education. We should have three strategies—one, a Long Range Strategy; two, a Middle Range Strategy; and three, a Short Range Strategy. Yet the most important quality in each strategy was discipline. Yes, discipline. There were many facets to discipline, but perhaps they might best be discussed as part of our three strategies: the Long Range Strategy, the Middle Range Strategy . . .

Jesus, that stack of papers is an inch thick, I said to myself. While the Short Range Strategy was being detailed, I looked curiously around at the rest of the class, the hundred and sixty-five of us, the best and the brightest.

Everybody looked almost excessively wholesome and normal—bright, eager, twenty-three-year-old faces, only a few beards, almost no long hair. About a third of us came from Harvard, Princeton, or Yale, only five or six like me were older than thirty, a quarter of the class was female, about a sixth black or Hispanic. The women and minorities were relative newcomers; thirty years or so before, neither would have been seen in that amphitheater.

Since I'd half expected a bunch of gnomes with inch-thick glasses, sunken chests, and calculators already in hand, the general appearance of the class was a distinct relief. There seemed none of those flippant, harsh, cynical expressions I'd gotten to know so well on the faces of doctors from my days in the hospitals. In fact, the principal spirit seemed to be freshness and enthusiasm.

Robin whispered in my ear, "Michelle and I were wondering if we should send around a petition about Saturday classes. What do you think?"

"Great!" I whispered back. Michelle composed it and handed it over for criticism. It read something like:

> The undersigned wish to inquire if the possibility might be explored of investigating the feasibility of transferring Saturday classes to some other time

period, if such a rearrangement of schedule could actually be effected at this time.

Respectfully yours,

Michelle leaned across Robin: "You think it's too strong? People won't sign it if it's too strong."

"No, it's not too strong."

We all signed it and passed it on.

The first few people read it, nodded vigorously back at us, and signed. The paper reached the end of the row and started coming back. Then it hit a fellow who read it carefully with knitted brows for five minutes, and handed it on unsigned. That seemed to start a chain reaction down the row—no one wanted to sign if his neighbor hadn't.

"Do these people want to spend all Saturday morning in lecture?" I whispered over to Michelle.

"I'm telling you, med students are very scared. They're afraid someone will take their acceptance letter away retroactively. I'll tell you about it later."

Finally, someone did sign, and that set off a couple rows of signatures. And so it went, in block fashion, finally reaching a guy a few rows down who was taking notes about the Middle Range Strategy. He glanced at the petition quickly, a painful distraction from the concentration of stenography, and slipped it under his notebook. That ended its circulation. Around noon, Dean Hastings finally wrapped up; we applauded politely, and I went down to pick up the petition. It had the signatures of about half the class. Not bad.

In a courtyard between two of the temples, a buffet lunch had been set up of punch, foreign cheeses, elaborate hors-d'oeuvres.

"What do we do with this thing now?" I asked Michelle, pulling out the petition and trying to keep egg salad off it as I sat down on the grass with my paper plate.

A tall fellow with curly red hair and one of the few beards in the class reached out and took the sheet from me. "I never even saw this. That Saturday-class business is ridiculous.

How come you didn't hand it around to everybody?" I gave him a pen to sign, and he introduced himself as Ron Kopell. His father, I learned later, was a professor of psychology at Harvard College. Ron had graduated from Yale and played oboe with a baroque wind ensemble before returning to school for the science courses needed to enter medical school. Like me, has was one of the four or five in the class with just the minimum background in science.

"I talked to Dean Hastings for a second right when we were leaving," said Michelle. "He said we should give it to Dean Chanesohn, since that kind of thing was the job of the dean of students and he didn't want to bypass him."

We looked around and spied Chanesohn's bald head surrounded by laughing students. He was gesturing high in the air with a petit four.

"Should we bother him at lunch like this?" asked Ron.

"When are we going to see him again?" I asked.

"We can just give it to him and ask for an appointment," said Michelle.

"I'll go with you," said Robin.

I started getting up. "We shouldn't have too large a group," said Ron. "He might get threatened."

I sat down and the two women went off through the clusters of faculty, functionaries, and students. From where we were sitting on the grass, we could see the pantomime.

Chanesohn turned with a smile on his face, started accepting the paper, then returned it quickly. More talk, much nodding by Robin and Michelle, some craning looks across the crowd, the paper offered unsuccessfully again, Chanesohn made a joke, everyone laughed, and the two women returned.

"Dean Chanesohn said he isn't in charge of that," said Robin, parting her long yellow hair. "He said he's just the dean of students. A Dr. Stone, the dean of academic affairs, should handle that."

"So where's Dr. Stone?"

"He isn't here right now," said Michelle. "He has an office over in Peter Bent Brigham Hospital. Why don't we see him tomorrow after those psychiatric evaluation tests we're all supposed to take?"

We started talking about the year ahead. "One thing it'll sure be nice not to have to worry about," said Ron, his head bobbing up and down over some salad, "is grades."

We all spluttered out food in an excess of unanimity. At Harvard, as at most medical schools, all courses were given on a pass-fail basis.

"But they do flunk some people, don't they?" I asked.

"Only four or five people out of the whole class," said Ron. "It's nothing to worry about, unless you really don't do your work. And if you do fail, somebody was telling me, they put you in a special class and go over all the material with you intensively, and let you take the exam again."

"But that would look pretty screwy on your record, wouldn't it?"

"It never goes on your record. Once you pass the course, that's all that shows up. The important thing to them is that you learn the material. That's why they print up copies of the important material in each lecture and distribute them to everybody. So you don't have to sit there scribbling like crazy and searching through zillions of different texts. All you have to worry about is their handouts. The important thing to them is that we learn medicine."

I leaned back on the grass. A pass-fail grading system, make-up tests, special printed handouts for each lecture. The dean was a light, humorous guy like Chanesohn, the chief student representative was Felipe, and I had classmates like Robin and Ron and Michelle. Maybe this whole enterprise could be exhilarating. Only one thing vaguely bothered me.

"Why do you think they keep telling us about crises and psychiatrists and counseling if everything's so low key?" I asked.

"I think they're genuinely concerned," said Ron, dabbing his beard clean with a napkin and leaning back on the grass. "You remember all the cannibalistic competition in pre-med courses. A lot of people just can't remember that's the past, we're in medical school now. They need help in adjusting. And for everybody, the whole process of becoming a doctor is a long, long haul. We're all going to need a little support. It's a lot of stress. I'm very impressed with the people running the medical school here—I think they're genuinely concerned, and I think they're committed to giving us that kind of psychological support."

That evening I was in my room, unpacking and going over how I was going to spend my money for the year. The class had been invited, en masse, to a reception at Dean Nathaniel Hasting's house, a palatial affair down the street from the Longwood Cricket Club. But with the rush of picnics, cocktail parties, and general festivities in our honor, I hadn't even had time to find my toothbrush or towels in the cartons that were stacked like an obstacle course around my bed. So I skipped the reception, and after arranging my belongings I was trying to draw up a budget for myself for the year.

In contrast to most of the class, my financial situation was simple. Both my parents were dead; I had no brothers or sisters, no rich relatives, and no money of my own. Whatever Harvard decided I needed, that's what I had to live on. And this nine-by-thirteen dorm room was home.

In the afternoon I'd visited the financial aid office, signed some papers, and gotten a voucher. Harvard fixed the yearly cost of attendance at twelve thousand dollars. It had awarded me a scholarship of thirty-five hundred and was lending me the rest. Which meant I'd leave medical school with a debt of about thirty thousand dollars. That amount was too large to be real for me. The most I'd ever made in my life was around a thousand a month; for long periods in the past, it'd been more like three or four hundred. Well, I'd worry about the thirty thousand later. Meanwhile, what did I have to live on now?

Financial aid had paid my dorm rent, then allowed me seventeen hundred to live on for the year. OK, let's say five hundred a year for books, clothes, telephone, soap, transportation and so forth. That left me with twelve hundred for food.

Or a hundred dollars a month, or about three dollars a day, or—just a second . . .

A dollar a meal? How was I going to manage that? A salad down in the dining hall cost two dollars!

Well, I was going to have to figure out some way. Maybe cook for myself in my room. And movies were certainly out, so were bookstores, trips out of town, and restaurants. Running and walking were cheap, so I could do a lot of that. It'd just take a while getting used to. A dollar a meal.

The next day, after taking a battery of tests designed to probe our personality patterns and sexual attitudes, Michelle, Ron, Robin, and I met in the lobby of Peter Bent Brigham Hospital to deliver the Saturday-class petition. Dean Stone's office was supposed to be on the third floor, but everyone there disclaimed any knowledge of him. We went back to the information desk, tried the second floor. No one had ever heard of him there either. It felt like I was back home. In every hospital I'd ever worked, no one ever knew who or what lurked behind the next door—administrator, operating room, or scrub brushes. It was comforting to know that Harvard hospitals were normal. By fanning out and trying everywhere, we finally located someone who claimed she was his secretary. The others were a little dubious since there was no name on the door, and the whole office seemed to be a cubbyhole. Harvard's dean of academic affairs worked here—where you could barely turn around?

The dean wasn't in. No, no one knew exactly when he'd be in. He has a lot of meetings. He was here till ten last night. Working very hard. A petition? She regarded it curiously. No, I'm afraid this isn't in his jurisdiction. He's dean of academic affairs—this seems to have something to do with the scheduling of your classes. The registrar—well, if Dean Chanesohn said that, then you should go and discuss it again with Dean Chanesohn. You must have misunderstood him. I know Dr. Stone wouldn't want me to waste your time by having me make an appointment. No, I can't accept a petition for him.

Robin, Michelle, and Ron were starting to back out of the cramped office into the hall. I was getting a little exasperated—this was the third dean we'd seen, and each one claimed the other was responsible.

"Where in the world are we supposed to go?" I asked. "It seems like we've gone to every dean at Harvard, and no one will even accept this piece of paper." I waved it around, egg salad stains and all.

The others were staring at me in dismay. But at that moment, an administrative assistant emerged from an adjacent office. Yes, she'd be very happy to accept the petition, and she knew the dean would be more than delighted to meet with our group—though she didn't know if he would be able to help us. An appointment for late next week, would that be soon enough for us?

As we walked back to Harvard, I felt pleased: we had our meeting. The others weren't so happy with how I'd behaved, and stayed a little apart. Near Vanderbilt, when we were splitting up, Michelle took me aside and fixed me with her intent eyes.

"Charley, you shouldn't have raised your voice with the dean's secretary."

I drew back. "I didn't raise my voice!"

"You know what I'm saying—waving the petition around. I've spent four years at Harvard, and I know what people are like here. They seem very relaxed and permissive, but they can also be very vindictive. We won't get anything that way."

"But we did get our meeting with Stone."

"That's what I'm talking about. If you start acting that way in the meeting, we'll lose everything. Plus get on their shit list. Which might not be so much fun."

"OK," I said, feeling mystified.

Back at the garden lunch, I'd talked with a pediatrician who'd been one of the two people to interview me when I'd applied. An older man with a gentle demeanor, he'd done more than anyone else to help me get accepted. I'd mentioned the Saturday-class petition.

"You're only here two hours, Charley," he'd said, slapping my arm and laughing. "Revolution already?"

"This isn't revolution," I said, a little shocked. "We're just trying to see if they could switch some Saturday classes to Tuesday, so we could have weekends free."

He looked at me, smiling. "But don't you know that Saturday classes are one of the old traditions at Harvard? You're asking for revolution."

Chapter 2

The Hand of Serendipity

Two years earlier: Mile 178 on the Colorado River in the Grand Canyon. A black column of rough basalt appeared downstream in the middle of the river—Vulcan's Anvil. Joey and I pulled our kayaks into the eddy behind it. On either side were the canyon walls, angling up half a mile in altitude away from us, the color of rouge dusted with an orangish pink. The 110° heat seemed to have filmed the sky with a translucence of white. Sitting in the eddy, we listened, trying to still even the gush of water under our boats. From either shore, there was the loud hum of cicadas in the mesquite and tamarisk. But below that sound was there another, a gravely ominous rumble?

"Do you hear it?" asked Joey.

"Yes," I said, not sure if I did.

We listened some more.

"I hear it," said Joey. "It's a mile and a half away and we can hear it. It's going to be a big mother."

"Yes," I said.

We waited for the other boats to catch up, then glided downstream in the idling current. I capsized and practiced rolling up a few times. The Colorado spread out, and now we were having to yell against the roar, borne by an upstream wind. Then we saw it and gave a whoop—a faint, telltale line where the river seemed to end, to drop over the edge of the world, and from down below, shooting up over the horizon, spouts of spume. We were there, the most famous rapid in the Western Hemisphere, the Mount Everest of white water, Lava Falls. We got out to take a look.

"Piece of cake," I started yelling, pacing up and down the shore boisterously, proudly confident. "Way overrated—piece of fucking cake." The others, more measured in their appraisal, let me lead off. I fastened my spray skirt and paddled eagerly out to the middle.

Lava began with an indolent tongue of flat water, flanked by subtly converging waves that nudged you with a show of unconcern into the maelstrom down below. After rains, the desert dust would be washed into the river, turning it the color of blood, but now the water was clear and blue, reflecting the sky overhead. As the current carried me closer, I shook out my hands and wedged myself tighter in the boat. Over the top of the V-waves, and I was hurtling down a roller coaster chute of water to a deep vortex of foam, the heart of the roar we'd heard a mile upstream. On either side, two exploding waves rose up, dwarfing me, shrieking. They crashed together, I aimed straight for that raging junction, nailed it, and the boat leapt out of the hole, half in the air. My paddle went right to brace against the current, but suddenly I was under water, river all around. Just below, I knew, were a rock and three enormous waves. My blade searched for the surface, I rolled up, but before I could inhale, a wall of water slammed into me and I went over. I could feel myself whirled and dashed about, upside-down. Again I rolled and again something hit me, and still I was under. The limits of my breath had been reached. A third try for the surface—there was just an instant of light before the river closed again. Water had filled my nose and mouth, I was starting to gag reflexively. My arms were feeling weak, and my lungs were screeching hysterically for air. Had I been trying to roll on the upstream side, the side where the current would drag me back under? Paddle and all, I swam in frantic slow motion over to the other side of the boat. I set up, heaved, and I was upright, stable, coasting up over one of the mammoth waves. I vomited out water and suds, inhaled air, and made for shore.

That evening we camped on a sandbar ten miles downriver. In the middle of the night, there was a lightning storm. With the rain pelting my sleeping bag into a soggy mess, and the blasts of thunder ricocheting about the canyon walls, it was impossible to sleep. I got up and stood naked on the bank of the Colorado, the rain water drenching off me, bursts of light illuminating great castles in the cliffs.

In two days, we'd be leaving the river at the Hualapai Indian Reservation. In a month I'd be back in the Lower East Side, working days in a state institution for the retarded, taking science courses at night at Columbia. My prospects for getting into medical school weren't good. For a class of a hundred and fifty at an average medical school, there were five or six thousand applicants. Among applicants over thirty, an average of one out of fifty got in. I hadn't been to school in ten years, and the last science aptitude test I'd taken back in high school had placed me in the fourth percentile from the bottom. But, I figured, if the hand of serendipity could pluck me up on that fourth roll in Lava, maybe it'd do something for me in the city as well.

Night classes at Columbia's School of General Studies—my first exposure to a grade factory—whole auditoriums filled with pre-medical students all with only one objective: to be among the elect, the ten or fifteen percent who get the A. Introductory biology: the lab bench at the front of the lecture hall piled high, bank upon bank, with portable tape recorders, almost concealing the professor. Verbatim transcripts would be typed up, then memorized intact. Grades posted in the hall, much tumultuous crowding about, identification by social security number to prevent cross-checking. Searching for the number, cold tingling in the stomach, teeth grinding madly, blanching faces, eyes fighting back tears, the fortunate ones knowable by that slow, smug smile gliding onto their faces. A professor's office hours: the line of students with disputes over marks stretching halfway down the hall.

Trying to do an experiment in chemistry lab: in sweeps the supervisor, shrieking at the top of her lungs, "I know you, the people who won't get into medical school! You're the ones who haven't even done your first melting point!" She paces up and down the rows, students' heads bent, terrified, over tubes and burners. She doesn't mean me, does she? Another lab, a lull while something is slowly precipitating out in a flask. I go over to a friend with whom I'd had a long, pleasant chat on the phone the night before. An hour ago, we'd gotten the last chemistry test back. I nod and smile through my safety goggles. Why is it that I miss the desperate gleam in the eye, the small twitch about the lips?

"How'd it go?" I ask.

"Get away from me!' The whole lab turning around and staring. "And don't try and find out my grades either!"

I go back to my Erlenmeyer flask, everyone following me with their eyes. There are the crystals, fine, lacy, faintly pink and delicate, slowly emerging from the liquid as it cools. Everyone is back to work in his own private, hurrying silence. I look at my friend; his back is to me as he too works over the glassware, but I can see that he is breathing fast and hard.

Overheard on the stairs: Professor A: "How are things in organic chemistry?" Professor B: "Average. Two attempted suicides." Laughter.

We were part of an empire of pre-medical students, ranging from coast to coast, all toiling incessantly, all possessed of a strange, maniacal fixation for percentage marks on pieces of paper. And Columbia night school was probably somewhat more habitable than other parts of the empire. All of us had already graduated from college, having concentrated in something besides science. Whatever madness betook us now, at least we knew that the world outside existed. What of those who, from the day they'd started college at eighteen, had disappeared forever from the ranks of men and become thralls in this strange realm?

In the momentary intervals between the constant tests, quizzes, midterms, and finals, I could catch glimpses of something else latent in the subject matter of science: the statistical aesthetics, the relentless naiveté. How lush it was, this new world thick with muons and neutrinos, massless particles, virtual particles. Electrons dancing from orbital to orbital, showering photons everywhere, two billion per cubic yard. Three dimensional fields interacting, constructing our fragile, tenuous existence; an infinitesimal shift of phase, of wavelength, and we would decompose upon the moment. What trend of the cosmos lay behind the fact that strong forces controlled the behavior of small entities like atomic nuclei, while weak forces dominated stars and galaxies? Very occasionally, I would get rushes of awareness, of recognition, but most of the time, I was marooned on the surface of things.

Every weekday, I'd get up at seven A.M., be at my job in the state facility for the retarded at eight-thirty. At five in the afternoon I'd take the train uptown—lecture till seven-thirty, lab till eleven. Back downtown on the subway to the Lower East Side, I'd crawl over the drunks who inhabited the stairway of my building, watch the mice and cockroaches scatter as I opened the door to my apartment, eat hurriedly, and crawl into bed at midnight. Then up at seven the next morning. Weekends were marathons of studying, from eight in the morning till I made myself a strong drink at midnight and fell asleep.

After a year of this, I'd had enough and went to the premedical counseling office to see about applications for medical school.

"You're a year early," said the advisor, a woman in her early fifties. "You've only had biology and chemistry. I don't care if you have an A and A+. You have to take calculus and physics and organic chemistry too."

"But I'll have finished those by the time I start medical school if I apply now."

"But the grades won't show up on your application. Which is the only thing that counts. And what about the Medical College Admission Test, the MCAT—how are you going to take that without physics and organic?"

"It isn't for three months. I'm pretty good at teaching myself things. I thought I could—"

"Now I've heard everything! You're going to teach yourself physics and organic chemistry over the summer? While you're working full time? Oh, and I notice you're taking a course in differential calculus over the summer, too?"

"Yes," I said. "But all I can do is try. If I get turned down, I get turned down. But I'm sick of working around the clock for years on end."

"And naturally you were thinking of applying to the usual twenty schools. Or would you like to apply to more?"

"I don't know anything about that," I said. "But the place I really want to go is the University of California in San Francisco. There were some doctors on the faculty there whom I admired."

She nodded briefly. There was a long pause.

"This whole thing is ridiculous. But I'll tell you what I'll do. We'll help you apply to that one school. Then you won't be wasting too much of my time. But I want you to know that even that is crazy. No one has ever gotten in the way you want to do it."

Over the summer, it swiftly became apparent to me that my task was not to learn organic chemistry and physics, but to teach myself how to do well on a standardized test. Much of college physics involves complicated mathematics; but calculators weren't allowed in the MCAT, so the math would almost certainly be simple. Much of organic chemistry is taken up with elaborate, multistage syntheses of exotic compounds; but the time limits permitted less than a minute per question, so ingenious synthetic sequences weren't going to play a major role. I worked with a high school review book in physics that had virtually no math and used a simple college organic text that concentrated on the properties of compounds, not the complexities of their reactions.

The MCAT took up a whole Saturday in October from seven-thirty A.M. till six-thirty P.M., and by the end it was clear that mental stamina was considerably more important than acuity. I got the scores back a month later, and was at or above the ninetieth percentile in all categories, including chemistry and physics. With two science courses to my credit, I had higher scores than the average for the entering class at Harvard. Yes, as I'd surmised, test taking was a skill unto itself.

At the last minute, I got frightened at the idea of applying to only one medical school and dashed off another application as a backup. Half at random, I chose Harvard. To avoid a squabble, I switched advisors, ending up with a courtly gentleman who, despite my paltry record, wrote me a glowing recommendation.

So off I went to my interviews, armed with my MCAT scores, dressed in a three-piece suit that was a refugee from high school graduation, lapels and cuffs all the wrong size, pants so short that large expanses of calf showed if I didn't keep pulling my socks up. Naturally, there was a blizzard in Boston when I arrived. I swam through mammoth drifts, my newly purchased $5.95 dress shoes from Grand Street already deteriorating at the seams. Water flying off me, I dashed down a hospital corridor, late for my first interview, banged open a door, sent a man in a white coat, the pediatrician, stumbling. He recovered himself.

"You must be one of the medical school applicants," he said.

There I stood, hair plastered down my face, already creating a puddle of snow water, eyes staring in mortal terror.

"How'd you guess?" I said.

At the end of the interview, we stood up, and I started donning my jacket and vest that had been drying in front of a heater.

"I still don't understand why you only applied to two schools. I've never heard of anybody doing that—it's always fifteen or twenty-two."

I shrugged. "Well, they told me I had no chance of getting in."

An eyebrow went up. And our eyes met.

Back at Columbia, consternation reigned supreme when I was accepted at both medical schools and wanted to turn down Harvard. People didn't do that. And besides, no one had ever heard of the University of California; the world ended at Hoboken. So I called up two professors of medicine at San Francisco whom I knew from my days working in a hospital there. They both told me to go to Harvard.

"Eleven of our twelve chiefs of service went there," one said.

"Sounds like Harvard's sort of the Eton or West Point or something of medicine."

"You could call it that."

In fact, the only one who urged me not to go to Harvard was a first-year student at Harvard. "Go to California," she said. "Anywhere but here. Don't get suckered by the neon H."

Chapter 3

Introduction to the Trade School

Medical school ain't that tough. Just a little confusing.

That summer, I'd gotten the course catalogue, which was the size of a suburban phone book. Harvard proudly announced that it specified no required curriculum for its students; everything was elective. I hadn't the vaguest idea what a first-year student normally took, and there were hundreds upon hundreds of choices: pediatric practice in rural Maine, tumor radiotherapy, orthopedics of ski injuries, tropical medicine, hypnosis. . . . At least I had some idea what those courses were about; others were total mysteries—major histocompatibility systems, biochemistry of glucoconjugates, hydatidiform mole and trophoblastic disease, synaptogenesis.

Best thing, I'd figured, was to get a good mix: combination of basic science, which I knew so little about, and practical hospital experience—morning on the wards, afternoon in the lab or library. I began flipping through the catalogue. "Introduction to hand surgery"—now that sounded like something useful. But, just a second, first you had to have something called "core clerkship in surgery." Let's see, clerkship meant hospital training for medical students. OK, I should probably get a solid surgical background first. I turned to core clerkship in surgery. Yes, I could begin that in September. But, aw hell, it required still another course, called "introduction to clinical medicine." This was getting complicated. I flipped again. But introduction to clinical medicine required "pathophysiology." What in the world was pathophysiology? And, Jesus Christ, there were ten of those pathophysiology courses! And each of them required biochemistry, gross anatomy, general pathology, and physiology. Screw hand surgery. I'll just start with "family practice with the Zuni Indians." But, dammit, that requires "core clerkship in medicine." And the whole same cascade of previous courses. Four hours later, I'd finally deciphered the nature of the elective system at Harvard: everyone elected to take the same courses: physiology, histology, biochemistry, neurobiology. And we'd be spending all our time in the classroom.

Physiology seems to concern the strategies of the body's big life support systems—breathing, eating, getting rid of wastes, and so forth. And this first week we're dealing with the mechanisms by which materials move passively or actively across living barriers, membranes and vessel walls. The lecturer, Hammond Warner, a lean, trim man with a bow tie, a long white coat, and distinguished white hair to match, is reported to be acting chief of the physiology department. I say reported, since who's in charge of what department, or even where the departmental offices are located, is largely a matter of rumor. What exactly is the chain of command at Harvard? No one seems to have a very clear idea about that either. One hears of faculty committees, deans, powerful professors, but who's over what? Somehow I get a strong impression of feudalism. It's even hard to tell who's running the course. According to the schedule, someone gives a lecture, then disappears for the rest of the semester; twelve different speakers seem to shuttle in and out. People say it gets worse next year where in some courses you never see the same guy twice in a row—a sort of scientific vaudeville show.

In any event, Warner, whether he is the head of the physiology department or not, is a great teacher—comprehensible, lively lectures, full of jokes, demonstrations, audience participation, and waggish slides. Now he's concentrating on the cellular sodium ion pumps, the body's main device for controlling water flow. An ion is an electrically-charged molecule or atom. While pure sodium is a soft, waxy metal, dissolved in body fluids the sodium atom loses an electron to become a positively charged ion and thereby acquires a jostling fan club of water molecules all interested in nestling up to that positive charge. A rule of thumb is that whichever way the body pumps sodium ions, there water follows, by osmotic pressure.

Warner demonstrates the importance of these tiny sodium ion pumps in the sides of cells by a series of slides of a cholera epidemic in Bangladesh. Cholera is caused by a microorganism producing a toxic substance in the small intestine whose net effect is to reverse the direction of the sodium pump. Thus the cells that line the intestine, instead of helping to retain fluid by pumping sodium into the body, pump it out. Water goes pouring off as diarrhea, resulting in rapid dehydration and often death. Given a couple days, the body can eliminate the infection with its own immunologic defenses. But how to survive the torrential outflow of water?

The first treatment is immediate replacement of the lost water directly into the veins to bypass the reversed pump in the intestine. To prevent the body's chemistry from going haywire, the water has to be salty to the same degree as the blood. Anywhere in the United States, a treatment involving only the administration of sterile saline solution would constitute no problem at all. However, in Bangladesh, there was far too little sterile saline solution to go around. Thus, for lack of what was essentially uncontaminated salty water, something that costs less than a penny a gallon in the United States, thousands were dying on the other side of the world.

Warner had gone over with a team of U. S. doctors. They'd improvised the tactic of using the short supply of sterile solution to get the patient out of coma, then enlisting relatives to give normal water continuously by mouth, hoping that some of it would get past the reversed sodium pumps in the intestine. The course of treatment was longer and chancier, but nonetheless the tactic worked. The photos were dramatic.

In the morning, a patient would be wheeled into their field hospital unconscious, with sunken cheeks and bulging eyes, unresponsive to pain. By that afternoon, he was awake, and the following day he was sitting up in the courtyard, features filled out miraculously, smiling and waving.

"It's one of the great satisfactions of being a doctor, effecting that swift a recovery from sure death," said Warner.

I could well believe it. I met Ron after the lecture. He mopped back his curly red hair. We both smiled.

"It's really good we start off with that kind of stuff," he said. "Imagine five million babies dying every year of diarrhea, mainly because they don't have any sterile water."

I nodded. "It's nice how he was able to combine the biochemical theoretics with an epidemic. It makes you want to learn more about the theories."

As it turned out, that was the last we were to hear of patients from anywhere but Harvard's own hospitals for a long, long time. In fact, as the semester wore on, it became apparent that the existence of sick people in general would play only a minuscule role in our education now.

Histology? It's the next course, and I've never even heard the word before. The dictionary said the Greek word *histos* originally meant the mast of a ship, then came to be applied to the upright staff of a loom, and finally was used in referring to anything woven. The seventeenth-century scientists who first examined living tissues under a microscope saw what seemed to be a meshwork of cells, a biologic fabric. So they called their trade, the microscopic anatomy of different tissues, histology, or knowledge of the fabric.

It's taught by a tall, young guy in blue jeans and a work shirt, named Jack Fineful. Every gesture, flick of the mustache, deadpan joke seems to say: tough guy. He'll slouch against the lab bench, one arm a pointer, and start ripping off a semi-ironic inventory of the types of cells in the body: "See this putting green, here? Bunch of microvilli all wiggling their poor little heads off. Here's a mast cell, ready to pop its rocks. And watch those vascular endothelial cells pull up their skirts when he does it. And this? No, if you say oriental carpet you're wrong—neuron processes. Golgi Prep." Then he's tearing at sixty miles an hour through cell biology and infrastructure. Despite this, everyone seems to sense that Fineful is warm behind the tough guy exterior—a six-foot-four-inch NFL lineman with an electron microscope and a heart of gold. By the scientists in the class, he's also regarded as a prodigy of nature—a hotshot researcher who actually likes teaching.

In the first lecture, Fineful had described what his own approach was going to be like. "This is a trade school," he said. "The material you're learning is not being taught solely for your intellectual advancement, even though that's part of our goal, but should eventually have a practical purpose. It should allow you to save lives."

The modesty of that term for medical school pleased me, an antidote to the "best and the brightest" notion. But whenever I repeated the phrase "trade school," I got an argument. It seemed to touch a sore spot, a nagging suspicion that we weren't real scientists, after all.

"No, no, no—we learn abstract science here. Basic science. That's a bad way of looking at it, trade school. You think we should act like a bunch of arc welders? I don't think of a patient like a girder with some rivets." So I suppose there is something to be said for the other side.

Following each histology lecture, there's a two hour laboratory session. I'd never seen a stereoscopic microscope, and I couldn't get the damn thing to focus. Finally, the fellow next to me, a slightly built guy with a touch of acne about the chin and a disturbing resemblance to Dr. Kildare, came to my rescue, and set the whole thing up in five seconds. I raced to catch up with the others. Yes, yes—there was the nucleus, the nucleolus, the brush border, some goblet cells, crypts, etc. Next slide, hmmm, stratified cuboidal epithelium in the sweat gland of a fingertip. Fingertip? I pulled the slide out from the microscope and examined it against the window light.

"Hey, Phil," I said to the guy next to me. He had majored in biology at Johns Hopkins; he should know. "Is this a real fingertip?"

He took it from me. "That's what it says. Does it look funny? Like a nose, or something?" He started putting it in his microscope.

"No, no—I mean, is this actually somebody's fingertip? They cut off a slice of somebody's finger?"

"It doesn't say monkey or anything. I guess that means human. There is a monkey phalanx somewhere in the box."

I held the slide up against the light again. There was the cross-section of the finger, red with translucent agate lines coursing through. Yes, that had once been someone's finger— it had felt coffee cups and pieces of paper and buttons, scalded itself, shook hands, gestured in excitement, caressed faces. Now it lived between pieces of glass in a box.

A small chill ran through me. "Strange," I said.

"Yeah, isn't it? Here's a piece of penis. A little later, you'll get to a salivary gland from someone's tongue."

I looked at him, my eyes widening.

Phil shrugged. "After a while, you just don't think about it anymore. Anyway, these slides are real old. You can tell from the way they're faded."

I started again, a little more slowly. If this was human flesh, however sliced, diced, dried, or stained, I should at least show it the courtesy of adequate attention.

Soon people began to leave for lunch. It was almost one; I was hungry, and another class started at one-thirty. I sped up: esophagus, testicle, intestine. . . . Where are those crazy terminal bars they say I should see? The heck with them, I'll look for them next lab. I got out another slide on the list, held it for a second, then put it back in the box. Can that too, I'm getting something to eat.

You get used to things fast around here, I thought as I locked up the microscope.

Biochemistry's supposed to be a relatively difficult subject, but with two years of chemistry behind me, I feel on somewhat familiar turf. Of the two or three principal lecturers, the main one seems to be Edwin Farrell, a tall, thin man whose long, white lab coat resembles a nineteenth-century schoolmaster's frock, giving him a vague resemblance to Ichabod Crane. Farrell's gray hair is trimmed down to an efficient crewcut, and though he makes dry jokes from time to time, I don't have the feeling he shares Jack Fineful's trade school approach. Early on, someone asks if we should memorize the structures of the twenty amino acids that are involved in biological processes. Though the question is addressed to the lecturer, Farrell gets to his feet in the back and answers preemptively, "In order to write Chinese, you must memorize thousands upon thousands of ideographs. A cultivated writer may know ten thousand. In this course, we will use as our vocabulary about a hundred and fifty or two hundred compounds. I don't think it's unfair to ask you to remember their structures, complex or not, especially since biochemistry is considerably more important than Chinese."

He gets roundly, though half-humorously, hissed for this and sits down looking disgruntled. But everybody decides from that speech that Farrell must be in charge of the course, so we better start memorizing like mad.

But what is it exactly we're supposed to memorize? The first lecture handout is filled with diagrams of the water molecule, complete with numerical specifications. Next handout—more diagrams, no explanations. Some equations for dipole-dipole interactions. What kind of dipole interactions? Where? What are we supposed to do with the equations? Third handout—first four pages are an enormous, fine-print table of fifty-eight proteins found in the blood, largely in incomprehensible serological shorthand. Give me a month and I still couldn't commit that table to memory. In lecture, it barely gets mentioned. What's the point? They're hitting us with an exam in two weeks, so I better get a line pretty soon on what's expected in this course.

My last course, cellular neurobiology, runs from one-thirty till four-thirty in the afternoon two days a week. And those are long days: the whole morning in lecture or lab, then three more hours sitting still in an amphitheater, listening and listening. I'm not accustomed to such nonstop passivity. The little I've managed to glean about nerves convinces me they're well worth some special effort. A nerve cell, or neuron, typically has a round part, the cell body, devoted to nutrition and metabolic control, while a long, thin tendril called an axon is the business end—it transports electrical signals. The round cell body will rarely be thicker than a ten-thousandth of an inch, but the axon it keeps alive can be three feet long— one infinitely fine cellular strand from your spine down to your toe, capable of relaying thousands of electrical messages each second. When the axon wants to communicate with another nerve cell, it stops about a millionth of an inch away and releases a signaling chemical. That junction between communicating nerve cells is called a synapse, and a single nerve cell can have as many as a hundred thousand synapses plugged into it. Evolution thought so highly of the synapse that it gave our brain a hundred trillion or so of them. What we consider self or mind, neurobiologists take pleasure in asserting, seems to be nothing more than the subjective experience of that inconceivably intricate synaptic architecture.

Everyone talks about Ron Genslip and Joe Peters, the two guys who run the course, in hushed tones—apparently they've been responsible for a whole bunch of breakthroughs in the theory of nerve physiology. But I'm hard to impress—if you've never heard about baseball, meeting Yogi Berra isn't such a memorable event. What I like about them is a Mutt-and-Jeff quality: Peters is younger, dark of hair, heavyset, while Genslip is thin, blond hair turning gray, a sharp dresser. One starts lecturing, the other sits in the audience, raises his hand, gets called on in turn, asks a question or adds a point, they wander off into a discussion of their own, then remember where they are and go back to talking to us.

There's only one problem for me—what the hell are they talking about? I know it's supposed to be about how a voltage gets established in a nerve cell, but they seem to assume you have a rudimentary familiarity with neuroanatomy ("easily the most complicated aspect of anatomy," confided one handout) and already understand those ion pumps backwards and forwards. My knowledge of neuroanatomy stops with an idea that the brain is located somewhere in the head, and I'm still trying to figure out those sodium ion pumps Warner told us about this week in physiology. But with nerves, things seem to be more complicated—besides sodium there are a whole bunch of other metals involved somehow, potassium, calcium, magnesium . . . And I can't report much progress with the lecture handouts: schematic diagrams of circuits, symbols for capacitors and resistors in series and in parallel, microelectrodes, oscilloscope tracings, potentials differentiated with respect to time, some plump little equations

$$V_M = \frac{E_{N_2} \, (g_{Na}/gk) + E_K}{g_{Na}/gk + 1}$$

I'm back in my room, it's one in the morning, I have two physics books and a text on electrochemistry spread around me. I look out my window—mine seems to be the only light on. Shit. How many years is this going to take me? I flip forward in the handouts to see what happens next:

During interval I, most of the loss is in the form of capacity current as in Fig. 7. Because less interval current passes B than passes A during interval I, a V_m is less at B than at A as shown at the right side of Fig. 6. During interval II, all of the loss is in the form of ionic current as in Fig. 8. Because less interval current passes B than A during interval II, the steady level of membrane potential that produces a balancing outward ionic current at B and regions to the left is closer to E_k than at A, as shown in Fig. 6. . . .

And so on. I scan all this fine print to see what the take-home message is. I can't find any. But, "If you compare this paragraph," the section summed up, "with the top paragraphs on pages 5 and 7, you will find only one idea not previously raised with reference to equivalence circuits, the idea in the eighth sentence." I wasn't about to look up the idea in the eighth sentence and find out what was so remarkable about it. Forty pages of this handout alone? I threw the handouts back on the shelf. Obviously, I needed a new strategy. OK, I'd find some book that had pictures of nerve cells, so I'd have some idea what they looked like. Then I'd practice a little electrical physics and chemistry, warm up my math a trifle. Get the ion pumps straightened out. Then start all over again. No sense in going to lectures or problem sessions meantime—just get me panicky and restless. Work hard, catch up. That was the way to approach things now that I was in medical school. Orderly. Methodical.

Robin came up to me in between physiology and histology. With her amber hair and warm, naive directness, I still got alarmed and tongue-tied when I spoke to her.

"Stone canceled out on that Saturday-class meeting," she said.

"What?" That kicked me out of my muteness.

"His secretary called Michelle and said he didn't have anything to do with Saturday classes. We should talk to Chanesohn."

"And Chanesohn says we should talk to Stone. These guys belong in civil service. We got to get together. After histo lab?"

"I'll tell Michelle."

We had lunch together in the Vanderbilt dining room, a one-hundred-foot-long, two-story hall with tall ferns, gilt chandeliers, and fireplaces suitable for roasting two or three wild boars. The price of the cuisine was way beyond my dollar-a-meal limit, so I made a sandwich in my room and brought it downstairs.

"Let's go back to Hastings," I said. "Far as I can see, he seems to be the supreme dean around here. He can assign it to somebody. Otherwise, we'll just keep getting the revolving door treatment."

Ron disagreed. "Tell Charley what Stone's secretary told you, Michelle."

"Well, I said we'd already talked to Chanesohn, and she said then she'd tell that to Stone, and she was sure Stone would call Chanesohn to get the whole thing cleared up."

"I think we should wait to give them time to work it out," said Ron with an earnest look in his brown eyes. "After all, they're the deans. They're in charge. We can't just go busting around. We don't have any power. If we offend them by coming on too strong, then where will we be? Our only hope is by showing that we're reasonable. If we put too much pressure on, it'll backfire."

"Just asking Chanesohn whether he or Stone is in charge is putting too much pressure on?"

"If Stone says he's going to handle it, then our barging in is too much pressure."

"But Stone didn't say that. His secretary said she'd talk to him about it, that's all."

Ron shook his head, and Michelle spoke up. "I agree with Ron. We have no power at all. We're not even elected by the class. What if they ask us if we represent the class? What can we say? Half the class didn't even sign the petition. All we can do is hope that they'll see we're reasonable, and they'll do the right thing."

"I don't understand what we should do then. We shouldn't even call Chanesohn?"

Ron and Michelle nodded. Robin didn't say anything.

"Just wait?" I asked. "We're going to have our first Saturday class tomorrow. Once things get going, it'll be like last year— they'd like to help us, etc., but it's too late now."

"We have to wait for them to get back to us. Anything else will just hurt us."

"They're not going to get back to us," I said.

"Yes, they will," said Ron.

"No, they won't," I said.

The next day Chanesohn called Michelle. Would it be convenient for our group to meet with him and Dean Stone the middle of next week?

Chapter 4

Act Reasonable

The second week, and a few rash souls have begun to ask questions. The entire class turns its head in wonder. Whispers—who is that guy? As time goes on, more hands are going up, but the class is becoming impatient with Smart Questions, the ones that instead of clarifying the material merely demonstrate the questioner's acumen. One tall, thin fellow in a varsity jacket that says "Mineola Softball" in large red letters has been identified as the worst offender. He sits in the first row, long, thin legs stretched out. Ten minutes into the lecture, his hand goes up.

"Question."

"Yes."

"Doesn't recent experimental evidence throw into question the inotropic role of parasympathetic neurotransmitters? Isn't acetylcholine's effect on contractility thought to be achieved solely through chronotropic mediation of end diastolic volume?"

"Excellent point. While controversy still rages over—"

The class disagreed. That kind of shit just isn't done here. Everybody checks the class book: Seymour Hantz. Queens College. Next time Seymour's hand comes up, some scattered titters. Seymour doesn't understand. By the next week, a few of the more confident types let loose a hiss or two as soon as

Seymour begins to cite *The New England Journal of Medicine.* That gives everyone courage. A barrage of hisses, growls, grunts, and sarcastic applause meet Seymour's further attempts. He knows something's amiss now. He moves back a few rows, cuts down on the Smart Question frequency. But the class, in its righteous indignation, is not to be appeased. We want Seymour silenced. By the end of the month, we have achieved our objective: Seymour has retreated all the way up into the last seat of the back row, and his thin hand stays at his side.

This class victory liberates the hiss as the principal mode of audience participation in the process of medical education, to be employed against lecturer and fellow student alike. How the lecturer or course director is to interpret the meaning of these sibilants, snorts, and gutturals is up to him. The important thing is that the class is not happy. Alternatively, a loud yawn while a lecturer is writing on the blackboard or the room is dark for a slide will suffice. The class laughs, the lecturer continues as if nothing had happened.

If Smart Questions are poorly regarded, few have the guts to ask Dumb Questions, the ones everyone has on his mind but can't find the courage to voice.

"You mean increasing the heart rate doesn't increase the amount of blood that's pumped out at all?"

How long it took me to realize that when I was completely confused, chances were everyone else was too, that group silence meant group bewilderment, not comprehension. But Dumb Questions are rarely asked since no one wants to Look Foolish in Front of the Whole Class. So the principal questions are those of the Moderately Intelligent variety.

"Wouldn't you anticipate a feedback effect there?"

The questioners are those who already understand the material from a previous course and so feel confident enough to ask for clarification on a minor point—even so, they are careful not to become too prominent and thus incur the ignominious fate of Seymour Hantz.

How many of the class seem to be repeating exactly the subjects they already took as undergraduates. Biochemistry majors insist on repeating introductory biochemistry; people with years of independent physiological research behind them opt for taking the elementary course over. And perhaps because most of the material is already boringly familiar, there's virtually never any discussion among the students of the content of a lecture or its implications, other than to label it lousy, boring, or pretty good. Already an esprit has evolved which has rendered general scientific discussions largely off limits; attempts to initiate them are regarded as ostentatious, pushy. If you mention having read an article on astrophysics, a slightly tense, pained expression slowly forms about the listener's face. Rather than respond to what you've said, he'll reply that he read an article too. About chloroplasts. And you look at each other. Next move.

But art doesn't occupy much of anybody's attention either. In fact, I never see novels, poetry, or books of any kind in anyone's pocket; nothing but texts line the bookshelves in dorm rooms. Conversation dwells permanently on school, occasionally wanders off to sports and movies.

I realize, too, that at the age of thirty-four, I approach everything here with much more wonder and innocence than do my twenty-three-year-old classmates: I've been exposed to science for two years, they've been doing nothing but for a third of their lives, no sloppy romantic sighs for them.

Nevertheless, even in these first couple weeks, I have managed to pick up some of the lingo of my peers and teachers. Now I understand that when the phrase "Basic Science" or "Basic Medical Research" is used, it refers to an activity where no practical result whatsoever is anticipated other than the production of papers in scholarly journals. A student indicates his interest in this highest form of research by an unquenchable desire to take multiple-choice and true-false tests. A lack of interest in basic science, on the other hand, is manifested by questions such as "Do we actually have to memorize that whole table?" or "What's the significance of all this data?"

"Culture," on the other hand, has a broad meaning for the medical student. It refers to any material that will not have to be memorized for the next test and thus can be safely ignored. Normally, this includes general theory behind the problem, historical points, social impact, cost factors, direction of future investigations, etc. When a lecturer announces this is for your cultural benefit, slip down in your seat, get your head nestled comfortably away, and ask your neighbor to wake you when it's over.

Other words are still more technically specialized. How long it was before it dawned on me that the word "harvest" had no connection with agriculture or food. Say you've been giving some rhesus monkeys massive doses of a drug. To assess the effects on their livers, you "harvest the crop." It would be unscientific if you said you killed them all.

As I began this process of intellectual acclimatization, class elections were held. For representative to the Curriculum Committee, the faculty body that determined how medicine was taught at Harvard, we selected a handsome fellow with a surfer's mane of auburn hair, a sleepy, West Coast mellow gaze, and a lot of inspiring talk about rural health care and family practice. Someone else had given what I thought was a much better speech, promising to work on improved course content, more intelligible handouts, especially in biochemistry, and an end to Saturday classes. But he made some critical errors: he carried *The New York Times* under his arm, a clear faux pas, and left before everyone else's speeches were over, implying that he had better things to do. The West Coast fellow, Marc Rensler, was already known to the class as one of those who asked Moderately Intelligent Questions, and to cap matters, was far and away the best disco dancer among us—to see him whiz in and out of those complicated moves was a caution. No contest.

By the time the speeches of candidates for the Committee on the Status of Women rolled around, most of the class had gone to lunch. The only people left were the three women running and a small audience of men. I'd only stuck around out of politeness to one of the speakers whom I'd gotten to know slightly, Cheryl Fredericks. She had short brown hair that parted on either side of enormous glasses and a glow of midwestern innocence and friendliness. At twenty-five, she was slightly older than the rest of the class, and had only a few more science courses than I had before arriving here. But, most important, she was one of the few with the courage to ask those essential Dumb Questions that no one else dared raise. Single-handedly, she'd straightened out more than one hopelessly confusing lecture. Out of gratitude for that, I was going to vote for her. The other two women gave pleasant, straightforward talks about how hard they'd work if elected. Cheryl said she thought the medical profession was saturated with sexism; at Harvard we hadn't had any women lecturers yet and in some courses we were never going to have any. Out of more than two hundred tenured positions at the medical school only seven were occupied by women, the percentage of women in the entering class had dropped markedly over the past few years, the system of medical education made it almost impossible for a woman to have children and still pursue her career—those were just a few of the things she wanted to work on. Cheryl felt she was best qualified to deal with these matters since she'd been involved in the women's movement for a long time, had worked for two years as a rape crisis counselor, and had written a master's thesis in sociology entitled "Systems of Sexual Stratification." All the men applauded. Cheryl was elected.

I went up afterwards to congratulate her.

"When I saw I was just talking to men," she said, "I thought I might as well go down fighting."

"But you won anyway."

Cheryl looked a little rueful, and pulled the brown hair away from her glasses. "I talked to some of the men—you know what they said?"

"What?"

"They said they decided to vote for me as soon as they heard I'd done that thesis on 'Systems of Sexual Gratification.' Because we sure needed more of that gratification stuff around here."

Indeed, the relations between the sexes at Harvard Medical School hardly seem to be shaping up as an unending social whirl. Such pairings as have occurred are mostly screened from public gaze, couples often sit apart from each other in lecture, wishing to avoid scrutiny in class. In the early weeks, there was a large women's meeting at lunchtime in Vanderbilt. En route to class, I met Shelley Prosser, a lively, black-haired biology major from Bryn Mawr, who was coming out of the meeting.

"So what'd you talk about?"

"A lot of things. Fact that we have almost no women teachers. Sexist jokes. Dating."

"Dating?"

"Yeah. The second-year class said all the men say we're bitches and just go out with nursing students and girls from Simmons."

Simmons was a women's college down the street. The men, for their part, grumbled unceasingly that the women in the class had, through their control of the Social Committee, prevented any joint dances or other festivities with The Simmons Girls, who seemed to grow more beautiful by repute with each passing week. Whether you believed the men or the women, The Simmons Girls certainly seemed to be bones of contention.

Nevertheless, the women in the class are starting to make their presence felt. Few are the lecturers who can get away with a sexual innuendo and not be hissed. Outside of Cheryl, only one or two women have risked joining the ranks of the questioners, but when a female voice is heard, all the women turn in unison and stare, some continuing long after the question has been answered. A lecturer's reference to reproduction or the distinctive anatomical features of women causes significant glances to be exchanged across the room.

In histology, one young research assistant gave what I thought was a perfectly fine lecture on blood cells, but got hissed unmercifully at the end and was reported to be unnerved and depressed at this rebuff. I happened to mention my bewilderment to Michelle.

"You know who was supposed to give that lecture," she replied.

"Who?"

"Grace Vanda. She's just about the only woman we'll see all year. She got called out of town or something, and he substituted."

"So that guy got hissed because he wasn't a woman?"

"That was a big part of it. I guess it's wrong, but it was such a big disappointment not to see a woman up there. Maybe I'll go and see him and tell him it wasn't his fault."

I ran into Kent Handel, the second-year class representative to the Curriculum Committee. He was a tall, lanky redhead, with the angular military bearing that came from four years at West Point. This year, for the first time at Harvard, Kent had assembled a booklet evaluating courses, part by question-naire, part by his own impressions. "Potentially exciting material," he'd comment on one course, "was reduced to the level of mediocrity by Dr. Smith's lifeless, disorganized lecture style." Harvard had paid Kent to publish it, and distributed the booklet to all students at registration.

Kent, a year ahead of our class, had, it turned out, been waging a war on his own for an end to Saturday classes. Without success.

"This place just fights to the death on that," he said to me, standing in the quad. "There's no necessity for it at all in terms of the schedule. I'm sure it's basically the same issue as those work shifts on the wards that last thirty-six hours without a break. Boot camp. Last year, our class went directly to the people who were giving the Saturday lectures second term and arranged with them to switch to a weekday. It was OK with the teachers and it was sure OK with us. But as soon as administration got wind of the change, it tried to move in to cancel the whole thing."

"Why?"

"The reason they gave was we'd bypassed them and so forth. But that wasn't the real reason."

"What's the real reason?"

He sighed and looked off. "Just hang around here for a while, and you'll figure out why."

"I can't figure this place out. They do that kind of stuff, yet they have Felipe greet us and they let you publish that course booklet."

"Of course!" Kent turned to me, his eyes suddenly bright. "That's Harvard. They'll let you say anything. They'll encourage it. The student newspaper attacks the medical school constantly, and Harvard pays them to publish it. Open your mouth, and in the twinkling of an eye you'll find yourself appointed to some committee, hobnobbing with luminaries and going to cocktail parties and having deans and famous scientists call you up at home to get your opinion on things. Whether Harvard will change is a whole other question."

"Well, this Chanesohn fellow doesn't seem so bad. He actually called us up to get a meeting. He was real nice in the talk he gave us."

Kent gave me a sympathetic look. "Yeah, Chanesohn's smooth as silk. Really beautiful to watch. Just beautiful. You'll go in all ready for blood, leave with less than you went in with, but he'll have you convinced you got everything you wanted and that he should be President of the United States."

I thought about that. "Maybe that's because you went in all by yourself as a class representative. I'd think it'd be hard to be one person, a student, and negotiate all by yourself with a dean. Maybe if you took more people—"

"No, I can't do that."

"Why not?"

"You'll see. I just can't work with medical students like that. Anything you do, they get terrified. They're in a permanent state of fear. Anything you try to do, they figure out forty-three reasons why it's a bad idea, and meanwhile there's a test in two weeks, and we got to go home and study."

"Well, we have a little group. If there is a Harvard method like you say, I'd rather meet it with other people, than try to do battle with it all by myself."

Kent smiled. "We'll see."

Michelle, Robin, Ron, and I had another lunchtime strategy session, before our meeting with Chanesohn and Stone.

"We have to have a plan," said Michelle. "We can't go in there completely unprepared."

We all nodded.

"We have to make a reasonable proposal to them," she went on. "Show that we're reasonable, willing to meet them halfway."

"But we're still going to ask them to switch the classes, right?" I smiled. "We're still in agreement on that?"

No one said anything.

"What do you have in mind?"

"You know how in histo, Fineful videotapes all the lectures so if someone misses one, they can go to the library and see it some other time?"

"You're not—"

"Let me finish. They could set that up in biochem Saturday mornings. Videotape the lectures."

"We needed a petition and a joint meeting with two deans to ask for that? One of us could have wandered over to audio-visual and set that up."

"But what's the matter with that?"

"You're going to have the whole class in the library every Tuesday, while Farrell lectures to an empty auditorium on Saturdays with a videotape machine going? Originally we wanted to switch Saturday classes to a weekday. Why have we changed our idea?"

"But Charley," said Ron. "You're missing Michelle's point. We have to show them that we're reasonable. That we're not crazy, that we're willing to meet them halfway. We have no power. We have to make some sort of reasonable proposal."

I looked at Robin.

She didn't say anything.

"OK," I said. "Why don't we explain that we just wanted to ask them why classes were held on Saturday. Ask them why. Wait and see what they do. Then if they aren't going to do anything, we can always ask if they could ask audio-visual for us to set up the videotape."

"That doesn't sound so awful to me," said Robin, speaking up for the first time.

Ron and Michelle looked at each other. "OK," said Ron,

reaching over to me with a friendly squeeze. "But you can't let off steam in there, Charley."

"I'm not going to let off steam."

"We could blow everything."

"OK, I'll keep my mouth shut."

"You don't have to do that. Just act reasonable."

Chanesohn's office was on the ground floor of the principal Roman temple that served as administrative building. We entered through immense Ionic columns, past a security guard, then into a two-story marble lobby with curving staircases, busts set into niches, framed portraits, and potted palms. A few more doorways, and our footsteps hushed into the deep pile of rugs. Things suddenly became intimate: old desks, deep upholstered chairs. Then Chanesohn himself appeared, that round, balding face turned into one large smile, and ushered us into the inner office. We each shook hands, he repeated our names back to us, looking us each in the eye. There were a couch and some chairs, and we distributed ourselves in them. Across from us, waiting, was Dr. Andrew Stone, dean of academic affairs. Though he'd graduated from Harvard Medical School in the same class as Chanesohn, he didn't seem to share the jovial expression. In fact, his thin face looked distinctly displeased beneath the perfunctory smile of greeting. Chanesohn pulled up a chair near us, so there'd be no desk intervening.

"I'm really happy this class is turning out so lively," Chanesohn said as he sat down. "A petition the same day you arrive. And following through too. As soon as I heard that, I decided I had to get to know your whole group in person. We must have chosen you well. If you're the examples of the kind of spirit we have, then this is going to be a great four years for all of us."

The stiff posture we had adopted began to loosen. Stone didn't say anything.

"Now to serious matters." And suddenly Chanesohn's expression returned to seriousness. I suddenly realized that face was quite capable of continuing right on to a terrifying glower. This man had range.

"The reason Andy and I wanted to meet with you jointly

was to avoid any kind of bureaucratic shuffle that's so easy to fall into when you have a bunch of administrators with overlapping functions. We're here to solve problems, not to pass them around." His face brightened again. "Now, who's your ringleader?"

Fear struck into the heart of us all. Pindrop silence.

"Come on, come on," he laughed. "I wasn't born yesterday. Somebody had to have the initiative to get this whole thing rolling . . . you, Michelle?"

"Well, I—"

"I'm not trying to intimidate you or single anyone out. It's just easier to get things going."

"I guess, yes," said Michelle, glancing at the rest of us.

"Well, we have this petition signed by about seventy-seven names that has to do with Saturday classes."

I looked at Chanesohn's desk, and there was a stack of photocopies. My lunch droppings had come out quite well, better than some of the names.

"We could have gotten more," said Michelle, "but we were just passing it around and it got lost, and—"

"No, I'm sure you're right. I'm sure your whole class agrees. But how would you like us to help you?"

"Our proposal," said Michelle, "is that Saturday classes be videotaped so those who don't go can see them in the library."

I sank lower in my seat. Chanesohn and Stone looked at each other in surprise. Each shrugged.

"You mean have lecturers talk to a videotape machine on Saturday morning, and your whole class would see it later in the library?"

"We—"

"I suppose we could arrange that for the lecture alone, but as you know there is a two-hour clinical presentation right after that lasting till noon. It's hard enough to get patients to come in and talk before a whole amphitheater of students. I'm certainly not going to ask them to be videotaped for posterity too."

There was utter silence for half a minute while Chanesohn and Stone stared at us expectantly.

"Could you explain why we have Saturday classes?" I said. The others turned around at me with worried expressions.

Stone replied, "As far as I know, we've had Saturday classes since Harvard Medical School was founded two hundred years ago. Up until a few years back, the country had a six-day work week, so students didn't think too much about it. Now many people work five days a week. So I guess that students periodically want to rearrange the whole schedule to fit their desires."

"Is there any reason why we couldn't have Saturday classes on Tuesday or Thursday or Friday?"

"There may be some scheduling conflicts. In fact, there probably are. It would require a tremendous amount of work now that the term has started."

"Are those scheduling problems insuperable?"

Chanesohn spoke up. "All these changes you're asking for represent a good deal of disruption for the school. I'm sure that, as mature people, you're aware of that. So before embarking on anything of that magnitude, we'd like to hear a little more from you exactly why it is so urgent that we change this two-century tradition for you."

Robin combed back her long hair with one hand and spoke with her shy elegance. "My family has a farm in Vermont. I'd like to go and spend a weekend there once in a while. Have something besides medical school all the time."

"I'm sure you could cut once in a while," Chanesohn said, smiling. "I did it when I was a first-year student here. More than I'll ever admit in public."

"But I don't want to miss every class."

"But you're not going to that farm every weekend, either?"

"No."

"It ruins your Friday nights," said Ron, opening his hands. "If you have to get up the next morning at eight, you can't very well go out and see friends, or go to a party."

"You're not seriously suggesting we drop a two-hundred-year-old tradition to allow you to go to a party and get drunk? Now, how would that look in the *Alumni Bulletin!*"

I decided to make a speech, whether I'd agreed to shut up and act reasonable or not. I raised my hand.

"Don't put your hand up," said Chanesohn. "When I lecture you can do that. There's just six of us here."

"For the last ten years," I said, "I've worked in medical facilities. And there's one memory that just keeps coming back now. I'd be sitting talking with a patient, in would sweep twelve coats, grab the chart from my hand, never introduce themselves to me or the patient, discourse loudly over the bed in technical jargon as if they were dealing with a hunk of beef, then sweep out without a word. On to the next case. Always in a rush. I don't want to become that kind of doctor. And what's particularly strange to me is that the people in my class here don't seem that way at all. Perhaps a little competitive, but that's about all. So the question in my mind for the past two weeks has been, what's the hamburger machine that chops up nice kids and turns them into the doctors I got to know? I don't have a lot in the way of an answer yet, but I can see a couple of clues. One is starting off by not having weekends like everyone else, then moving on to continuous round-the-clock work shifts on the wards. Combine that with an isolated setting, intellectually and emotionally. Eight or ten years later, you emerge. You're in your thirties. You never really had your twenties. You realize you never had a youth. Everyone else did. But you didn't. So how do you start treating the cause of this irretrievable loss, the patient? You treat him angrily, bitterly. you resent your job, you resent sick people. Maybe you decide that the only thing you can get out of this ordeal is cash. Isn't there some way we can figure out to make a tiny inroad into that process, like switching a Saturday class to give people weekends?"

Chanesohn had turned completely around and was listening earnestly. "That's really an extraordinary statement. I don't think I've heard anyone, much less a first-year medical student, summarize exactly what I've seen myself about what medical education can do." He nodded, then looked around. "Mr. LeBaron certainly put his finger on what I consider the number one issue here: how do we turn out physicians in every sense of that word, and not just inhumane technicians."

I started feeling pretty proud of myself. It had been a good statement, hadn't it? This guy Chanesohn was OK.

"I agree with Dr. Chanesohn on those points," Stone broke in. "But I can't see what all this has to do with Saturday classes. You just have to face up to reality—sooner or later, you'll be in hospitals working, not just Saturday mornings, but whole weekends, days and nights on end without a break. What are you going to tell people—come back some other time because you're afraid you might lose your youth?"

"Andy here is, of course, playing the devil's advocate," said Chanesohn before any of us could reply. "But there is a large proportion of people here, major members of the faculty, people who care deeply about good patient care, who do espouse those kinds of ideas. I've never found a way, myself, to answer them, but what you've been telling me here today clarifies my thinking a great deal."

Robin spoke up. "Is there any chance we could do something on this Saturday business?"

"I certainly think we can look into it," said Chanesohn. "Don't you, Andy?"

"It would involve rearrangements for the entire school: inventorying class lists, polling professors, determining conflicts. The registrar will have a fit."

"Why can't we just move the class from one empty time slot to another?" asked Robin.

"Andy's just giving you an idea of some of the work that's involved," said Chanesohn. "These things are not always as simple as they seem. But that's our job, cutting through red tape and getting things done."

"What kind of time frame are we talking about?" I asked.

Stone shrugged. "I have no idea what the registrar might be able to do and—"

"I mean a week, two weeks?"

"Perhaps."

"So do you think we should set up a meeting for two weeks from now so we can—"

Stone looked at me over his glasses. "You're pressing me awfully hard, Mr. LeBaron."

Ron and Michelle said "Come on, Charley."

Chanesohn nodded. "I think we should try to be flexible about this. A two-hundred-year-old tradition doesn't die that easily. What do you say we let Andy handle the technicalities? And I'll handle you rabble-rousers."

We all laughed and, following Chanesohn, stood up.

"So should we call you the week after next?" I asked.

"Come on, Charley," said Michelle and Ron.

Chanesohn gave me a friendly bang with his shoulder. "This class is going to be great, isn't it, Andy?"

Stone looked at us all and smiled.

Chapter 5

The Negentropy Eaters
—or—
Envelopes of Anti-Time

Every day, I try to trot a couple times around the Fenway, a park a block or two away from the medical school. How amazing it is to me now that nature still exists out there, beyond the libraries and laboratories and lecture halls—the extravagant, gaudy, almost indecent blaze of a New England autumn. A wind blows and splotches of hot color come raining all around me, festooning my hair, catching in my clothes and shoelaces. Wheezing like a vintage locomotive, I hurtle into a dip of the path, an explosion of gold and maroon sails up knee high, settling slowly after I pass.

But how long I can continue to find the time for even these small excursions is becoming questionable. I've started making long lists and schedules, trying to apportion tasks so I can finish blocks of material. Even when I make them up, they seem too ambitious; a week goes by, and I have to rip up the list. I make another schedule, cut corners, still fall behind. The day no longer has enough minutes in it; I race through dinner, throwing frozen foods into my toaster oven so I won't waste valuable moments cooking. A close friend gets married in New York—no question of being able to attend. Lack of money is now a boon rather than an inconvenience—with it, I might be tempted to go to an occasional movie instead of staying at my desk till midnight Fridays and Saturdays. Other than those daily jaunts around the Fenway, I haven't been more than three blocks away from school since I arrived.

Edwin Farrell, the man who told us to get cracking on memorizing those two hundred chemical compounds, is delivering the biochemistry lectures now. Always appearing before us in that same knee-length white lab coat, he has a weathered, melancholy expression, an almost weary cynicism to his voice, occasionally enlivened by dry humor. But what is biochemistry?

We get pictures of proteins that twist around like an endless piece of spaghetti knotted up on itself, all sorts of numbers and arrows scattered in mysterious places; detailed charts of multienzyme complexes, though what those complexes do ain't so clear. The pivotal course in the pre-medical curriculum, organic chemistry, had been almost entirely given over to the theories of industrial reactions, and it had been an enigma to me why a detailed knowledge of petroleum cracking and the synthetic sequences of plastics was considered so important in preparing you to deal with human suffering and death. But industrial organic chemistry was simplicity and relevance itself compared to what we're getting now.

Introductory lectures on "the Embden-Meyerhof Glycolytic Pathway." "Overall reaction deceptively simple," we're informed at the outset in the lecture handout. Then there's page after page of chemical gobbledegook. But just a second—what is "The Embden-Meyerhof Glycolytic Pathway"? Are we synthesizing something, breaking it down? Does it take place in the ocean, outer space, crayfish, where? Does it start things off, end them? In short, what's it all about? Silly concerns. Just plunge right ahead and start getting it all down cold while you have some minutes to spare:

> Rabbit muscle aldolase—Class I, Type A, MW 160,000, four sub-units of MW 40,000; Formula: Alpha-2, Beta-2, but isozymes of varying ratio Alpha/Beta are found. Mechanism: Horecker et al., *The Enzymes*, 3rd ed., Vol. VIII, p. 213-258. See hand-

out. Consider reaction in *direction of synthesis* of hexose-P.

What reaction? What have rabbits got to do with this? Are we really supposed to look up the eighth volume of an encyclopedia of enzymes and memorize forty-five pages of mechanism? Who knows? A point arrives where you stop fatiguing yourself with those kinds of questions. You just slog away till the wee hours, surrounded by texts, rewriting the sentence fragments of the handouts, tediously deciphering reactions, trying to memorize tables and charts. What in the world is the test going to be on?

Ron thinks I'm overreacting. "We're in medical school now, Charley. We're not back slaving away to get an A so we can get admitted somewhere. How many people flunked last year? Four or five?"

"Maybe your memory's better than mine. I'm slow at this brute recall stuff."

"Nobody's good at it. You're not by yourself. But I like to see a movie on Saturday, get up at ten on Sunday, instead of seven-thirty. What's the matter with that?"

"Nothing's the matter with it."

"Have someone over for dinner once in a while, I don't see why I have to give that up."

"I'm not arguing with you."

"What kind of doctor am I going to be if I start hating this? I want a chance to see the woman I live with once in a while. Half an hour a day I play the oboe. How much more am I going to learn by giving those things up?"

"I'm not saying you should give them up." The more Ron talked, the more I decided he was a good influence on me. What an arid life I'd been leading the past month. But I still couldn't shake the feeling that this wasn't a question of doing well, but of survival.

"The biochem people aren't insane," Ron went on. "They know we're taking other courses. They know there's people like you and me, who've barely had any science, mixed in with people who've spent all their lives in labs. I think the only people they flunk are the people who goof off. I'm putting in a solid hour and a half, two hours a day on this stuff. Besides going to all their lectures and classes. I'm not interested in getting an excellent, all I'm interested in doing is passing. And I think I'm doing about ten times as much as I need to do that. I'll bet when you see the test, you'll see I'm right.

"Boy, do I hope you're right," I said.

The test is on a Thursday. During the weekend and early part of the week, I've done virtually nothing else but biochemistry. Wednesday, I stay up till three A.M., drinking tea and honey, closing my eyes and in the jangled darkness trying to whip processions of facts across my consciousness. At six-thirty, I get up for an hour's refresher dose of diagrams and graphs, and in the amphitheater I give a last look at my scribblings, but they suddenly seem to be alien hieroglyphics. That scares me; I take a Tums, and put them away. Farrell, tall and thin in that white coat, comes in and distributes the tests.

"Christ! I don't know any of this!" is my first reaction. Then I calm down and start writing. A couple pages of detailed short-answer questions, some calculations, then two longer questions—one on saturation curve shifts of hemoglobin, the other on the kinetics of enzyme catalysis. Not so bad. I keep writing till the bitter end, just to be safe.

Walking out of the amphitheater into the sunlight of the quad, I'm exhausted, lightheaded, but relieved. It'd been a little easier than I'd anticipated. Other people didn't seem to agree. Cheryl said she wasn't going to think about the test till the grades came back. Ron didn't say anything. I walked down the street to celebrate with an ice cream cone. The next battery of tests was in less than four weeks, all the courses together. I wasn't going to be able to put in this kind of effort for each of them simultaneously. And I was behind as it was. But later for that stuff. Now for a maple-walnut double with jimmies.

The following week, the tests came back. I'd gotten all the short answers right, lost my points on the long questions, though no one had bothered to make any notes on my paper as to why. I discovered later that the graduate students who graded the tests worked, in effect, with a list of fifteen or so facts that you were supposed to have regurgitated in toto—if you mentioned only ten, then two-thirds credit. No room for ingenuity or analysis.

Since letter grades were technically forbidden under the pass-fail system, most course directors marked papers with numerical grades, then posted a big chart giving elaborate statistical data on the distribution of those grades in the class. All of which had the same effect as if they graded and ranked you. So after each exam, there tended to be a jostling crowd around the bulletin board where "the curve" was tacked up. But despite the helpful efforts of the faculty, only a few zealots worked out their exact positions. For almost everybody the big question came down to: was I above the median or below? In the top half of the class or the bottom?

I learned later, to my surprise, that my seventy-seven on the test was well above the median for both the science and non-science majors in the course. But more important, there was some breathing room between me and the passing grade of sixty. I asked Cheryl, who was taking an even heavier course load than I was, how it had turned out.

"Just barely," she said, making a motion to wipe her brow. "But that's all I wanted."

Ron came up, staring at his paper in disbelief. "They flunked me," he said.

But why is it, in this developing atmosphere of grade fear, with the vanishingly small time I have at my disposal, that I can't keep my mind from straying into distracting questions of what biochemistry is all about anyhow? There seem to be assumptions underlying the whole discipline of which I'm entirely ignorant, most deriving from a branch of physics called thermodynamics, which is the study of heat, and more specifically, a concept which relates to the way heat flows, called "entropy," or disorder. So while I dutifully memorize everything that's placed in front of me, I also begin trying to read up a little on this entropy business and related matters—

if no one will explain them, perhaps I can learn about them on my own. This project, or private alternative curriculum, continues long past the end of the course, through the following semester, into the summer beyond, and never really finishes. And what little I do discover astonishes me: there seems to be emerging a unified scientific model for the nature of life, a phenomenon which has hitherto resisted all efforts at rigorous analysis. A revolution in science was taking place all around us, and no one ever bothered to mention it. It was as if I were studying physics in the twenties and was never told of relativity or quantum mechanics.

If you were strolling by Central Park Lake, and suddenly some of the water formed itself into a long tube, jumped out on the bank, and started chasing you, chances are you'd be a little surprised. If the self-assembled water tube continued to pursue you through the crowds on the Mall, down Broadway all the way to Times Square, caught you at a broken subway turnstile and proceeded to munch on your leg, using as teeth pieces of broken beer bottles it had picked up en route, you'd probably be even more surprised—such events don't seem to happen very often, even in New York. If someone proved to you that there was enough energy from the sun in those molecules of water to do all that and more, you'd still be a bit amazed that the event occurred—not very likely, you'd say.

It turns out that science doesn't have much more to say about that kind of event than you or I do—except science likes numbers and can quantify the kind of improbability that only surprises the rest of us. And science likes technical names for the things it quantifies, so it called disorganization by the term "entropy" (from the Greek, meaning "turning") and discovered a law that is rather obvious, at least to big-city dwellers, that things tend to get more disorganized as time goes on. Entropy increases. Mountains, skyscrapers, billboards tend to fall apart after a while. Smoke drifts away, bicycles wear out, fires burn themselves cold. Parts of Central Park Lake don't spontaneously organize themselves into tubes and chase people across Columbus Circle. In fact, everything around us appears to be following a progress toward structurelessness, and we gauge the rate of that progress by twisting up pieces of flexible metal and letting these structures untwist slowly, so they push on the arms of clocks and watches. It's the relentless increase of entropy that creates the unidirectional flow of time.

The only problem is that one very, very tiny part of the universe—negligible by any standard of mass, size, energy, or influence on other objects—does appear to be departing from that universal trend toward disorder. Instead of growing more disorganized, it has become more and more orderly at the expense of its surroundings, until now it boasts the most complex objects in the known universe. Scientists are always interested in exceptions, no matter how minuscule, and this localized, upstream flux of increasing organization does touch on some personal concerns as well. This minute *negentropy* rebellion against the universe is life.

You and I would be inclined to dismiss the question: given enough time (say the age of the universe) and enough matter (say all the particles of the universe), accidents are bound to happen—baboons typewrite *King Lear*, water-tubes jump out of Central Park Lake, cells self-assemble in some ancient ocean, and here we are. But scientists like numbers. So they examined a typical, simple bacterial cell to see what the probability was of its components getting together by accident. The probability wasn't very big—it would take the lifetimes of a billion universes just to get one bacterial cell to assemble itself by chance. Well, this put the statisticians of entropy in the position of the apocryphal French aerodynamic engineers who proved beyond a shadow of a doubt that the bumblebee couldn't fly.

So in the 1940s a number of physicists who had helped overthrow classical Newtonian mechanics deserted to biochemistry, convinced that there must be some unknown but fundamentally special force at work in the processes of living things. The first conceptual step they made was a fairly simple one. If you take a container of air, it's very unlikely that left by itself most of the air will end up on one side of the box. But if you place the container between something hot and something cold, the gas on the hot side expands and pushes over toward the cold side, so you end up with most of the air over on the cool side—a simple, structured situation that wouldn't have happened without the heat flow. Thus events which are very improbable at equilibrium become quite probable when energy is allowed to flow through. That "thought experiment" became the standard model for a whole new branch of thermodynamics, called "nonequilibrium" or "steady state." The sun is the heat source, outer space is the heat sink, and the surface of the earth is what gets organized as the heat flows from one to the other.

In 1953, a graduate student named Stanley Miller took the logical next step. In a container, he put some salt water and the postulated components of the earth's primeval atmosphere—methane, ammonia, water, carbon dioxide, carbon monoxide, and hydrogen sulfide—then heated the container and passed electricity through it for a week. To everyone's astonishment, when he ran an assay on what he'd cooked up, a large array of the building blocks of life, such as amino acids, had been synthesized. It began to look as if the formation of basic organic compounds, at least, wasn't a once-in-a-billion-universes affair, but a quite normal event when the right materials are around and an energy flow is available to help structure things.

Three and a half billion years ago, by most theories, conditions on earth bore a certain resemblance to that container. There was a constant blast of highly energetic ultraviolet light from the sun, and the oceans became, in effect, a dilute "hot broth" of organic molecules. Those molecules predominated which had the most stable bonds. Carbon, an element which is extremely versatile and promiscuous in its chemical bondings, also has the peculiar property of being able to form long chains of identical subunits. Those types of chains became most populous which could release some of those subunits to go off and lengthen themselves. Other kinds of chains which didn't tend to replicate in this manner gradually comprised a smaller fraction of the molecules in the hot broth. A point was reached when the easily utilized, free raw materials for chain lengthening and replication were used up, so only those molecules continued to proliferate which could rip off molecular spare parts from their brother and sister chains. Defensive and offensive weaponry developed— simple enzymes to yank out needed molecules, and a surrounding wall or membrane, both to give protection from being ripped off and to hold the assembly of offensive weaponry in place. So these molecular accretions of structure were starting to regulate their own environments, to segregate their working parts from the forces of time and disorder.

One problem existed: as these molecular organizations became more complex and specialized, spontaneous self-replication by every component of the entire assemblage became harder and harder to arrange. Certain molecules called nucleic acids were peculiarly efficient at self-replication. Their usefulness as structural elements or catalysts was negligible, but proteins were efficient at those jobs. The molecular organizations which became most numerous were those which achieved a symbiosis, or interdependence of types of molecules—proteins as enzymes and architectural components, nucleic acids (particularly DNA) as specialized replicators. A nucleic acid molecule can replicate itself—but how can it direct the assembly of a complex protein?

The expedient of symbolism was hit upon: use four different kinds of DNA, each representing a "letter," three letters will make up a "word," and this word will symbolize an amino acid, the building block of proteins. Put a particular sequence of triple-letter DNA words together and you've spelled out symbolically a particular protein. So there arose a universal convention of DNA symbols—a biologic language, the genetic code—which took the revolt against entropy, disorder, one step further: the flux of heat from the sun to outer space across the earth's surface was no longer stashed merely as the energy of chemical bonds, it was stored as information.

This storage of sunlight as sequences of symbols permitted

molecular structures to become no longer merely objects, but forms, possessed of an existence independent of the specific materials that composed them at any given moment. A sequoia can be four thousand years old, yet no individual cell in it will be more than three years of age. The organic structure specified by the genetic language remains while materials flow through it.

But superimposed upon the thermodynamic flux which produced aggregations of structure, then storage of information, was a kinetic gradient which propelled these complex, self-replicating, compartmentalized molecular assemblages (cells) into increasing degrees of cooperativity and intimacy in order to survive. Once multicellularity caught on, six or seven hundred million years ago, there was an explosion of life forms, which swiftly went about the task of specializing their constituent parts for the detection of crucial information about the environment—pressure, saltiness, magnetic fields, vibrations, light, dissolved chemicals, velocity of movement, humidity, etc. Effective utilization of this sensory data involved communication systems among the cells of the organism—whose structure as a whole was now the life form—finally allowing the construction of simple models or functional images of selected aspects of the environment. Memory carried the revolt against entropy and time another step further by permitting the organism to refine its evaluation of the current state of the environment by comparing it to symbolic information about the past, about entropic states which no longer existed. Finally, a particularly effective architectural system of nerve cells evolved which, when wired together, battery upon battery, permitted the organism to create complex predictive models of the surroundings, construct images not only of the present and the past, but the future as well. This most recent product of the steady-state flux of sunlight across the earth to outer space is the human brain and the symbol-based society it created. With its hundred trillion synapses, the human brain offers the highest density of order and information, or negentropy, of any object in the known universe.

From the cyanide molecule which formed the building block of amino acids to the human frontal cortex in three and a half billion years, evolution is the most complicated, extended chemical reaction known. But to what might seem to be largely a "local question," the astrophysicists added their own cosmic perspective. Carbon, the essential element of life, was created from the fusion of helium nuclei in the cores of immense primeval stars. When those stars exploded as supernovas, the carbon atoms and other heavy elements necessary for life were seeded out into the thin interstellar gas. As typical "second generation stars" like the sun collapsed into existence out of that gas, the nascent radiation blew carbon and the rare heavier elements into a concentrated ring a few light-minutes out. From that ring, the earth was formed; its thin, tenuous biosphere is literally a web of ancient stardust.

So the essential metals of the human body—potassium, sodium, magnesium, cobalt, zinc, copper, which exist in barely calculable quantities in the universe at large but whose delicate balances determine whether we live or die, controlling even our emotions, aspirations, flights of fancy and sorrows—were forged in the hearts of collapsing stars and exploded out as supernovas before being concentrated by a flux of sunlight into our blood.

An unheralded revolution seemed to have taken place in how scientists regarded living things. Biological creatures weren't the lonely products of some supreme accident, the absurd denizens of a rock moving through a trackless void, poor items of awareness imprisoned in a clock that's running down, at best poltergeists that can shriek, weep, bang, and issue cries of meaningless doom and alarm. No, the galaxy was an immense broth of stars, orbited by isolated pinpricks of thermodynamic eddies, oases of growing structure and organization, which were resisting the great flux of time toward disorder and stasis. Biological systems were not random fluctuations in an equilibrium assemblage, but inevitable corpuscles of sentience, floating iridescent and defiant in a waste of hydrogen.

So what I was so diligently studying, like a half-literate medieval scribe copying out the New Testament, barely reading or understanding it, did have scope, grandeur, even a terrifying beauty. And the biochemical analysis was extremely thorough going, incorporating thermal physics, statistical mechanics, information theory, and organic chemistry into a single conception that saw living things as localized turbulences at the interface of probabilities, whorls and upstream eddies in an entropic torrent, portable envelopes of semiliquid negentropy that spontaneously developed pattern-recognition and image-formation capacities in their efforts to survive the effects of time.

Much of this was in the standard texts, but Harvard biochemistry scrupulously avoided references to those topics and kept us busy with the details of one synthetic pathway after another. If we had to learn "useless things," couldn't they at least be concepts which awakened our awareness of the natural world?

I knew the letter of biochemistry. But had I understood the spirit? Since it was a rare lecture that mentioned anything but the isozymes of rabbit muscle aldolase, I was on my own.

Chapter 6

Jailhouse Rock

An animal experiment in physiology on the circulatory system. Our team of four students reports to a lab, and there, splayed out on their backs with their limbs clamped to metal tables, are four dogs. Ours is a black mongrel that seems to be part Labrador retriever. She'd gotten a dose of morphine and anesthetic earlier, so she's asleep already—a nod to our sensibilities; we'll never have to observe the dog awake and possessed of a personality. Part of her abdomen is shaved, so there's a lot of rosy flesh to be seen, moving rhythmically up and down as she breathes.

Ron inserts a rectal thermometer, sets up a heating lamp to keep her warm. We do some tests for depth of anesthesia, then set up the ECG leads. She's already dribbling some smelly urine down the drain in the table into a bucket. Ready to go.

Someone uses a forceps to tent up the skin of her hot abdomen; with a scissors, I slit out an elliptical opening, nudge deeper into the thin muscular layers, find the femoral vein, succeed in tying it off after a couple tries, then make an angled snip halfway through it. Blood's all over the place, on our fingers, rivulets on the abdomen, then stops. I insert a plastic tube into the vein, with a clotted string manage to tie it in place and hook it up to some saline solution.

Our machine operator points to our dog's chest. "Respiration's up." It does seem to be rising and falling more quickly.

"Stress," says the lab instructor, a young experimental physiologist with a beard. "That's usually what happens." Back to me. We're going after the femoral artery now.

I root around with my blunt dissector, finally free it up. You can see the pulses of the heartbeat going through its walls as tiny waves. I put a clamp on one end, tie a string around the other, then make an angled incision.

Blood bursts out, hits me in the eye, runs down my face into my mouth. Clamp's not tight enough. I wipe the blood off, try again.

The dog wakes up. First there's a general stirring of limbs. Then she twists her head around and looks at me. Our eyes meet. Then she starts howling. The hubbub in the room collapses to aghast silence, everyone is frozen in movement, and the howling continues, horribly loud in that sudden emptiness.

I'm trying to hold on to the clamp on the artery, blood is filling up the wound, everything's gone slippery, one back leg has come loose from its moorings and is thrashing about. Ron and someone else grab it and hold it down.

One of the physiology lecturers comes charging into the room with a syringe, jabs it into the tube to the vein. A pause, the struggling lessens, the howling becomes a mournful whimpering, and dies out. I get a better grip on the clamp and the blood flow stops. The room is only slowly returning to its former noise level.

"Why'd she wake up?" someone in our team asks the lecturer.

"It didn't wake up," he says. "That's a reflex."

"A reflex?"

"Yes. Don't worry about it. She wasn't feeling any pain."

"Why was she howling and struggling?"

"It's a reflex. There's no awareness. There's no consciousness. It happens in surgery. Afterwards, people don't remember a thing."

We look at each other. We'd like to believe it.

"Just keep the anesthesia a little heavier." The lecturer

walks off, we mop up, I get the clamp tighter and manage to get a tube in the artery and tie things off.

Since the experiment lasts six hours, we go out in the hall to take a break. I can't bring myself to eat the sandwich I'd brought in a brown paper bag. There's the familiar childhood odor of wet dog all over me. I stand there in silence listening to the conversation.

Back inside, we run some controls on the machines, start taking measurements, moving a pressure gauge up and down the aorta.

The dog wakes up again. A few restless whines, then up comes the head, trying to see its own belly; again dazed surprise in its eyes, and a long, piercing, heartsick howl that seems to ache through all the rooms and halls.

"What the fuck is going on over there?" another table says.

The dog begins to try feebly to bite at my hand.

The lecturer barrels in and jabs the syringe again. "Remember to watch that level," he says to our instructor as the dog falls back.

"This mutt just doesn't want to stay asleep," says our instructor. "It's had three times the anesthetic that every other pooch here has had."

Our dog is still feebly moving, so we wait. And while we do, another across the way starts yelping. The lecturer, syringe on high, goes over, and things calm down there too. I can see why the other teams had started getting angry with us. That raw, animal sound of pain seems to burn its way into your soul.

"Is there anything we can do to keep her from waking up again?" someone from our team says as the lecturer walks by.

He stops. "It didn't wake up, it wasn't conscious. That was just a reflex. It happens a lot."

"It'd be hard to convince somebody who didn't know anything about physiology that she wasn't conscious."

"Yes, and do you know that we can't even publish pictures of our research in scientific journals because someone might think we're being cruel? Here are experiments that may save people's lives, and we can't even demonstrate our experimental protocols to other researchers in the field. Do people want another human to die a death of incredible, prolonged agony, instead of sacrificing a white rat humanely to find out how to prevent that death?"

"Is there any animal research technique you wouldn't use?" someone asks.

"There's a perfectly lovely golden retriever in the other room I really wanted to save. He had such big brown eyes and such a cold little nose. But I wasn't able to. Meanwhile, you guys better get back to work, or you won't be finished till midnight."

Two hours and one more howling incident later, we'd completed all the basic experiments.

"You want to see what's inside?" asked the instructor, and everyone nodded.

Out came a saw, and with a soft, then grinding sound he tore away at the breastbone. Some tugging, a crack, and both sides of the rib cage had fallen away. There were the lungs, orange somehow, tiny, inflating in and out with the pressure of the pump. Some careful tearing of skin and tissue, and there was the heart, small, pinkish red, now going at incredible nervous speed, almost vibrating rather than pumping. Evidently from all over its body, messages were flying in— Danger! death is near!

"Feel it," said the instructor. "Try and squeeze it and feel how strong it is."

I reached in hesitantly. It was slippery on the outside.

"Squeeze it—go ahead."

Yes, it was solid and hard and strong, much firmer than any muscle of mine. The pressure of my hand alone didn't seem capable of stopping its beat.

"OK, now watch this." He took out two electrodes and shocked the heart. It fluttered madly about in its soft cage for a moment, then resumed its vibrating.

"You see that?"

We all nodded.

"Just a short jolt, and the heart can go back to its normal

beat. OK, *now* see what happens." He gave a prolonged burst. Wild flailing about, then the heart resumed vibrating.

"Boy, this pooch. She doesn't want to kick the bucket."

The next time, he held on for twenty or thirty seconds. When he removed the electrodes, there were a few unsynchronized pulses, then stillness. The dog was inert now.

At Vanderbilt there was a sign: "Dog Tired? Come to the Dog Days Happy Hour in the Commons Room! Drinks 75¢." The weekly happy hour had been steadily growing in popularity with the class—you started drinking immediately after lab Friday afternoon, with Harvard subsidizing the booze. This Dog Days Happy Hour seemed to have drawn a particularly large contingent. People were standing around on oriental carpets or leaning on the grand piano, laughing and joking. Later, I talked to other people about the experiment.

"Once we got going, I didn't think anything about the dog," said one fellow. "I just got wrapped up in the physiology. It really showed us how things work in there."

A woman I knew was more emphatic. "I thought it was beautiful. Actually reaching in and feeling the heart—it was so strong. I'd much rather do that than read and go to lectures." A subsequent class poll identified the dog lab as the most popular single event in the physiology course.

That wasn't my reaction. I went upstairs, threw my clothes in the laundry bag, took a shower. But nothing could seem to get that doggy smell out of my nostrils. It was dinner time, I hadn't had lunch, but it seemed impossible to eat. I'd play some rock on my clock radio, then start memorizing some circulatory and renal equations. But I sat down on my bed in my underpants and thought for a while in silence. You came to medical school to learn how to heal people, save them pain and maybe even their lives, I said finally, half out loud. And it sure doesn't seem likely there's ever going to be a place where you'll have to explain things. But if you do wake up somewhere years from now and much to your amazement they want explanations for why you tortured and killed a dog today, you better get your story all good and rehearsed, because you'll have a lot of explaining to do.

I'm allowed little time to squander on such mawkish reflections. In the twinkling of an eye, it's midterm week, four exams in jackhammer succession. Two A.M., and I'm sitting at my desk, surrounded by notes, handouts, books. Out the dorm window, I can see others pacing up and down their rooms, holding index cards, or bent over papers with fluorescent light silvering their faces. Twelve hours of nonstop efforts to commit stray facts to memory, and my mind is beginning to wander sleepily. I put my feet up on my desk and lean back in the chair.

It's been more than a month, and we still haven't heard from Chanesohn and Stone about the results of all that inventorying of class lists that was supposed to take place preparatory to moving Saturday classes to a weekday.

Last week, Ron, Michelle, and I had run into each other between lectures.

"What do you say we call them up and find out how things are going?" I asked.

"I have good feelings about that meeting," said Ron. "It's really good to know that someone as sensitive as Chanesohn is second is command at Harvard."

"So I'm sure there'll be no problem if we wander over there sometime and find out how all that polling of professors and so forth is coming along."

Ron held up a palm. "They said they're working on it."

"You mean we shouldn't even ask how it's going?"

A serious, responsible expression had filled Ron's bearded face. "I think we impressed them that we're reasonable. If we sacrifice that, we might lose everything."

"How about if they don't contact us at the end of the next week, we call them?"

Ron and Michelle looked at me, then each other, half-amused, half-exasperated.

"OK," I'd said.

I rub my neck and gaze at all the texts that line the shelves above me. Among the obvious lessons of the early weeks had been the discovery that those lecture handouts were not enough, unless you'd taken the course already. I'd bought only the books recommended by each course director and later tallied up the cost—two hundred and seventy dollars for one semester alone. How was I going to buy clothing, linens, paper, pens . . . ? Was I going to have to try for seventy-five cents a meal? One problem at a time. Something should be done about following up on that Saturday-class business. But what? Ron was so passionately devoted to the idea that the people up top are slaving away night and day for us that he'd never go for another meeting. And Michelle is so convinced that those deans are dangerous folk, all ready to do us in, that she'd support Ron.

I sighed. If this was what was involved in moving a class from one day to another, what kind of obstacles must be faced by people trying to do something about those round-the-clock shifts on the wards? How about Robin? Robin might go for a meeting, but I'd have to supply the initiative, the energy. And did I have any of that myself?

I glanced up at that two-hundred-and-seventy-dollar row of books, all staring at me, multicolored and intimidating. Then I looked out at the windows of the Vanderbilt court where my classmates paced with their flash cards. My eyes felt sandy and the lids were starting to droop.

"You win," I said, lurched up, grabbed a book, and started pacing back and forth myself.

We never heard another word from Chanesohn or Stone and Saturday classes remained.

Next day, everybody in the class suddenly seems to be whirring with fear. Rumor now informs me that physiology flunked twenty-five people last year. *This* is the big one. I'd put twice the effort into neurobiology and biochemistry— megamistake, I'm informed. Well, shit, I'm still sleepy. What with graduate students and dental students and miscellaneous unfortunates, the room is completely packed. I manage to get an aisle seat, but next to me is a Black guy from

Yale, Alex Starr. Alex and I are in competition for tallest in the class. So we keep banging knees and elbows trying to get arranged in our seats. I put my spare pencils on the floor. Someone steps on them and breaks all the points. People are muttering equations, like Hail Mary's: renal plasma flow equals concentration in urine of PAH times flow rate over arterial minus venous concentration, resistance is proportional to the reciprocal of the fourth power of the radius . . . Raymond Marcus, a tall, pudgy, black-haired fellow, alleged by many to be in charge of the physiology course, circulates about the amphitheater with an armful of tests. Row after row falls silent.

This mother's a telephone book, I say to myself as I get one. There must be ninety pages! I look at the first question: if someone takes aspirin, where does most of it end up? Then there's a list of all sorts of body fluids. Well, how the hell am I supposed to know that? I leave it blank, go on. More short-answers, a few I know, the rest I leave blank. This is getting serious. What's this? What's the normal concentration of urea in the urine versus plasma? On top of all those equations, we were supposed to memorize normal concentrations for all those blood and urine components—they weren't even in the handouts!

"Motherfucker," says Alex next to me and bangs my knee with his by accident. The room is stone silent. I finish doing the questions I know and start going back, but I don't have enough information even to guess intelligently. I'm going to flunk my first exam here, I say to myself. Why, oh why, didn't I spare some time from neurobiology and let biochemistry slip a little? I go back to the aspirin question. I look at the clock—five minutes to go. Shit, shit, shit.

"Marcus's a motherfucker," I hear Alex mutter again. At least maybe I'm not alone. Or am I? I start slashing through, putting down any answer that comes to mind. One minute to go, back to the aspirin, that's one fifth of the test, and I'm drawing an utter blank. I dash down a bunch of guesses—if there's a trick, I sure won't have time to see it.

Marcus is trying to pick up the tests, people aren't letting go, attempting to scribble down one last answer. He comes to me, I break in mid-sentence and give it to him. Who cares? I failed anyway.

In stunned silence we hear the histology people tell us about the lungs, then go to lab. In the hall, one guy keeps saying, "Let's cut this shit! Go and get drunk right now!" But his friends barely listen, keep walking automatically. Jesus Christ, I think, this place isn't for me. I go through the motions of looking through the microscope, but most people aren't even doing that, just commiserating with each other. I shut down early and go back to the dorm and start vacuuming. Get rid of reminders of the past. I make lunch for myself on a door that I use as a counter, then drag myself over to neuroanatomy, the next installment of the neurosciences series.

It's taught by a husband/wife team. The husband, Hansen Bates, is supposed to be famous in the field of neuron electronmicroscopy; he's in his fifties, conservatively attired, cultured, pleasant, but somehow a little vague. His lectures are delivered slowly, with many pauses for breaths, sighs, extraneous recollections. It seems as if we have only half his attention. His wife, Elizabeth Ching, is in her thirties, beautiful, wears T-shirts with pictures of the cerebral cortex and messages that say, "Ask me—I'm the Brain!" She's a frantic bundle of energy.

The class isn't ready for either of them. First, Liz Ching gets up, charges back and forth madly along the lab bench, telling us that neuroanatomy is the toughest part of anatomy, and we have only six weeks to learn it, but we'll do it somehow. Everyone groans inside. On she goes, lecturing up a storm.

Why didn't I go to California? I say to myself. Pure stupidity.

"And you're going to work your heads off," she finishes. "You're at Harvard now."

Everyone hisses.

Hansen Bates walks slowly to the podium, takes five

minutes or so to arrange his notes, then puts a slide of the brain on the screen. It looks like a bowl of uncut macaroni. Bates isn't helping things any.

"Moving posteriorly along the sylvian fissure, we encounter the supramarginal gyrus which comprises a significant portion of Brodmann area 40. While posterior to the supramarginal gyrus . . ."

Biochemistry and histology tests coming up, and I got to memorize this incredible tangle of bumps, loops, niches, estuaries, chasms, and humps? He's just spent more than an hour on that slide alone, and I can't remember a single squiggle.

Someone raises a hand. "Are we going to have coffee and cookies?" Genslip had always arranged for a coffee break at midpoint in the long haul from one-thirty to four-thirty.

Bates shakes his head. "I'm sorry, that can't be arranged."

Hisses and howls of fury fill the amphitheater: "Assholes— what do they mean, no cookies? How do they expect us to sit through three hours straight? I'm boycotting this course!"

Observing the class's somewhat less than tractable mood, Bates has the sense to cut the lecture short and let us go home early.

Thirty or forty years ago, some sociologist or another came up with the idea that in the melting pot of American society, it was extremes of stress—pain, grief, and the like—that tended to unmask latent ethnic behavior. Well, who was to say that in this moment of crisis the WASPs weren't reverting to a tight-lipped, emotionless reserve, or that the Jews weren't alternating between brilliant volubility and morbid depression, or that the Chinese weren't excelling everybody but at the cost of working themselves around the clock to utter exhaustion?

That might all be so or not, but the Irish had decided that enough was enough. Yes, the small contingent of boys from Fordham and Xavier and St. John's were fed up. This whole question called for something more than mere studying—it required some serious drinking.

So, on the spot, they formed a society dedicated to that express purpose. Now, there already was a surfeit of rather elegant societies at Harvard—Cabot, Peabody, etc.—named after various prominent or wealthy physicians, mostly dead. Rumor, no doubt malicious, had it that these organizations were enclaves of the hereditary Harvard element, and that their members spent most of their time sitting about in deep armchairs, wearing old school ties, sipping sherry, considering weighty thoughts, and pointing out to each other articles in *The Wall Street Journal*.

The Irish dubbed their new group "The Walter B. Cannon Society for Social Deviation," after the imposing figure who inhabited the deathless portrait that greeted incoming classes in Amphitheater C. As a professor at Harvard around the First World War, Cannon had developed the theory of a pre-programmed response of the organism to danger—increased heart rate, more blood flow to the muscles, less activity of the digestive tract—and called that constellation of physiological effects "fight or flight."

The Irish then proceeded to elect as their president a Pole, Kosciusko Rostopovski, a short, corpulent Harvardian with an enormous handlebar mustache, nicknamed Devo, since punk rock blasted continuously from his dorm room. Devo's specialty was wearing women's sunglasses to lab and leaving tests half an hour early yelling, "Beer!"

And so, smack in the middle of midterm week, the Walter B. Cannon Society for Social Deviation was pleased to announce that a costume party would be held that night in the Vanderbilt dining room, entitled the Cannon Ball. To everyone's gratification, Harvard was more than happy to supply the beer.

Attracted by the promise of free booze and pretzels, half the class showed up, most dressed as Arabs since that only took a sheet and a belt around the head. But, among others, Alex Starr went to greater pains, dolling himself up in a tight sequined dress, Veronica Lake shoes, pancake makeup, blue eyeshadow, and copious mascara, contriving to prance about like a six-foot-four queen of 42nd Street. Unable to think of anything better, I put on my mountaineering knickers, helmet, and glacier goggles.

Apparently cognizant of class discontent, the whole physiology department turned out in full regalia, including Marcus dressed as a samurai. Later a rumor raged about the class that little Byron Vitellino, the biophysicist from MIT who arrived in a muscle shirt, motorcycle jacket, and ducktail, had pulled a knife on Marcus, indicating in no uncertain terms what would happen to him if we got a final like the midterm we had just taken. So what? Marcus could've defended himself, was the general reaction. He had a sword, didn't he?

By two A.M. most of the faculty had departed, judging the ambience to be a trifle coarse and the hour a bit late. So it was just the hard core left to swill and dance. Devo, pacing about in rimless spectacles and a long, gray lab jacket to impersonate Cannon, held a bottle of beer like a dispenser of holy water, baptizing the mob with a solemn expression. A cowboy on roller skates was doing the Lindy with Alex, whose mascara was starting to run down his face in sweaty rivulets. Climbing hardware flinging about, I was engaged in an uncoordinated facsimile of the funky chicken with an amoeboid creature of indeterminate sex that kept banging its pseudopods into my knees. Careening around the periphery of the strobe-lit dance area were some Jewish Bedouins, specters on a carousel gone mad.

Some reveler kicked out the plug by accident, the music ground to a soggy halt, and we all stood there, orphaned in the sudden silence and darkness. After some curses, amplified pops and scratching, a hundred and twenty decibels of rock roared back. And it was the King!

Went to a party at the county jail!

And suddenly, by one accord, the whole Walter B. Cannon Society for Social Deviation was down on the floor, writhing and kicking their feet in the air, under the disapproving gaze of all those nineteenth-century portraits.

Everybody in the old cellblock, dancing to the jailhouse rock!

The crimson curtains and gilt chandeliers whirled, and there I was on the floor too, kicking upward, limbs intertwined, rolling giddily about one part of that topsy-turvy centipede of legs, arms, pseudopods, roller skates, sequined dresses and high heels, all gyrating furiously in the transcendental incandescence of the strobe.

Then it was ten the next morning, light streaming in my window, my alarm sounding disconsolately away. Still in my climbing knickers, I was sprawled half-across my bed, my glacier glasses twisted around my nose, nearly strangled on a Prusik, with a headache seeming to screech echoes and reverberations from one side of my helmet to the other. I got up, tottered about, then sat back down again and put my head in my hands.

Chapter 7

In the Trenches

Let us leave the mysteries of the iodoacetate inhibition of phosphoglyceraldehyde dehydrogenase, the intricacies of the ten synthetic steps leading to pre-squalene pyrophosphate. Travel with me, if you will, two hundred miles from the Roman temples of Harvard Medical School, with their coats of arms, the oak leaves dimidiated upon an eagle rampant. We are in the warehouse district of the lower west side of Manhattan, on the outskirts of the Village. From the streets comes an incessant roar of trucks, but one building in the midst of all this commercial din does not seem to be a warehouse. It has bars on all the windows. It is the Lower Manhattan Rehabilitation Center, a residence for a hundred and fifty or so retarded people who have been relocated from Willowbrook, a colossal, scandal-ridden institution in Staten Island. A "community facility," it is designed to "return the developmentally disabled to the mainstream of life."

Four P.M., and I am sitting in the fluorescent glare of my small, social-work assistant's office on the second floor. The cinderblock walls are covered with pictures I've clipped out of magazines, of waterfalls, trees, snowbanks, mountains. I push some forms aside. The sheltered workshops let out half an hour ago, and most of my people should have made their way back home by now. I walk down the dark hall and take the elevator upstairs.

As usual, the elevator stops at the wrong floor. It is a blackened shell, a strong odor of damp smoke still pervading the halls. Some time ago, a young man, José, had been transferred to our facility from Manhattan State, a public mental institution on Ward's Island in the East River. There had been some interfacility dispute as to whether José was primarily retarded or disturbed. The State Department of Mental Hygiene in such cases invariably chooses retardation as the primary diagnosis, since conditions in mental hospitals are somewhat less idyllic than ours. José, however, didn't want to live with "no stupid lowgrades."

So at ten A.M. every day for a month and a half, I could set my watch by an enormous bang outside my office, as José shook himself free from the aides in charge of him, threw open the door to the administrator's office and demanded to be able to return to Manhattan State. Some attempted calming talk about how there were many procedures to be followed, forms to be completed, approvals to be obtained, joint conferences to be scheduled, evaluations to be made . . . more yelling, and finally José would be dragged kicking and flailing and shrieking back to his classroom. All things considered, José was relatively patient—he gave the administration six weeks to rectify matters by conventional methods. Then, when no action seemed to be forthcoming, he burned down the sixth floor. The next day, the red tape was miraculously cut away and he was transferred back to Manhattan State.

The elevator rises to the seventh floor where the higher functioning residents live. The floor is divided into two areas, termed "apartments"—one locked, housing the most violent retardates, the other a largely open unit for the better behaved. The bedrooms are alcoves, with four beds each and assorted lockers for personal gear. A few of the lockers are lassoed with an intimidating assortment of chains, combination locks, key locks, twisted coat hangers, and miscellaneous contraptions suitable for repelling the James Gang. These precautions are well advised since virtually every article of value belonging to a retarded resident, from clothes to toiletries to portable radios, is immediately stolen by staff members as soon as the resident obtains it.

The elevator doors open, there is an enormous hullabaloo of rock and roll, a television blasting soap opera, people yelling for no reason at all other than that it feels good to yell hour after hour in the absence of anything else to do. Fourteen residents descend on me, arms outstretched, ready to hug. They do this to anyone who gets off the elevator. Instead, I shake hands formally all around, saying their names, insisting that they say mine in return. At the last one, something gooey. Sure enough, feces that someone had forgotten to wipe off. We both go into the bathroom to wash. Another resident is standing over a toilet bowl flushing it again and again, yelling incomprehensibly to himself. He'll do that all afternoon till called away to dinner. On the way to the open living unit, I pass a stairwell; there's the smell of dope where some aides are congregated. On the whole, the effects of that seem preferable to those of Ripple and Thunderbird, the other drugs of choice, since alcohol tends to create more violent incidents.

The professional staff are all downstairs in a meeting. Professional staff are in meetings four days a week, from one-thirty till four-thirty. The state has decided that all is not as it should be in facilities such as Lower Manhattan Rehab. To correct this problem, it has devised a thirty-three page form which must be filled out on every resident every twelve weeks. In addition, there are a host of satellite forms in which each professional is to keep an hour-by-hour log of his activities for each client. Then there are control forms, and forms to control the control forms . . . Since the volume of paper work is so enormous, psychologists and teachers and speech therapists are pulled off their regular duties and made "case managers," a role which involves essentially nothing but form completion.

At the door to the open living unit is a young man with blond hair. Though he is sitting there endlessly rocking back and forth, he is not retarded. He came from a broken home and suffered such severe emotional disturbance in childhood that he was institutionalized before he even had a chance to start school. It wasn't until he was a teenager that testing revealed his normal intelligence. By then, he had been left unattended for so long in giant wards on Staten Island that he began staring at the sun. Now he is blind.

Or watch as Butch, the six-foot-three, two-hundred-pound resident swaggers down the hall—hordes of smaller residents scatter fearfully at his approach. Nothing out of the ordinary. Hierarchies of force are endemic to Lower Manhattan Rehab. The aides, rather than buck the system, use it. A resident acts ornery, won't take his pills, won't go to dinner—why stand there cajoling or arguing when a step or two takes you to Butch's room? Butch is more than happy to oblige, knowing that you will return the favor eventually. He stalks into the recalcitrant resident's room. That is all that is usually needed—an actual blow would indicate that Butch's reputation was on the wane.

I take out my key and go into the locked ward. It's perpetually dim, with some sooty sunlight filtering in past the barred windows. In one of the alcoves is Enrique, a tall, strong, heavily built man of twenty, Puerto Rican, with a straggly three-day's growth of beard, and mussed-up black hair. Headphones are clamped tightly on his head while Joe Bataan blares from a record player. Another resident, Albert Jones, the owner of the phonograph, is capering madly about the room vaguely in time to the music. Enrique looks at me, then looks away, keeping the headphones on.

"Why don't you take those off, Enrique?" I say loudly.

"What you say?" Instead of its usual low, gravelly tone, his voice is high and squeaky.

"OK," I say, and start to leave.

He takes them off. "Why'd you want to see me, Chas Debaris?" Enrique has trouble with my name; it wavers in a spectrum between Lavoris and Debareass.

"I want to have a talk with you, Enrique. Where there's quiet. Why don't we go down to my office?"

"Nossir, Chas Debaris, I'm not going down to your office. Nossir." He starts to put the headphones back on.

"Why not?"

"Nossir, Chas Debaris. I'm busy."

"OK. Then I want to see you in my office at nine tomorrow morning." I start leaving again.

"Wait, Chas Debaris." Enrique puts the headphones down and gets up. "What do you want to talk to me about?"

"We can talk about it in my office tomorrow."

"Why can't you tell me now?"

"I can. But I want to go to my office where it's quiet and you and I can talk in private."

"OK, Chas Debaris." And we go off downstairs together out of the racket and crowds of the wards. Enrique is walking bent slightly to one side.

"Ribs hurt?"

"Yeah. Side hurt me all last night. Couldn't sleep. Staff member."

Enrique's parents were drug addicts whose whereabouts were now unknown. At age two, he'd been hospitalized for multiple contusions about the head and body; he was released a couple of weeks later in the care of his parents. When he came back to the emergency room with burns on his legs, he was placed in a foster home, temporarily. An aunt claimed him; he showed up again in the emergency room six months later, this time for malnutrition. He went through a succession of foster homes. At age five, moderate retardation was diagnosed, and he was taken out of the foster home and placed in Willowbrook. And there, one of hundreds in vast warehouse-like wards, he grew up. Episodic violence was a familiar pattern among the institutionalized retarded. At best, it produced some spoken words and food; at worst, even a blow was better than total neglect.

A couple of days before, Enrique had left his own record player unattended for a moment or two. He'd returned to find it smashed. For six months, he'd saved his sheltered-work-shop earnings of twelve dollars a week to buy that phono-graph. He had come shrieking and crying into my office; I'd managed to talk him down. We would use his next paycheck to help repair it. But the next day at workshop, there'd been some bookkeeping foul-up, and his check would be a week late. Enrique had overturned a workbench, shattered a glass window, and rushed into the street.

Sometime later, as I was sitting in my office, there was a crash, wood splintering, and screams. It was Enrique. He'd invaded the secretarial area, picked up an IBM Selectric, and hurled it through a partition. Two secretaries were hurrying off down the hall, one was hiding behind her desk. Enrique threw over a file bin, and hurled a metal in/out stand at a running speech therapist. All along the corridor, administrators' doors slammed shut. This kind of event was not unfamiliar. They would call security; in ten or fifteen minutes or so, the institutional police would stroll up one flight, the place would be in wreckage, perhaps someone hurt. A month ago, a twenty-two-year-old man, who'd killed someone at a previous institution, had demolished the classroom that was next to my office, sending two other residents and three staff members to the hospital. Incidents of this sort were so common it required weekly meetings of an "Incident Review Committee" to keep up with the steady flow of lacerations, broken limbs, scrapes, cuts, sprained backs, etc.

Enrique had picked up another Selectric. I waited till his back was to me, then slipped in behind him with a full nelson. It was a good hold, since unlike the choke (which was preferred by most staff), it didn't have to be painful or do damage. The Selectric crashed to the floor.

"Cool, Enrique, quiet," I said in a low voice behind his ear. One of the principles that I'd evolved in dealing with violence was that the method by which it was subdued was as important as the fact that it was subdued. If there was much angry yelling and blows, the resident learned that you were no different than he was. If you were quiet, calm, and used a minimum of force, he remembered that afterwards. But Enrique was too upset to respond immediately. He started kicking about wildly. I sank backwards to the floor, enclosing his legs in a scissor lock that immobilized him. I kept repeating, "Quiet, Enrique, it's all over," in his ear.

"They're fucking with me!" he said breathlessly. "They're fucking with my check! Fucking with my check!"

"I know," I said. "But right now cool, cool. Just quiet. We're going to take a rest right now." Another principle was never offer to solve a grievance, however justified, when someone was being violent—all he learned was that violence solved problems.

"Chas Debaris, they're fucking with my check. How I'm going to fix the record player? Motherfuckers. I'll fuck them up."

"I know," I said. "But we're resting right now. After we're all rested we'll go into my office and have a talk. But right now, just rest."

Administrators' doors were opening timidly now. Enrique was still breathing hard. I just hoped that he had calmed a little before they could get to us.

We weren't in luck. A deputy director, with a doctorate in psychology, arrived with a whole bunch of unfamiliar faces in tow—a state review team down from Albany, the kind of people who had devised our thirty-three-page form, and who reviewed things by finding fault with how completely we filled it out. This noisy episode must have been a disagreeable intrusion. There Enrique and I lay, half under a desk with broken typewriters and strewn files all around us.

"Very excitable young man," said the administrator benignly, indicating Enrique. "You're OK now, aren't you, Enrique?"

"They're fucking with my check."

"Well, your social work assistant, Charley, will take care of that for you right now."

Reward violence on the spot.

Security had now arrived, billy clubs dangling, pistols on the hip.

"You can let him up now, Charley," the deputy director said.

"I know him," I said. "He's still excited. He'll blow as soon as I let him up."

"They're fucking with my check!" said Enrique.

"Cool," I said softly behind his ear. "Cool, cool, cool." I looked up at the administrator. "Give me six, seven minutes, he'll be down." Half that, I thought, if you'll just clear out and stop giving him attention.

"No, I'm sure he's fine now." The deputy director looked

back at the state review team with a reassuring smile. This certainly didn't look good for Lower Manhattan Rehab: the very citadel of the administrative area itself in wreckage, a social work aide twisted up with a retardate in some ungodly looking wrestling hold down on the floor. No, the state review team wasn't pleased at all. They were shaking their heads and talking to one another. The deputy director took my arm. This was an order now. "Let him up now, Charley."

"Cool, Enrique," I said and relaxed my grip. We both got up. I kept one hand on his shoulder, massaging it.

The seventh-floor psychologist arrived.

Enrique swept me off. "You not putting me on punishment!" he screamed and lunged forward.

The state review team fled in terror down the hall. The psychologist was bowled back into a wall. Fists flying, security dove in, a pall-mall rampage as Enrique went down, surged up again, chairs broken, swearing. Finally, a guard got a billy club against Enrique's neck and started to squeeze. Enrique's features contorted, he spluttered uselessly for air, tongue hanging out, face going blue, they keeled him over with a crash, put on a hammerlock so his eyes bulged out in pain.

The administrator was on the phone. "I want a nurse with stelazine down here, right now."

A guard, holding one of Enrique's arms, grinned. "The needle, Enrique. You hear that, the needle!"

A momentary thrashing that failed as the club tightened against his neck.

A Filipino nurse appeared, holding a syringe. Some struggling while Enrique's pants were pulled down, the injection, and everyone breathed a sigh of relief. In ten minutes, Enrique was feeling drowsy. Three aides led him upstairs, swaying and docile.

He was out of commission for two days while they shot him up with heavy drugs. Even now, as we walked into my office, he was a little dull and lethargic. We sat down.

"OK, Enrique. You remember what happened three days ago?"

"They dope me up," he said in that absurd tenor he'd acquired from the billy club choke hold.

"Why did they do that?"

"You putting me on punishment?" He rubbed his side. "They kick me when I upstairs too. Staff members."

"No reason at all?"

"They fuck with my check."

"So that's why they doped you up, they fucked with your check?"

"No."

"Why, then?"

"I don't remember so good."

"Come on, Enrique."

"I threw something. I don't remember. That's what they told me. Albert Jones. He say that."

I sat back and sighed. The usual results: after massive sedation, no one was very clear on what happened before. An injection was easy to arrange; working out plans to help change someone's behavior was almost impossible—that involved the thirty-three-page form, case conferences, all sorts of levels of approval. The net effect was that no consequences ever attended a resident's violence—just some massive medication and everything forgotten afterwards. If I'd been able to hang on to Enrique for five minutes more, if administrators hadn't arrived, I could have brought him down, gotten him in my office, told him exactly what privileges he was losing and why (all in private since I'd have to bypass the forms), made violence and its results immediate and obvious. A few days later, when the connection between throwing typewriters and restrictions had sunk in, I could have straightened out the check and the phonograph problems, leaving it clear that violence had just served to delay things. Now everything was hopelessly muddled; anything I did would just seem arbitrary to Enrique. This time, we'd gotten off lightly, the seventh floor psychologist just had to have some skull x-rays and a few days off for a mild concussion. Sooner or later someone was going to get killed.

"Chas Debaris?"

"Yeah."

"I want to go to workshop. I want to be cool. But they keep bothering me. Motherfuckers. Keep bothering all the time. Break my record player. Steal my clothes. They make me crazy. I get crazy in this place."

"Yeah, I know, Enrique." Were I living on the seventh floor amid the extortion rings and thefts and homosexual rapes, how much stelazine would I need to keep me from throwing typewriters?

"Chas Debaris? Other people get out of Lower Manhattan Rehab. You get other people out. Put them with families. How come I can't go to foster home?"

"Why do you think, Enrique?"

"I throw things."

"That's right."

That was the main barrier now, but it wasn't the only one. Even if Enrique became the Mahatma Gandhi of Lower Manhattan Rehab, there was still another hurdle. Back on Staten Island, a group of research physicians had decided to test some hypotheses concerning serum hepatitis. So they injected a large number of retardates with the virus. Enrique had been among the "subjects" intentionally infected, and now he was a Hepatitis B carrier. Direct contact with blood or secretions (a punch? a kiss?) was required for transmission, but what foster home would accept a hepatitis carrier of Enrique's size, build, and record?

"But Chas Debaris, you got to get me out of this place. It makes me crazy. While they have me doped up, somebody break into my locker, take all my clothes. Staff member. Now I got no winter clothes. They take my baseball glove too. Now I got nothing. You got to get me out of this place." He started sniffling.

I came around my desk with a box of tissues. Enrique began crying in earnest, his shoulders shaking, mucous running down over the mustache that was starting on his lip. I put my hand on his shoulder and rubbed it, then looked down at his battered sneakers. If I managed to get him back into workshop, that's what he'd be wearing through the snow; no coat or sweater, just a couple shirts. What could I say? You'll never get out of Lower Manhattan Rehab, Enrique, they shot you up on purpose with a virus and now you'll never leave?

"You got to be cool, Enrique."

"When I going to live a life, Chas Debaris?" Enrique put his arms around my leg, his head against my thigh. "When I little, they put me in Willowbrook, they hit there. I just sit around, rock all day. Now I here. They steal all my clothes. I got nothing to wear when it's cold. They break my record player so I got no way to listen to my records when I sit around ward all day. When you going to get me out of here, Chas Debaris, so I can live a life?"

I put my hand on his head, tried to straighten the dirty, knotted hair. I looked through the bars of the window at the warehouse across the street. "You just got to be cool, Enrique."

But, you ask, what has this to do with Harvard Medical School? And the answer is nothing. Or more precisely, Harvard Medical School has nothing to do with all this. No, I discovered as I delved deeper and deeper into the complexities of lipoyl transacetylase, scrupulously memorized the location of the acidic carbon in the thiazole ring of thiamine pyrophosphate, prepared myself for regurgitation of the prochirality of the meso form of citrate, that there was no danger of my finding any answers at Harvard to the problems of Lower Manhattan Rehab. No, Harvard did not dabble in that sort of thing—though it was more than happy to make use of the Staten Island hepatitis experiment. The different kinds of hepatitis, I learned later in a virology handout, had been the subject of "controlled human transmission studies." While such studies had been "criticized on ethical grounds" (what these quibbles might be was anyone's guess), such human experiments "have established the basic epidemiological facts," which were then detailed for our memorization.

But even this tangential, intellectual contact between the world I'd left and the world I lived in now was an extremely rare occurrence. Harvard had its circle of private hospitals, its network of research grants. If I wanted something a tad less elegant, the catalogue gave little clue as to how I might obtain that training. And, in fact, in the three years that I was at Lower Manhattan Rehab, we never saw anyone from Harvard, or Columbia, or Cornell—but the list could go on endlessly.

And going to Harvard I began to understand in my guts what I'd always sort of realized in my head without thinking it through too much. This place was to produce generals. And generals might wish to be on Right wing, or fashionably on the Left, but on one issue they were unanimous: generals do not fight in the trenches.

Chapter 8

Citgo or Bust

One morning before physiology lecture, a Black second-year student, Jerry Hearn, stood up before our class. He was slight, almost frail, very dark, and spoke with a New England accent. He'd graduated magna cum laude from Harvard in biochemistry and, like Felipe, leaned with a negligent grace against the lab bench. We all hushed, knowing vaguely what was coming.

"Now you've been hearing a lot about minority admissions since you arrived here," he said. "Probably more than you want to hear—flyers, meetings, things in the student paper. And by now you're probably getting just a little bored with the whole thing."

Yes, that was us, all right. We'd been here almost three months, and by now we were a little world-weary, a little jaded. It'd take more than your average issue to get us involved.

"So you're wondering why there's another guy up here, taking up lecture time, to give us another rap, telling us there's another meeting we should attend, when we'd much rather be home in front of the tube."

A guffaw went through the class, people pointed mock-accusing fingers at each other. Yeah, this guy's OK. He ain't a fanatic like some of them.

Up until 1968, the medical school had admitted an average of three-quarters of a Black student a year. Then, with the assassination of Martin Luther King, about half the student body signed a petition asking that Harvard try to do a little better. A Minority Admissions Subcommittee had been established, and the next year more Blacks and Hispanics began arriving. There was no quota, ninety-three percent of all minority applicants were rejected, a predominantly white Central Admissions Committee made the decision on who actually got in, and, in our class at least, half the Blacks came from Harvard, Princeton, or Yale. Nevertheless, the new medical school administration had decided that the Minority Admissions Subcommittee had to be eliminated. Efforts toward that end had provoked petitions, leaflets, and a mass gathering in the administration building in September. Then the issue had disappeared from view for a month or so.

Suddenly, we learned that during this interval Archibald Cox had been imported from the Law School, and he and Dean Hastings had drawn up a "compromise"—the Minority Admissions Subcommittee would be retained but converted into a pre-screening body. Minority applicants, unlike white applicants, would first be evaluated by the Minorities Subcommittee, ranked, then distributed to the other subcommittees where they'd join the rest of the applicant pool, to be reevaluated and reranked all over again. In effect, minority applicants would be singled out for double screening, and could be rejected at any step. To handle any legal challenges the minority students might offer, Harvard put a private law firm on retainer.

Mobilizing quickly, the minorities hired their own attorney, brought over two other professors from the Law School to dispute Cox's contention that the current minority admissions procedures were illegal, convinced the Central Admissions Committee not to implement the double screening plan, and began an effective campaign of organizing the students against the administration. What Harvard had, no doubt, hoped was going to be a swift, silent rearrangement of admissions procedures seemed on the brink of turning into a major public embarrassment.

To date, the minorities had had uncontested access to the students; somehow the Harvard administration had to counteract the propaganda that was fed almost daily to the medical students against the new admissions proposals. Perhaps a question-and-answer meeting with Dean Hastings? For once, Harvard and the minorities were in agreement. Organizing for them had been difficult since the enemy was invisible, a dean who rarely emerged from his office and lab. A meeting, yes, but where? Hastings wanted it in a small room in the administration building; it would be intimate, a chance for back-and-forth discussion with influential students and opinion makers. The minorities wanted it in the biggest amphitheater available, allowing a large group of students to become directly exposed to the question. And the minorities had one bargaining chip which they had selectively withheld: going to the press. When the dust settled, the minorities hadn't called a press conference, and Hastings had given in on the location, though he decided to bring along Cox to help bear the brunt of the confrontation.

Now that the minorities had Amphitheater E, they had to fill it—a half-empty room meant serious problems in claiming support. The third- and fourth-year students were off in the hospitals and would be impossible to organize. That left the second-year students and us. For that mass meeting in September, not many from my class had shown up. And the minorities absolutely needed us if they were going to fill that auditorium.

"And that goes for me, too," Jerry went on, still slouching against the lab bench, "I'd rather be in front of the tube with a little brew watching a Bruins game myself. You think it's any different for those of us who are involved in this issue? We're sick to death of it. But let me tell you something." Jerry moved out of the slouch and his hand went up to point at all of us. "There are subtleties to this minority admissions question that no leaflet can communicate."

Subtleties? We picked up our ears. Subtleties were our specialty.

"And only by attending that meeting are you going to grasp those nuances, understand this whole question in its essential complexity."

Complexities, yes. We were good at those kinds of things. That's why we were here.

Jerry's hand had turned now, seeming to hold some delicate, immaterial object. "The ramifications of this whole matter are not at all obvious at first glance. Of course, to those of us involved, we'll be in a very difficult situation if no one shows up—the whole idea of minority admissions at Harvard, even across the whole United States, may be finished. And many of you may come for that reason. But the rest of you might wish to consider how vital it is to comprehend the shadings, the refinements of the question. For that reason, if for no other, I'm asking you to join me in Amphitheater E to meet with Nathaniel Hastings and Archibald Cox."

Wild applause, students who'd never read a leaflet were standing up, clapping over their heads. "I'm going to that one," I heard around me.

That night, I had a large studying assignment and, in the course of boning up on Sharpey's fibers, managed to get the times mixed up and arrived an hour late. Afterwards, I pieced together what had taken place before my arrival. Dean Hastings had distributed what seemed to be a lecture handout and proceeded to read it for a quarter of an hour. He expressed his personal dedication to expanding the number of minorities in medicine and explained that the double-screening proposal manifested that intent. "Together in commitment to goals which we all seek," he summed up, "I am certain we can fulfill our legacy. Toward this end, I pledge my service and hope that you will pledge yours."

Archibald Cox then declared that the current medical school admissions procedures "are illegal as hell," and argued that the double-screening plan for minorities would assure everyone equal protection of the laws.

When I arrived, the auditorium was packed, and I had to squeeze into a seat on the steps. Felipe was chairing the meeting, pointing out questions, while Hastings and Cox sat on chairs in front of the lab bench with beleaguered smiles on their faces. There was the special prosecutor himself: tall, lean, bronzed, white hair crewcut, bushy black eyebrows, elegant in a vest and pinstripe suit. The students seemed to be getting all tangled up in amateur efforts at forensic duels with Cox but I couldn't see that he was doing that great either. It became increasingly obvious to me that Cox was unfamiliar with the actual situation at the medical school.

Throughout these disputes over precedents and points of technical jurisprudence, Jerry Hearn had had his hand raised quietly, and finally Felipe called on him. In a soft voice that made everyone hush to hear, he began with a review of the history of minority admissions. As he went on, the softness departed, and his tone grew relentlessly stronger. No, we weren't going to get any more statute casuisty.

"Over and over, the same pattern of behavior is apparent here. Meetings we're 'invited to attend' after they've already been held. Massive plans sprung on us with a day's notice, representatives elected to one committee only to be told they actually belong to another."

Cox began slowly getting to his feet to reply, creating a ten-foot orb of presence around him.

"Do you think I'm finished?" said Jerry. "Well, I'm not. Do you even think we want to do this? Take so much time from learning medicine to write leaflets, staying up half the night in meetings, getting into wild arguments with each other over what's possible and what isn't? There's only one reason why we're going through all this—you are forcing us. We didn't initiate any of this. We're only fighting for our asses, fighting to survive."

Applause went through the crowd, and Cox sat down, smiling benevolently.

"You ask us to trust you. Before the Minority Admissions Subcommittee, we trusted you. And do you know what that trust got us?"

"Not a damn thing!" someone yelled.

"Three-quarters of a Black person a year! Right up until ten years ago. All during the sit-ins and freedom rides and cross-burnings of the Sixties, that was the best way Harvard could figure out how to serve the country. We couldn't even trust you to get one Black or Hispanic a year. No one seemed to care whether that was as 'illegal as hell' or not."

"Shit," I heard around me.

"Well, now we got maybe sixteen, eighteen percent of the class Black or Hispanic. That ain't much, but it sure is better than three-quarters of a person, and we're going to hang on to it. We ain't trusting nobody to take care of that kind of stuff for us no more."

Hastings's hand was up to begin a speech of his own, but a "Right On!" went through the audience, and he lowered it.

"So you might just as well know that you're going to have to tell us about meetings because we're going to get there somehow and take care of business. I don't pretend to know why you've decided to do all this. But I can tell you something about us, something you should remember when you get together in your offices and try to work out a strategy to beat us: we're not fighting for some abstraction that we read about in a book somewhere, we're Black and Hispanic people and we're fighting for our asses. And remember that one thing: when people are fighting for their asses, they don't give up."

Jerry sat down, and the Blacks and Hispanics in the audience had already jumped to their feet, yelling and applauding. Again, Hastings was trying to say something, but now even some of the whites were rising and cheering too, caught up in the mass emotion, and he was drowned out. The standing ovation continued for ten minutes, while Cox and Hastings sat there, alone in their chairs at the bottom of the amphitheater, silent, trying to smile against the roar.

In the midst of all this excitement, the bottom has fallen out from medical school. I'd managed to survive my Cannon Ball hangover and limp through midterm week, actually scoring in the top half of the class again in biochemistry and garnering a couple of excellents in histology. In neurobiology, I'd presented my sorry plight to Genslip, and he'd immediately arranged a tutor, and I'd managed to squeak by the final, discovering en route that I wasn't even supposed to be in the course since I lacked some of the prerequisite science background. And the physiology test had turned out to be so equally a disaster for everyone that I was almost exactly at the median.

All of which should give me a provisional sense of security, but why is it that everyone everywhere is suddenly talking utter gibberish? No longer do the biochemistry folks bother giving us handouts with any words on them—just page upon page of diagrammatic reactions lifted without explanation, and sometimes without title, from various texts. Since the lectures clarify nothing, you often must figure out a plausible name for each reaction, then go searching through indices to find out where you might get a clue as to what's up. That name-and-find process alone can take an hour.

And the Bateses seem to regard neuroanatomy as one of those "begat" sections of the Pentateuch—an endless recitation of names—while their handouts get distributed sporadically, if at all.

And as the coup de grâce, for our unit on respiration in physiology they've honored us with Randolph K. Wurstblau, who is reported to have almost won the Nobel Prize three times and is the department's celebrity in residence. He's a small, thin, almost emaciated man, with a quick, harsh voice. The class consensus is he could be mean if he wanted. Right in the middle of midterm week with everyone still in shock, he starts off with a two hour "demonstration." What's being demonstrated no one's quite sure, but somebody's in a stationary bicycle peddling away and is breathing into a tube; numbers are flashing on and off across an impressive array of machines; technicians are scrambling about, pressing buttons and flipping switches; semilog graphs are being traced; Wurstblau is talking away a mile a minute; and equations such as

$$P_{AO_2} = F_{IO_2} (P_B - 47) - P_{ACO_2} (F_{ICO_2} + \frac{(1 - F_{IO_2})}{R})$$

are being scribbled on the board for our edification. True to Harvard tradition, no one raises a hand and explains that we just finished two exams, have two more coming up and don't know a thing yet about breathing. But perhaps it's just as well—Wurstblau doesn't look like the type who's used to listening. So we copy down number after number in boxes labeled "BTPS," "V_{DCO_2}," "V_E (ATPS)." What these boxes signify, no one has the faintest idea. In lieu of anything else to do, we egg on the guy in the bicycle: "Go! Go! Go!"

Exams finally over, we go back and start reading the handouts; they consist almost entirely of equations of the type that were jotted on the board, along with table upon table of figures. Using all of this, we're supposed to perform elaborate computations, but no examples are provided to show us how to begin. I try one—it takes me three and a half hours and nothing comes out right. Even the physiology majors and Ph.D. candidates are in a panic. We go to the first conference. Exactly no one has gotten anywhere, much less finished the assignment. The conference leader tries to get through the first question; two hours later, we adjourn for lunch, the question still unanswered.

Next demonstration. Wurstblau must have gotten the word by now. But if he has, there're no signs. A dog lung is inflated and deflated. We're given oscilloscope tracings and assorted graphs. From these we're supposed to determine a whole alphabet soup of values—MVV, $FEV_{1.0}$, PEF, R_L near FRC. We go to another conference. We try that first question of last week for another two hours. Again no progress.

Third demonstration—something about carbon dioxide levels. We're given one hundred and seventy-seven boxes to fill in with figures, then told to put that data to use in plotting the medullary respiratory center's sensitivity, determining equivalent altitude, reason our way to the subject's blood pH, estimate a host of parameters we've never heard of. We spend a whole extra conference just defining what the various abbreviations mean and never get to the questions. Wurstblau returns to his lab, leaving the rest of us scurrying about, reading text after text, trying to figure out what breathing is.

Now even the class mood seems to have changed. Back in

September, you could go up to almost anyone, stick out your hand, introduce yourself, and make a friend. The same approach now elicits only politeness and a penetrating glance—"What's this guy really want from me?" Prevarication is at an all time high; everyone denies furiously that they're studying at all, but one glance out my window at one A.M. shows me how many windows are still lit. People yell angrily, urging someone else to "Relax! Relax for God's sake!"

Cheryl decides she can't take it anymore, but, more sensible than the rest of us, flies off for a weekend with a boyfriend. No books, just a change of clothes. She comes back feeling much better.

"But you can't believe the reactions I got around here," she says, blinking those innocent eyes behind her big glasses. "People were shocked—they told me I was committing academic suicide, going away for a whole weekend. I'm certainly glad I did it, though."

"They were probably the same people who say they haven't studied anything and haven't the vaguest idea what's going on, meanwhile they've memorized the whole urea cycle ahead of time."

"The same ones," she says, nodding.

Just barely, I hang on to jogging a couple of miles each day after classes. Even then, I'm preoccupied. Flecks of starlings whirl in ellipses in the sky at sunset. Gene pool control, I say to myself; semisynchronous action of billions of cerebral microcontrol units. They cruise back in an immense, smooth curve over the lake—just like seeing a servomechanism change a missile's course in midflight. Running in a daze, I cross the Fenway Drive, a terrifying screech almost on top of me, a bumper skidding larger, I leap forward. *Not now!* I cry to myself. Not after all this work! I speed home, realizing that I am not a life anymore, a sentient entity with a finite number of moments to experience before I wink out of existence, but a passive receptacle of knowledge, an inconsequential vase bearing a precious fluid of facts.

One Friday night, Donna Danzig, a classmate who lived in

Vanderbilt, and I shared a dinner in my room. Like me, Donna was short on cash, but in her case her parents, who were well off, had refused to pay the contribution that the Harvard Financial Aid office had decided they owed. With no one budging, Donna ended up living in the cheapest and smallest room Vanderbilt had to offer, barely large enough to hold a bed, dresser, desk, and person at the same time. She was an attractive, slender woman with wavy blond hair and a turned-up nose. Yet somehow it seemed difficult for her to smile, much less laugh; her brows were often knitted into an expression of faraway, almost melancholy concentration. I'd noticed her first out the window of my dorm room. Alone among all the class hurrying back and forth across the courtyard, she took the time to glance about her, examining the sunlight on the shrubs and walls, the birds flitting hither and yon about their nests in the eaves and coats of arms. Anyone who still maintained an interest in her environment after three months at Harvard must be worth knowing, I'd decided.

Donna spread out a salad, while I started layering up a small homemade pizza for my toaster oven. But in whatever manner a conversation started, it was impossible to keep it off school for long, whether you wanted that topic to come up or not.

"You know, I spent three years working in an institution for the retarded," I said, chopping up a tomato more and more definitively. "And there was never a time there that was as intellectually deadening as now. I've never been in a place where the students have so little interest in what they're studying and so many of the teaching staff seem totally uninterested in generating that interest. Look at biochem—I counted seven separate stages in that pyrimidine synthesis. What's it all mean? Why are we memorizing it? Just copying out an intelligible account of that thing took me three hours. Why do they have to be so lazy? Why can't they just take a couple minutes out to write what's going on, what they want us to know, in plain English?"

"Of course, they're lazy with us," said Donna. "They have a

right to be lazy. They have important research to do. They can't spend a lot of time with us."

"So if they can't spend a lot of time with us, why don't they at least teach us something that has to do with medicine, with patients?"

Donna shrugged. "I hear this is just the beginning. When we get taught about drugs in pharmacology next year, it'll just be about different people's theories of biochemical mechanisms. They even announce that the course has nothing to do with patients."

I put down my knife. "But how can they do that? We're going to spend most of our careers pushing drugs off on people. Why can't we get at least a couple months of formal training on what they're used for and when not to use them and what drugs are bad together and so forth?"

"We're supposed to get that in the hospitals."

"But I've seen how things operate in hospitals—everything on the run. If we're going to spend two years sitting in classrooms, why can't we use that time for getting ready for dealing with sick people?"

"It isn't considered important."

I spread out some tomato sauce and grated cheese. "Well, I don't care anymore whether it's important to them, it's important to my morale. I'm getting to the point where if I heard just one fact a week that had to do with a patient, one practical thing a week, one thing that I know I won't forget the second after I leave an exam, I'd be happy."

"Why do things have to be practical?"

This was an old argument. Bewilderment with what was going on in your medical education was generally considered a sign of scientific anti-intellectualism. Discussions normally degenerated into disputes over whether knowledge, any knowledge, was good for its own sake. But stubbornly I decided to pursue the question anyway.

"Don't you think things should either be practical or have some theoretic significance? You think we should memorize reactions just to memorize them?"

"How do you know there isn't any theoretic importance?"

"Because I can't see any, and they haven't pointed out any."

"But there could be. I don't think everything we learn here should be just practical."

I put the pie in the oven, and we sat down to Donna's salad, which was a cornucopia of miscellaneous fruits, nuts, seeds, and vegetables, covered with chickpea sauce.

"OK," I said. "When I was studying physics back in night school we calculated the mass of the Milky Way, did all sorts of problems with harmonic motion, nodes and antinodes, blackbody radiation, quantum energy levels, that sort of stuff. Maybe you can tell me how I'll use that in a hospital, but I can't. I can't see that it has any practical value. But it seemed to me that measuring the mass of a galaxy was fun, revealed some principles about natural phenomena, and showed how accessible immense and faraway objects could be to mathematical analysis. So I know why I was there, whatever the teaching or the tests were like. Memorizing the seven steps of pyrimidine synthesis just to memorize them doesn't give me any sense that I'm doing anything but wasting my time and developing a contempt for the subject matter and the people who are teaching me."

"Maybe there's a theoretic significance that you don't see?"

"So why don't they point it out?"

"Perhaps they assume we see it."

We both munched on our nuts and spinach for a while.

"Fine, let's say it's of tremendous significance," I said. "Let me give you an analogy. The rose window in the north face of Chartres Cathedral is extraordinarily complex and beautiful. When I visited Chartres, the guide turned his back to the rose window, faced us, and proceeded to describe in exact detail each image on each shard of glass, the symbolism of the colors, the mosaic pattern of the panes. Never once turning around. But he'd devoted his life to Chartres. If instead of explaining the rose window to us, he'd forced us to try and memorize all the images and recite them back by rote, the whole thing would have been worthless and unpleasant. At the very best, we could only have parroted what he'd said himself. Now let's say one of these cycles is a rose window of biochemistry. Should we just memorize it, recite it, and forget it? Or should we be taught how to understand its meaning and roles and interaction in life?"

Donna thought for a while. "I know people who can memorize these things and realize their significance too."

"People who got taught biochem somewhere else first."

She shrugged. "Other people too." Donna had completed her calculus requirement for Harvard while she was still in junior high, and blazed her way in a similar fashion through Swarthmore, doing independent research in physiology. She'd decided that if she didn't know more than everyone else, everyone knew more than she did.

"I'd like to meet these other people," I said, getting up to take my pizza out of the oven. "I sure haven't met any."

"Well, I have."

We sliced up the pizza and gingerly started eating it, trying to avoid scalding our tongues. I decided it was time to get the conversation off this rehashed question.

"One thing that struck me today," I said, "is these guys never mention patients they've treated. If I were teaching, I couldn't stop myself, I'd be using real-life examples all the time."

"Their patients?" Donna smiled.

Those smiles were so few that I stopped in the middle of a munch. "Yes, their patients."

"They don't have any patients."

"OK, some of them spend most of their time in the lab, but they must have—"

"They're not doctors."

I burned the roof of my mouth. "What do you mean they're not doctors?"

"Farrell isn't a doctor, Wurstblau isn't a doctor, Genslip isn't a doctor—"

"So what are they?"

"Biochemists, or some other scientific degree. They never had any patients."

"How about Fineful and Vanda and—"

"No. They're Ph.Ds. They never worked in a hospital."

"Well, somebody has to be a doctor around here."

"Some of the physiology people are, but none of them treat patients now. They're just in labs."

"Why'd they get M.D.s?"

"To do human experiments, I guess."

"So no wonder we don't hear anything about patients. These guys just work with glassware and Bunsen burners. Are you sure about this, Donna?"

"Of course. You must be the only one who doesn't know it. But you don't have to be an M.D. to teach medicine."

"No—I wish everybody was Fineful." I explored my burn with my tongue. "But it sure explains why we never hear anything about sick people around here. This place is pure test tube research. Harvard pays them, and sets up their labs for them, and they're required to teach us in return."

"Harvard doesn't set up their labs."

"What are you talking about? They're all over in Building C and D and—"

"Harvard barely pays a cent. It's the federal government. Almost every cent for everything around here comes from research grants. The researchers aren't really dependent on Harvard."

"So why do they bother coming here at all? Why don't they just do their research and leave us in peace?"

"Harvard's how they get their grants. They get on the faculty, that way they have the name and prestige behind them when they ask for money. You don't think they could get a grant operating out of their kitchen or garage?"

Carefully, I took another bite of pizza. "So Harvard doesn't really employ these guys at all. Being on the faculty here is just a system for getting grant money. They never see patients, and teaching us is like a minor annoyance. No wonder everyone gives a different lecture—they spread it out."

"Sure. That's why we get tests like the Physiology mid-term—everybody who lectures writes in his own question. The course director isn't going to knock out a question or change it—that'd be challenging someone else in his own field. How could you not know this?"

"Maybe if I'd been around science more I would have." I wiped my chin. "No wonder everyone wants us to memorize their specialty. That's all they ever do. They can't possibly imagine that you could function in life without it."

"We get some very famous people that way."

"Like Wurstblau?"

"He's very renowned in all sorts of fields. He almost won the Nobel Prize three times. He has some new research coming out on hormones."

"I wish he'd do some research on teaching about breathing."

"He's world famous. You can't ask him to spend a lot of time on us, trying to come down to our level."

"But we're not talking about Sassanian influences on Byzantine ivories—sooner or later, people's lives are going to hang on what I know or don't know about breathing. And I don't know a damn thing."

"I know some people who did his problems and said they were easy."

"Did you?"

"I couldn't do a single one. But I know people who did."

I laughed. Back to the old argument again.

At Swarthmore, Donna had written some poetry and short stories. She'd brought some over, so we sat on my bed and read them together. It seemed to me there were some beautiful images in them.

"Are you doing anything now with this?" I asked.

"How can I?"

I nodded. "It's all I can do to squeeze in a little running each day."

"I can't even do things like that. Once, I got over to Kenmore Square, though." She picked up her things.

"Where's Kenmore Square?"

"You know—over by that big Citgo sign."

"The one you see when you go down to Star Market?"

"Yes."

"You went there?" I was amazed—I still hadn't gotten any further away from school than those same three blocks. "How'd you find the time?"

"This was during orientation."

"Oh." I walked her to the door. "But what's there?"

"Oh, not much, some stores, a bookstore."

"A real bookstore? Not a medical bookstore?"

"No, a regular one, and some other stuff. B.U.'s near there. It's actually a little seedy."

"Wow!" A whole blazing world existed out beyond the Harvard quadrangle and Vanderbilt Hall. And someone had actually reached it. "Gee, maybe I can walk there."

"I wish I could find the time now," said Donna, standing in the middle of the hall. "Since school really got started I haven't gone anywhere."

"But at least you got there once," I said enviously. "I wish I could have done that."

The next day, I made a quick trip with my shopping cart down to Star Market for the week's groceries. Yes, there it was, blue and red and white and towering over everything, a triangle inside a square, the Citgo sign—as far away as the Grandes Jorasses had been from the Dent de Géant when I was climbing last summer in the Alps, stupendous in the distance, defining the horizon. So that was where life was lived out beyond the pale of pyrimidine synthetic sequences and pulmonary function tests. With a full cart, I hurried back to my room and spent all Saturday night in fruitless efforts to memorize the converging routes by which isoleucine and valine are degraded to succinyl coenzyme A. My morale was dropping.

Sunday morning I got up early, made breakfast on my hot plate, and got to work again. The day wore on, but I was getting less and less done. I'd scheduled fifteen hours of studying today, seven were gone, and I was nowhere near a quarter through. Outside, it was the clear, crisp afternoon of late November, the cirrus clouds gliding in distant wisps across the sky, gusts blowing dead leaves about the courtyard. And here I was, inside my room as usual, with eight more hours of memorization ahead of me, then tomorrow up at seven-thirty and a full day's classes lasting till four-thirty. And more studying the following evening, rushed and behind. Would I even be able to get outside for a couple of minutes today?

I looked up at the two immense, black looseleaf notebooks that held my collected biochemistry and physiology handouts. Each was fatter than the Manhattan phone book. I threw a book at the door, then put my head down and started to cry. I'd never get out of this little room. I'd never make it to the Citgo sign. Then with tears coursing over my hands, making blotchy stains over my diagrams, I thought of Percy Wendt and his clogged shunt.

A few years before, I'd been completing my alternative service as a conscientious objector in a large public hospital in San Francisco, and had been assigned to the communicable disease division and respiratory care units. Aside from the drug addicts and attempted suicides, almost all of my case-load, a whole building in fact, consisted of floor upon floor of tuberculosis patients. Most of these patients were Chinese; they lived in overcrowded, underventilated rooms, worked long hours, and were frequently undernourished. Afraid of the possibility of deportation, they didn't come to the hospital until their cases were far advanced. So we often had whole families—parents, children, even uncles and aunts—all in the same building. For reasons which weren't clear to me, the hospital never allowed families to stay together, though hospitalization might sometimes last a year. Husbands were put on one ward, wives on another, children in another building entirely, in the same ward that housed the adult drug addicts. The children had spent all their lives in the same room as their parents, barely spoke English, and were unaccustomed to American, let alone public hospital, cuisine. I'd go by their rooms and see them wailing hopelessly away, refusing to eat. During "visiting hours," parents would be permitted to come down and comfort their children, try to feed them mashed potatoes and roast beef with chop sticks. Since this was a public hospital and patients had no alternative place of treatment, the amenities tended to get short shrift. The waiting room for the intensive care unit was taken over by a university research lab, so relatives had to stand in the hall through the long, dreary hours to see if their loved ones lived or died.

But Percy Wendt stood out in my mind because among other things he was not the typical TB patient at all. He was in his twenties, a college graduate. How he'd caught TB was anybody's guess, but he showed up at the emergency room with a bizarre set of symptoms—bulging abdomen and mental disorientation. A friend of mine was interning in the emergency room at the time. The usual diagnosis in these situations is the half-waggish "acute belly," and the standard procedure when all else fails is to open the belly up surgically and see what's going on in there. As part of the preoperative routine she inserted a catheter through his penis and began draining urine. She noticed that an amazing amount of urine was coming out and that simultaneously his acute belly was becoming less acute. Obviously something was blocking the reflex that automatically voids urine when the bladder is full, something that was also interfering with his sensation of pain from that area, perhaps disorienting him as well. The operation was canceled, and a diagnostic workup revealed tuberculosis of the spinal cord.

Percy ended up on one of my wards, and I went to talk to him in my usual gear—ankle-length gown, face mask, surgical cap. Percy couldn't see much of me, or anyone else who treated him, besides the eyes, but I could see him. He was a good-looking young fellow, a little pudgy, black hair thinning out, a slow smile that eventually broadened across his whole face.

"When can I get out of here?" was his first question.

Draining the urine seemed to have cleared his mental state.

"Have to ask your doctor," I said through the mask.

"Who's he? These guys come in and out all in a pack, never say who they are."

"Let's see, the resident is Dr. Devlin and your interne is Dr. Schmidt. You want me to write those down?"

"Could you? I've been here three days, and I have no idea who's in charge of me."

"That's pretty much usual here," I said, writing the names on a sheet of paper and adding my own. "But if you feel well enough, don't be afraid to ask questions."

"OK. What're you doing here?"

We laughed.

"First, I'm supposed to see if you have any insurance, and second if I can get you any benefits that'll give you money."

"I don't have any insurance and I don't have any money," he said putting his palms up. "Ninety dollars and a bunch of books and a bicycle. You can have the books. I've read them all, and they're heavy anyway. But you're not going to take the bicycle away, are you?"

"No," I said. "If you don't have any money, there won't be any charge. But it sounds like you might be eligible for some disability benefits. Why don't I ask you some questions and fill out the forms for you?"

"Shoot. I got nothing to hide."

After processing the paper work for a variety of disability programs, I handed the case on to the medical social worker. But from time to time I'd drop in on Percy, and we'd chat. He was trying to work his way through The Magic Mountain. Somewhere it had been discovered that he had an IQ of 160, so he was known through the Communicable Disease Division as "the patient with the 160 IQ."

Percy's tuberculosis proved resistant to treatment, and he was still in the hospital two months later when a disability program sent out a psychologist to administer some tests. I lent her my office and escorted Percy to and from the tests. Afterwards, she took me aside.

"I see some definite neurological impairments," she said. "Definite signs of some sort of brain involvement, particularly in the language area. They're a bit elusive in conversation, I don't think they'd even be noticed, but they showed up on the tests that I gave him. Are his physicians aware of this?"

"Gee, I never heard about anything like that since he was admitted."

"Is there some way I can speak to his doctor?"

Paging got a hurried Devlin on the phone. "Look, I just got two barb ODs one after the other in ICU. We're flailing away here. I haven't got time for that kind of stuff."

"Could—"

"Got to get off stat. Sorry." Click.

"Well, he was too busy right now," I said.

"I really want to talk to him," the psychologist said.

"I'll get a hold of him when he's not busy and have him call you at your office."

In general, it was hard to interest the young doctors in the TB patients and their problems. As a disease, tuberculosis wasn't much of an intellectual puzzle nor did it follow a very complicated course. Patients came in reporting weight loss, night sweats, a phlegmy cough. You took an x-ray, maybe a skin test, sent the phlegm off to the lab to see what grew up in a culture dish. To treat it, you gave them a good diet, some streptomycin, and left them alone. Pretty hard to impress your attending with that—the flashy action was over in Intensive Care.

But the next day I managed to run down Devlin emerging from the pneumonia ward. He was a tall, blond man with a floppy mustache. Ward staff said he knew his medicine cold; he was quick, articulate, and confident. And as usual, he was in a hurry. Anticipating that, I'd already written out the psychologist's name and number.

"Late for grand rounds," he said. "Got to run."

I charged down the stairs after him. I was used to the fact that doctors don't stand still for anyone but other doctors, and I was so low on the hospital pecking order I couldn't get an orderly to stand still for me.

"You know Percy Wendt?" I said as we rounded the next landing.

"Guy with the 160 IQ in 54."

"Yeah. I had a psychologist come out. She gave him tests. She thinks there's a neurological involvement."

Devlin started laughing uproariously. "What the hell you think he's in here for? He's got TB of the spinal cord. Don't you read the charts?"

We hit the access hall to the main wing. "Yes, right. But what she's talking about—I don't know anything about it technically—but she says there's some sort of mental disturbance."

"No, no. That was when he came in. Long ago. His BUN was through the ceiling, his electrolytes were all screwed up. But once we got that bladder draining, no problem. We had a neuro consult. It's in the chart."

We were racing along the hall, passing gurneys and wheel chairs and prisoners clanking along in their leg manacles.

"Well, she thinks there's something there. I don't know what those other things mean. Here's her name and number. Could you call her?"

"I'm late for grand rounds. Schmidt's sick. I was on all last night. Those barb ODs are still half-croaked. Bunch of new students tomorrow, and now I'm supposed to call people."

"Could you take her number? It shouldn't take too much time to call her."

"What's the point? We did a neuro consult. They gave him a clean bill of health. So some half-assed psychologist thinks otherwise."

We were at the door to the auditorium. Inside I could see a blizzard of white coats, while someone was up front with a pointer. That was privileged territory. I stopped.

"Late for this thing," Devlin said. "See you around." The door closed behind him, and I stood there out of breath with the telephone number still in my hand. I tried to corner Devlin a few other times with the same results. I put the number in the chart in the off-hope that someone might have a free moment to use it. But Percy was transferred as a convalescent patient to the city's long-term care facility shortly thereafter, and gradually I forgot about the incident.

A few months later, I was walking through the main hall of the hospital when I saw Percy again. Now he was in a wheel chair and seemed to have some dressings around his neck. I went up to him.

"Hey, Percy," I said. "How's it going?"

He raised his head slowly and focused his eyes on me. "Who're you?"

"Charley, the intake worker, when you were on 54."

He looked at me for a while, not saying anything.

"So what're you doing here?" I said.

"I don't know, man." His voice was rough and the words slurred. "I don't know, man. I don't know what's happening."

I looked at the nurse with him. "Is he on sedation?"

She shook her head.

"What service?"

"Surgery."

"What are they doing?"

She shrugged. Percy's head had dropped down again.

I read the chart. Percy's mental status had begun to deteriorate at the long-term care facility. He'd been transferred back here, where it had been found that the TB had ascended from his spinal cord to his brain. Now they were installing a plastic tube, a shunt, to try to drain some of the fluid in his cranium.

I last saw Percy a month or two later when he was transferred temporarily to one of my wards. The shunt had clogged repeatedly. When I entered his room, he was lying on his back in the bed, staring vacantly at the ceiling.

"How're you doing, Percy?" I said. "Remember me?"

He didn't move.

I put my hand over and squeezed his shoulder. Slowly his head came around to face mine. He didn't say anything. Spit started to drool from one corner of his mouth.

"Aw, fuck it, Percy!" I said out loud, clenching my fists.

"Fuck it all!" I squeezed his shoulder hard, then gently, and left him, still leaning to the side, staring at the wall now.

For the past three months, I thought, weeping over my biochemistry diagrams, have I been anything other than late for grand rounds? Quick, snappy, one-phrase answers were the best I could provide. Give me two years of endless short-answer tests, then put me on round-the-clock shifts, and how many Percies would I accrue?

I stood up, scattering pulmonary function equations and dog lab notes and leucine degradations to the floor. My cheeks were still wet with tears.

"You motherfuckers!" I said. "You got one less victim now, assholes. I'm making it to the Citgo sign!" I kicked aside the book I'd thrown at the door, slammed noisily out of the dorm room, and banged down the stairs out into the deepening November twilight.

Off I went, without a coat, running past Star Market, dark warehouses, billboards, cars, garbage, a McDonald's. I got lost in some jumbled streets, but kept pushing forward, ever forward, across an immense, roaring expressway, down a short hill—and I was there!

Kenmore Square with the Citgo sign colossal above it. I'd broken through, and here was life in all its exuberance and fleshiness and hope. A pizza parlor—two of them! Bright signs, a Howard Johnson Motel, a discotheque, some derelicts in the street, a Dunkin' Donuts. I wanted to own it all, blend my soul forever with this seamy world. I went skipping down the street, tried to leapfrog a parking meter, knocked myself in the crotch, and reeled onward, half bent over and giggling. Traffic was honking, unshaven types were hanging out on stoops. But my blood was boiling with delirious joy. I dashed across the square and put my hands against the cold stone of the building that supported the Citgo sign.

"No more victims, you motherfuckers," I said. "You can fucking fail me a hundred times, go through all your terrorist acts, but you've had your day. I made it, assholes. Find yourself another personality to reconstruct with your dog labs and liberal deans and nice psychiatrists and carnitine acyl transferase. Maybe you won't notice it at first, maybe you won't notice it at all, but you got one victim less."

Part Two

REVOLT IN MICRO

Our current concepts of thermodynamics are rooted in the industrial revolution and the attempts to determine how much mechanical work is available from heat engines. Entropy provides a measure of the work that is unavailable because of our lack of knowledge of the detailed state of the system. The whole structure acquires consistency only because it requires work to obtain information. If this were not true, a Maxwellian demon could indeed continuously violate the second law of thermodynamics. The second law and the entropy measure tell us as much about the observer as about the system. This accounts partially for the difficulty of the entropy concept. In steam-engine thermodynamics we do not require very detailed knowledge of the state of the system; however, in biology the case is entirely different as the phenomena depend on molecular detail. A misplaced methyl group can eventually kill a whale. The relationship between the observer and the system may thus achieve considerably more importance in biological thermodynamics than in previous considerations of a more coarse-grained type.

This introduces a very subtle point, since in biology we have the possibility that the observer and the system will, in fact, be the same.

—Harold J. Morowitz, *Energy Flow in Biology:*
Biological Organization as a Problem in Thermal Physics

Chapter 9

Repose in the Midst of Chaos

I went over to Cambridge and used half of a secret emergency stash I'd reserved in case I broke my leg to buy a new ten-speed bike. I rode it back without the slightest idea how to operate the gears, grinding them unmercifully, ecstatic anyway, proud of my new toy, my ticket to the world. Tag still fluttering, I met a classmate in the lobby of Vanderbilt.

"Got a new bike," I said, grinning like the Cheshire cat.

"Jesus, that looks expensive. I thought you were poor or something."

"I am, but I can blow money too," I retorted with pride.

"Where're you going to go in that thing?"

Hmmm . . . I hadn't given that much thought. "The Green Mountains."

"The Green Mountains in Vermont?"

"Sure. I been there. They're nice."

"You're crazy. This is December. It'll start snowing here any minute. There's probably a foot already in Vermont."

I shrugged. "Or somewhere else. Anyway, I got a bicycle now."

Sure enough, it started snowing a week later, and the bike hung vertically in my closet all winter. But every day, I looked over and stroked it lovingly. It was there when I wanted it. In the spring, the second time out, someone stole it.

But I didn't feel too bad—it had served its purpose there in the closet all winter.

Relativistic effects are becoming apparent. The structure of time is collapsing under the weight of approaching finals. But that's their problem, not mine. This is the post-Citgo era. Alone among course directors, Jack Fineful in histology is tapering down the work and giving us review sessions. Last week, he'd handled the microstructure of the male reproductive apparatus, swaggering up and down before the lab bench, stroking his mustache, pointer held high. Then Grace Vanda stepped in for the female side of things. One of our few women lecturers, she's in her late thirties, has an alert, infectious smile, bright gray eyes that seem to open impossibly wide. Everyone says she's a brilliant teacher, but it's hard for me to say. I just think she's beautiful. All through the blood and lungs, I'd sat there, ignoring the slides, just dreaming and palpitating away. And after every lecture, I'd follow her off to the labs, two steps behind, not daring to ask a question or make my presence known.

And for this lecture on the ovaries, uterus, and vagina, Grace arrived wearing a T-shirt that said, "Catch Beaver Fever!" The guys in the class were cheering and yelling for more. The women looked mortified. Lecture started, Cheryl raised her hand, announced she found the T-shirt offensive to her and all women. Groans and shouts of "shut up!" from the males—those dumb-ass women's libbers!

Grace said, "Oh, really?" and proceeded to peel it off in one sinuous wriggle, revealing another T-shirt underneath that said, "Anything boys can do, girls can do better!" Raucous cheers and applause from the women. Boos from the guys. When all that had quieted down, a lot of male hands went up, demanding that Grace remove the final T-shirt since it was an insult to them. She seemed to weigh the idea for a moment, then to sighs of disappointment from the men, decided to go on with the lecture.

But I have more than mock battles of the sexes on my hands. I have Céline. Twenty-two years old and French and arriving, by her own proclamation, smack in the middle of finals. I'd met Céline by accident in a Paris post office five years before; for three years, we'd exchanged occasional correspondence, and for the last two summers, visits. Though half-Scandinavian, with cobalt blue eyes and blond hair, she'd been born and raised in Paris and did not lack for Gallic subtlety or fire. She required one hundred and ten percent of your energy and time, and made you love every minute. But how did that fit into medical school finals week?

Vainly, I tried to explain the situation to Céline in letters— if she could arrive just three days later, I'd be free, waiting for her to emerge from airport customs. Céline dismissed these arguments as the transparent lies they obviously were; the real point was: what was I attempting to conceal from her? Céline had completed her fourth year at Necker, the most prestigious medical school in France by common report. As in most of Europe, students went straight from high school to undergo seven years of medical training before becoming doctors. Now Céline was taking some law courses, while still keeping up with her medical studies. If she didn't pass the exam for judge, she'd go back to being a doctor. Things were different in France.

But what kind of elaborate hoax was I trying to perpetrate upon her? What? I couldn't study for exams if she moved into my room with me? What absurdity!

Since letters had not resolved things by mid-December, Céline called me at three A.M. from Paris. Twelve years younger or not, Céline was more skilled in such negotiations than I. When we hung up, an entente had been reached: rather than arriving the first day of exams, Céline would arrive the second. As far as I was concerned, that was a victory; another five minutes on the phone and I'm sure I would have found myself that night on a transatlantic jet, having used the remains of my emergency stash for a one-way ticket to Paris.

The consequences of all this could be serious, since no one can figure out what to do about physiology. Wurstblau is long gone, we're deep into hormones, but the class is still having conniptions over what, if anything, we're supposed to remember about respiration. Should we really memorize those supertanker equations and learn by rote the numerical values for the concentration in the blood and urine of all those gases, ions, proteins, metals, sugars, acids, bases. . . ?

Ron and a biology major from Princeton named Adria and I went to see Marcus, the tall, plump fellow who, most people think, is course director. His office was a tiny, cluttered alcove off a crowded lab. There didn't seem to be any door to close and lab techs kept rushing in with test tubes and questions. Over Marcus's head was a chart of some of the major biochemical pathways in a mammalian cell—all nine square feet of it was tapestried with diagrammed reactions in microfilm-sized print.

"You should be familiar with those pulmonary equations," he said smiling. Marcus, with his round, young face, was so jovial and friendly in person that it was hard to believe he'd actually inflicted that midterm, then Wurstblau, on us.

"So we should memorize them," said Ron, stroking his beard with some concern.

A look from Marcus said, "Don't push me on details."

"Or should we just know how to manipulate them if you give them to us?" asked Adria, a short, black-haired woman who had the reputation of being a hard worker.

Marcus ran his hand along the desk. "You should know what they say."

"So we should memorize them?"

He sighed and sat up. "I wouldn't get bogged down in respiration. We're into the endocrine system. You shouldn't ignore that. Actually, it should help you synthesize a lot of what you've learned."

"It's hard to synthesize if you don't know what's going on in the first place," I said. "And I wasn't able to do any of those problems on the pulmonary function tests. The result is I don't know anything about breathing. But I'd like to learn, even if it means more work. Could you give out some questions about material you'd expect us to know?"

"I think you put your finger on it. The class has had too much work already. In fact, that's been the chief complaint.

And I'm inclined to agree. More questions would just be the straw that broke the camel's back."

"Along those lines," broke in Adria, "could you tell us what blood and urine values we should remember? So we don't have to run around trying to memorize everything."

"Just the important ones. Don't go overboard."

"Which ones are those?"

"I don't want you to get bogged down in a lot of sterile memorization."

"But could you give us a list of the important ones?"

"Many people differ in what's important, and each hospital has its own definition of what normality is."

"So what should we do?"

"You should try to get a strong grasp of the essentials."

"But I looked in the back of a book, and there are hundreds and hundreds of numerical values," said Adria.

A lab tech came in, and there was some unintelligible discussion between her and Marcus. When she left, he turned back to us with a thoughtful expression on his face. "One of the things I've realized lately is how difficult a period this is for all of you. All of you have been at the top of your classes before coming here. Now someone has to be below the mean. That can cause a great deal of stress, I'm sure. Even psychological trauma."

"But we're not talking about grades and curves," I said.

"No, no," Marcus nodded sympathetically. "No, I'm sure you're telling the truth. But I'm also sure that for a large part of the class, this change in the image they have of themselves is very stress-provoking, a very, very difficult transitional time for them psychologically. So I do agree with you that we all have to work together to help people over this period of adjustment."

"But wouldn't giving people a clear idea of what was expected on the final—"

"Absolutely. Absolutely. That's a big part of it. And we can't forget the human aspect either, the incredible strain each and every one of you is under. And I appreciate you mentioning all this to me. This is the kind of feedback that course directors need. I'll make an announcement to the class next lecture to say we understand the kind of problems of psychological readjustment you're going through, and we'll do anything we possibly can to help you through."

True to his word, Marcus made his announcement the very next morning, saying he understood how each of us felt about not being number one in the class anymore. Only one person could be number one. But we should all know that our feelings of disappointment were natural, entirely normal. Nevertheless, we shouldn't become overly concerned or overwrought—because that might just hurt our performance on the final. And put us among those who failed.

Someone asked if we'd have more time for the final than we'd had for the midterm. Marcus said he hadn't wanted to get into specifics, but we should be advised that the whole physiology department stood behind us one hundred percent.

Someone else wanted to know if we could get an inventory of the blood, urine and respiration values we'd be expected to commit to memory. A woman in the class, Marcus replied, whom he didn't feel at liberty to identify, had compiled a list of numerical values. He didn't think he should state whether they were the important ones or that the figures were right. But if the woman in the class wished to identify herself to us individually, we might use her values. Of course, they might not be significant or correct. Alas, the woman with the values never identified herself to me.

Though we have the usual assorted lecturers for the hormone block, the guy in charge seems to be Jonathan Silverman, a youngish fellow with a Vandyke and a penchant for plaid jackets. As a medical student at Harvard, barely out of his teens, he is supposed to have done some path-breaking genetic research. Inspired by this success, or perhaps finding patients less interesting than test tubes, he deserted medicine for Basic Science, and now is said to be the dauphin of the physiology department, Wurstblau's heir apparent, as the man who might someday receive that telegram from the Swedish Academy. What for, nobody seems to know—perhaps it's just

right. It was tough. But I had guts, all right. Better to act modest, though. "Well, it isn't all that bad. I can manage."

"But you must certainly have gotten depressed once in a while over the past few months."

"Once in a while."

"And women friends? Do you have women friends?"

"I have a friend who's coming in from Paris."

"Oh, that's so far away. None closer?"

"Well, I've tried to make friends with some of the women in the class. My luck's been variable, I guess."

"Why is that?"

Just a second, I thought, this is all very nice, but aren't we getting a little far afield? "Really, why I'm here is that physiology lecture. Someone said during orientation you wanted to act as our ombudsman?"

"Oh yes. My job is to be of help to all students here."

"Do you think scheduling a lecture during finals period is a good idea?"

She paused, choosing her words. "I would certainly like to find out why it was necessary."

"Could you call someone over in the physiology department and ask? I guess nothing can be done this year, but maybe next year they'll be able to come up with a better idea."

"I certainly want to reduce the amount of stress people feel here. Anything I can do, I will do. As far as I'm concerned, as dean of students I'm your representative to Harvard, not the other way around. But I am concerned for you, Charles. We have a little group—it's only eight to ten people, who are first-year students and discuss their problems. Personal problems with adjustment to a new life in medical school. It's already been formed, and I'd have to ask their permission—it's their group, not mine—but perhaps you'd like to join us?"

"I'm pretty busy," I said. "But maybe you could let me know about your talk with Dr. Silverman or whoever. I'll write down my phone and room at Vanderbilt."

"Yes, I'm glad to have that. But Dr. Feinstein, my husband, and I are having a few of your classmates over for dinner. Nothing formal, just three or four people, perhaps you'd like to join us? Right after exams. People who aren't going home for the holidays. I hate to think of people sitting around in the dorm, getting lonely. Holidays can actually be very trying times. And I'd like to get to know you better, and I'm sure my husband would be fascinated too."

"That sounds wonderful," I said. "But I really can't think much past exam period right now."

"You can bring your French friend along, if you wish."

"I'll check with her. But, meanwhile, I guess I can expect to hear back from you in a day or two about the physiology lecture?"

"You can be sure I'll be getting back to you. This has been very exciting for me, Charles. But I feel I only know part of you, and there's so much more to know. I really hope you'll be able to come back when we can have a *real* chat."

I never heard anything more about the physiology lecture. But I did get a written invitation in the mail to come to dinner.

Still, if the amount of grumbling was the only indication, more complaints than mine must have been filtering back to the medical school administration. Dissatisfaction with the disordered state of our medical education had reached the point where, for the first time, I actually heard people muttering occasionally about petitions and meetings.

And one morning, who should appear but Dean Myron Chanesohn. With a bow tie and white jacket, it was obvious he'd broken off from pressing matters at the Peter Bent Brigham Hospital. That broad, waggish face adopted a serious expression as he strode to the lab bench up front.

"It was just about this time in my first year, sitting right where you are now, that I decided that Harvard Medical School was not the place for me. I'd done just terribly on a histology exam—then, we had grades—and there was a note from the professor: 'Come and see me if you want to discuss this.' Of course, the last thing I wanted to do was discuss anything with him."

We all laughed heartily. So Chanesohn knows about that kind of stuff, too!

"But I finally got up the courage and dragged myself to see him. He went flipping through his class list. 'Chanesohn? Oh yes, Chanesohn. You're the sociologist, the fellow who got in here with almost no science. I didn't know what to do with you.' Of course, at that point I didn't know what to do with myself either. All I wanted to do was to become a psychoanalyst and get away from things like histology as fast as possible—but I couldn't very well say that. Then he looked at me hard: 'You know, Chanesohn, it's a crime they let people like you in here.'"

Howls of laughter. And now he's dean of the medical school!

Allowing a smile to broaden across his face, Chanesohn held up a hand and we quieted.

"Well, it may have been a crime, but Harvard had already committed it, and there I was. So I left school for Christmas— at that time finals were in January—and spent time with friends in New York and came back and passed all my courses, including histology.

"Now the reason I came over here to see you is this: the crime has already been committed in your cases, too. And if someone like me could do it, so can you. We picked you because we knew you'd be the best doctors in the nation. And when we pick people, they don't get away from us. You're here at Harvard, and you're going to stay at Harvard. And no course, or bunch of courses, is going to change that."

As the class rose to its feet, clapping and cheering, Chanesohn whisked out the door with a big wave. There wasn't much talk about petitions or group actions after that.

And even the boys from biochem have decided to talk nice to us.

"I've been approached by several of your representatives," Farrell said at the beginning of one lecture, "who're concerned about the amount of work you have now, that everything has turned into moment-by-moment crisis management. Well, I want to assure you that we don't expect perfection from you, just normal performance."

Very pleasant, I said to myself. But talk's cheap. Let's see if your final is any different from those midterms. Nevertheless, I've stopped working in biochemistry like I used to. With two high passes behind me, I got some leeway. The material is also vaguely familiar from my one course in general biology—the molecular structure of chromosomes, DNA, RNA, the genetic code.

A sugar molecule in the form of a five-sided ring is stuck onto a six-sided ring containing nitrogen, some phosphate is attached, and we have one of the letters of the genetic code. What are the peculiar properties of these rings that make them so specifically useful as the quanta, the alphabet, the minimum units of information storage in all biological systems? We never learn, but there must be something extraordinarily meritorious about them, since the three-letter words those rings spell out can suffice to create, self-construct in a turbulent world, every salient aspect of an artichoke and dragonfly, porcupine and dandelion, orchid and parrot feather, ladybug and octopus eye. And in the nucleus of each cell in each of our bodies resides an inconceivable battery of such ring-letters than can assemble in a jouncing sack of salty water in a woman's belly, at rates which approach one-quarter million cells a minute, the hundred billion precisely organized neurons of the human brain.

After the final lecture, Farrell puts down his pointer, shuts off the slides, and with his melancholy eyes fixed on the back wall, sums up his impressions of the science that he's made his lifework: "The extraordinary fact about living creatures, living processes, is the structure, the order, they manifest in the midst of disorder. Each process is interlocked, each life depends on another, the prey upon the predator, the predator upon the prey, cycle upon cycle, pathway branching into pathway in a web of inconceivable beauty. We don't exist as units alone in an inanimate world but as part of that intricate web. It is this sense of location in the midst of loneliness, repose in the midst of chaos, that constitutes the aesthetic and the real reason for the study of the chemistry of living things."

There was some perfunctory applause. I didn't join in. I sat there stricken as people filed out, hurrying off to the library. I thought again about the rose window at Chartres. Farrell was down by the lab bench, putting away chalk, gathering his things.

You son of a bitch, I said silently, staring at him, while almost alone high up in the amphitheater. I can understand being so immersed in the day-to-day world of test tube research that nothing larger ever invades the mind. But if you know, if you see that beauty, how could you defile it by teaching it to us in this way?

Chapter 10

$

—or—

The Red Van in the Sawtooth

One night, right as finals were about to begin, I decided to squander thirty-five cents on a Coke and went downstairs to the soda machine next to the Vanderbilt lobby. I put my money in. Nothing happened. I hit the coin return. No money back. I banged, kicked, swore. Nothing—just those dioramas of dewy cans staring implacably back at me. Then I remarked a torn piece of paper off to the side which warned: "This machine is a thief! It rips off money!" Beneath, someone else had left the commentary, "What do you care? You'll be ripping people off for plenty later!"

I wasn't in the mood to be broadminded. I wanted my soda. I kicked the machine again, then scrawled a reply next to the commentary, "And you're the reason, asshole."

But, trudging upstairs, reconciling myself to a glass of water, I thought of that red van of two years ago. One warm June morning, I'd found myself sitting on the grass of a campsite near one of the forks of the Payette River in Idaho's Sawtooth Range. Around a bend, up one of the Payette's other forks, the most famous wildwater kayaker of our time, Dr. Walter Blackadar, at whose home I'd had dinner the night before, was to drown, his head driven slowly underwater by his own boat that had wedged under a sunken log. But that was a year hence. Here was the dappling of sunlight, the smell of pine resin, squirrels leaping noiselessly around heaps of duffs and cones. Paddles and kayaks were strewn about randomly. Our group of ten or twelve boaters was taking the day off, lying naked in some hot springs down by the river, drying off on rocks in the clear mountain sun.

Earlier in the season, on a wilderness stretch of the Chattooga River between Georgia and South Carolina, I'd run a rapid named appropriately by the locals "Sock-em-Dog." The Chattooga was up at flood level, and rumor had it that the body of a rafter, who had gotten swept off a few months before, had jammed in the rocks of the final waterfall of the rapid and hadn't been recovered for four months. So I approached Sock-em-Dog with a modicum of caution—easing through a maze of rocks and side currents, then over the side of the falls, down with a splash and paddling frantically to free myself from the backwash. Then an unearthly hand of foam reached out and yanked me back in. And an inhuman force, more water than I'd ever felt in my life, was blasting down, plastering me back against my boat that was doing end stands in the hole. That force ripped the paddle from one hand, banged me on the head with it while I madly strove to hang onto it with the other; it flailed away from me, but I managed to twist to the side underwater, diving down for the outward current that was somewhere below, my helmet caught it, tugged me, I grabbed the loose end of the paddle, was swept out upside down and rolled up.

Though breathless and relieved—it hadn't been a difficult rapid, just a dangerous one—I was even more astonished at the cataclysmic dimensions of the water force that had held me twitching and immobile in a rage of current, that had driven itself up my nose, ripped my eyelids open, sightless but scoured. And for a while afterwards the world seemed strangely new and fresh. I sensed myself a guest under the sky, an earthly tourist with so much still to see, an indigent lodger to whom unexpected hospitality had been extended, a child in a new home, seeing with the eyes of a child.

But, given these intermittent awakenings, what was I doing

alone and disgruntled up by the road, while everyone else was dozing or frolicking in the sulphur springs down by the Payette? Why wasn't I down there too by the river, basking in heat from the molten roots of mountains, rejoicing in silence and praise for life's seamlessness, kaleidoscopic mutability, winsome charm, majestic glare? No, I was sitting at the back of my fifteen-year-old Volkswagen bus that had broken down for the two-hundredth time that year, fiddling randomly with wires, first trying one in one socket, then another, then tying the two together in a bow knot. Nothing worked and there wasn't a service station for fifty miles.

When in pulls the doc from Kentucky who'd gone back to the town of Stanley for supplies. Yes, there it was—oh what a lovely van, all red and simonized and big and purring. That thing never broke down nowhere, banging around on the worst access roads Idaho could provide, it'd never conk out on you in the middle of a dirt road in the Adirondacks in February.

Now there's a racket, I said to myself: that guy gets two months off, three if he wants it. And the two weeks I get for paid leave from Lower Manhattan Rehab would barely carry me to the Rockies and back. And he can buy a nice new red van like that and not have to worry about upkeep. Shit, and here I am trying to splice together wires and who knows if it'll ever start. A car like that, and I'd be basking in that hot spring right now, thinking clear, beautiful thoughts, measuring the design of the universe. Yessir, that's the racket to get into: medicine.

When I got back to Lower Manhattan Rehab from the West, I found my desk piled high with forms to be completed and the news that they were laying off a third of the staff while increasing the number of the retarded residents of the facility by one half.

Fortunately, I'd been on the job just long enough to be spared, but there was a steady stream of about-to-be-unemployed speech and recreation and art therapists coming in to say goodbye. Their farewells served to remind me that I might not even have my poor, decrepit bus for long.

A soon-to-be-jobless psychologist dropped by my office with the "Help Wanted" section of the *Times*.

"Look at this," he said. "Can you believe this deal?" He showed me the ad: "'Emergency Room Physician. $50,000 a year, four-day work week, three months vacation.' Can you believe that?" he repeated. "They could get four of me for that. Three day weekends, whole summer off plus a month in the winter. What a deal!"

I saw a better deal later: the average specialist, three years after completing his residency, grosses nearly a hundred thousand a year. I wasn't greedy. Nope, not me. I didn't want that much. Just enough to afford a red van like that doc from Kentucky had. And maybe enough money to have a family someday. A little farfetched, but why not? It'll take some work—what is medical school, three years or something? But I've been screwing around long enough. I should look into that.

So I looked into it, and here I was drinking my glass of water in my dorm room at Harvard. First, I'd go through four years of this kind of delightful stuff, then three or so years of internship and residency where I'd be on those round-the-clock shifts. When I get out, I'll be in my early forties and have to start paying off a thirty-thousand-dollar debt. But, after that, the red van and all its attendant Technicolor pleasures!

Thing is, I mused as I finished off my glass of water and started back to work, I wonder if this might not be a pretty roundabout way of buying a car?

Chapter 11

To the Green Mountains

Saturday night, Dean Hastings and Chanesohn have scheduled a finals-eve party for us in the Vanderbilt Commons Room. Initially, we're all insulted. Me? In the dorm studying Saturday night? Why, I'll be out painting the town red, as usual.

But ten P.M. Saturday arrives, and sure enough I'm studying. Sheepishly I go downstairs. Chanesohn has stationed himself at a tank of ice and is busy popping open Heinekens and handing them around. A group has surrounded Hastings but there aren't that many people in attendance, only twenty or so, including some freeloaders from the second year. I accept a beer from Chanesohn who's in chinos and a sweater.

"Hi," I say. I figure he'll remember me as the first-year student who made the most memorable statement he'd ever heard about medical education.

"Hi," he says back, not showing any signs of recognition.

"How's it going?" (Isn't he supposed to ask me that?)

"Pardon me." He reaches around and gives someone else a beer.

"So, have you gotten used to the change from California?" I ask. Before Harvard, he'd been chief of medicine at Stanford.

"Completely." That round face with the great expanse of bald forehead is sweeping around the room.

"You don't miss things from there? Lying around in the sun?" I'm sort of shuffling back and forth from one foot to the other. "Always being mellow?"

"No, I didn't like that. Didn't like that at all. I'm glad to be back."

"Oh."

Silence.

One of our class reps arrives. The cordiality of a sudden smile breaks over Chanesohn's face. Much enthusiastic hand-shaking and proferring of multiple beers. I get edged to the periphery.

"Where've you been keeping yourself, Meredith? We never see you anymore."

"No, these finals have got me pinned down. But that was a nice talk you gave the class last week, Myron. Lot of people really appreciated that."

From the cafeteria, there had been the sound of rock music. So I went across the lobby and, lo and behold, the Peter Bent Brigham Hospital's pathology service was having a Christmas shindig: tables loaded with food, colored lights blazing on and off, a band pumping electric chords into the immense volume of the hall: No sooner had I started sampling some of the hors d'oeuvres, than, one after the other, four different women tried to pull me by brute force on to the dance floor. The situation for them at the Brigham must have been awful for me to get all this attention, but I hadn't had enough beers to let myself be seen lurching and tripping about, so I retreated in disarray back to the deans' party, collected another Heineken, and joined a group, informing them of big doings across the way.

"Shit, I'd really like to see a few new butts," said Nick, who had a rep as the fastest backcourt ball handler on the Vanderbilt basketball circuit. "I never seen so many goddamn militants as we got here in my life. Shit." A couple more bottles, and we were all emboldened to invade the pathology fling, when Dean Hastings walked up. Suddenly, everyone was on best behavior. Standing next to him, I was struck by how short he was—I towered over him. With the close-cut brown hair and trim, light physique under an English hunting jacket, he had an almost military bearing, except that his eyes were a trifle vague, as if he'd just removed some spectacles. Perhaps he had.

"So are you boys working hard?" Hastings asked.

"Oh yes," we all nodded. Then someone held up a beer ironically, and we all quickly followed suit—we might be studying Saturday night, but we weren't maniacs. Nossir.

"Well, that's what this whole thing is for," said Hastings. "I remember what it was like for me first year, living in Vanderbilt, taking most of the same courses you boys are taking. I appreciated a break once in a while." He shook his head and smiled.

We shook our heads and smiled.

But, beer in hand, I was still examining him. So this was someone who was responsible more than any other single person for the character of the semester I'd just gone through. We were a foot or so apart, but how wide the gap really was: here I was cooking my one-dollar meals on a hot plate in my ten-by-twelve dorm room after a decade in the lower echelons of public institutions, now in my first contact with science, occasionally inebriated by concepts, mostly floundering in endless sloughs of facts. And there he was, one of the Brahmins of medicine, whizzing constantly about the world giving lectures and attending meetings, conferring with cabinet officials in that giant office with the antique furniture. It was important suddenly to reach across that gap and speak. And it seemed my responsibility somehow. But how?

"You do research of your own, I understand?" I said, gesturing with my beer. Hastings wasn't drinking.

"Well, when I have the chance." He looked up at me with those vague blue eyes. "They don't let me have much time." A smile that said, "We both understand how it is, don't we?"

"What's your field?"

"Lithium transport."

"Lithium like in the drug for schizophrenics?"

"Not for schizophrenics. Depressives. Manic depressives."

The group nodded solemnly and repeated "depressives" while glancing at me as if I were a dunce.

"So you're trying to find out why it works."

"Not that ambitious. Mainly, how it's transported across cell membranes. If we can elucidate that, then perhaps someone else can show us why it works with depressives."

"Depressives," everybody said again.

There was a silence. I hadn't exactly done it, had I? Someone had once told me that Hastings had never really practiced medicine—just completed his year of internship then hurried back to the labs. Was it true? I couldn't figure out a polite way to ask. If so, were immunoassays and restriction enzymes and standard deviations and NIH grants and standing committees all he knew about? If he'd never practiced, would he know about things like clogged shunts, or Chinese kids with TB crying in the empty night of hospital corridors, or sun-blinded teenagers locked in institutions for the retarded, or orphans shot up on purpose with serum hepatitis? If he didn't know, there must be some way I could tell him. But there were so many things, I couldn't get any of them out; so I stood there looking at my beer bottle, confused.

"Well, I have to move on to some other groups," Hastings said.

We all thanked him for the party. He thanked us for being there. We thanked him again. He joined another group. We ran over to the path party.

By one A.M., the med students had made off to their rooms with every single bowl, tureen, and casserole dish of food that the Brigham people had brought, and I was drunkenly stumbling about the dance floor with a lighthearted, red-tressed nursing student named Jessica.

"There's one thing I can't stand," she said, pointing out another couple.

"What's that?" I said, moving in to dance close.

"Doctors who try to get nurses drunk, then put the moves on."

"But, Jessica, what do you think I'm doing?"

"That's OK. You got yourself twice as drunk first."

"Let's go upstairs," I said. "Where it's quiet. And we can talk."

"Watch your step," she said, taking my arm.

Four hours later, I woke up with three quarts of beer wrestling eighty-three hors d'oeuvres to a draw. It was five A.M. Sunday. Tomorrow morning was the biochemistry final. Tuesday, histology and Céline. Wednesday, neuroanatomy, which I hadn't looked at for a week. And Thursday, the big one, physiology. Jessica was certainly going to want a slow breakfast and lots of good talk. This was pushing the spirit of Citgo too far. What was I going to do?

After half an hour of thrashing about in indecision, I'd so thoroughly destroyed the bedclothes that Jessica couldn't sleep either, called a cab, and went home. I had a Bromo-Seltzer, set the alarm for eight, and curled up around my pillow.

The biochemistry test was the usual wasteland of rote recall. Most questions seemed to have been lifted from miscellaneous texts, and this time they hadn't even bothered to retype them—just cut, paste, and photocopy—so the first page was a mishmash of different typefaces and angles of print. I got my usual grade, Ron and Cheryl surged well up above the median, but the relief to all of us of finally being free of that course was hard to describe.

To everyone's astonishment, our friends in histology gave us some impossibly hard slide identifications and a trick essay question that revolved around a point of gross anatomy never discussed in the handouts. But even the people who did badly weren't panicking, just worrying.

"When will we know whether we passed?" asked one.

"We got a case of Colt 45 over in the refrigerator in my lab," said Fineful, stroking that mustache. "These things should be graded before we have to call out for another."

The worrier's eyes opened in pure terror, then Fineful gave a wink, and the expression dissolved into relief.

"Take a vacation," said Fineful.

146 / Charles LeBaron

*　　*　　*

Céline called me from Logan Airport that afternoon as I was trying to cram chapter after indigestible chapter of neuroanatomy down my mental gullet.

"I am arrived," she said, sounding tired. "Are you content?"

"Of course I am content, my Céline," I said in French. "I am very, very content."

"Then why are you not here?"

"As I wrote, Céline, it is absolutely necessary that I study without cease today and tomorrow."

"As usual. Very well."

"I will tell you how to come here by bus and subway. If you have too many heavy things, I can pay for a taxi."

"I have many presents for you, but I will manage on the subway."

An hour later, she arrived in the lobby in high-heeled sandals, white socks, and a loose, flower print dress, carrying a sack full of other flowery dresses, and with a Prisunic shopping bag containing croissants, a *baguette moulée*, and some paperback science fiction books for me to practice my French. We kissed, then started upstairs.

"This is agreeable," Céline said. "Each person has his own room. In France, there are many to each room, the women are separated from the men, and no one can visit. I like this place."

I showed her my room. She sat down on the bed.

"Now I will show you your room," I said. "We have much luck. Someone moved out on the third floor, I spoke to the concierge, and I was able to obtain this private room just for you for the next two days. Is this not great luck?"

But Céline was not to be deceived. "Of what need do I have for a room? This room is sufficient."

"This is for your benefit, Céline. When I study, I am most restless. I stay up late. You must be quiet. You know that is difficult. This room is quite small. I—"

"No. I do not wish it." She began unpacking her things. "I stay here. I will be quiet. You can study."

"But just for two nights, Céline. Then—"

"No. I do not wish this other room. Stop with your pleasantries."

"I must insist, Céline. I cannot study while you are here."

"Then I return to France!" She began picking up her bags. "You may keep your presents."

"Céline."

"No. First you do not meet me at the airport. Then you throw me from your room. You are hiding something. I do not care to know what it is. I part for France."

"I hide nothing."

"Why do you lie? You are not good at lying. I leave."

"Don't leave." I got up and stood in front of the door.

Céline put her hands on her hips. "I will scream."

We looked at each other. I was a foot taller and fifty pounds heavier, but there was no doubt who was tougher.

"Will you be very quiet? Not say anything?"

"I have said I will be quiet." She tossed her yellow hair proudly.

I looked at my neuroanatomy. I didn't believe her. But. . . . "D'accord," I said and helped her unpack.

For a while, things looked bad as I kept getting peppered with questions about soap, bathrooms, places to hang clothes, schedule tomorrow, who was cooking dinner. But around seven-thirty, there was a sudden calm. Jet lag had caught up with Céline. Serendipity was smiling on me again.

The Bateses gave us a long, complicated test in neuroanatomy; but it was open book, so everyone carted in wheelbarrowsful of reference tomes, then carted them back to the dorm after the exam, not that much wiser for having taken the course. It's obvious that if I'm ever to learn anything about the structure of the human nervous system, I'll have to teach it to myself sometime in the future.

So it all comes down to physiology. The number rumored to have flunked last year is increasing geometrically. In the limit, it will approach the size of the entire class. But there isn't enough time to reach that limit. Only fourteen hours of studying left, some of which may or may not be allocated to sleep. I've averaged three a night for the last week.

Before plunging in, I make dinner for Céline and me. She is finally willing to concede that all this is not an elaborate alibi.

"But this is very ridiculous. In France, were there no grades, only pass and fail, no one would work at all. Why do you work? They could not make a French person work like this for no grade," she said, blue eyes flashing.

"Imagine a foot race, Céline," I said, "in which only the last ten people lose. Everyone, all one hundred and fifty, except those ten, wins. We all start slowly—what is the chance of my being one of the last ten? Then you discover that others are going faster than you, and you are among the last ten. So you speed up and get to the middle, leaving someone else in the last ten. Then those people speed up, and soon everyone is running as fast as they possibly can."

"In France, we would band together."

"In America, people are not accustomed to banding together in such a manner."

"Then Americans are stupid."

"Do the French think of Americans as stupid?"

"No, you are right. They think they are barbarians or very intelligent children. But not cultivated and not adults."

"But even children and barbarians can be ambitious. That is why everyone runs so hard. If you fail, they put you in a special class with the others who have failed and give you the test over again. No one wants that. No one says it aloud, but it is considered a humiliation. More of a humiliation than any grade could ever be. It implies that you are not intelligent enough to be here. And everyone at Harvard seems secretly worried that they are not really intelligent enough to be here."

"But these things you must memorize," Céline pulled over some of my handouts and gestured at them with disdain. "These have nothing to do with intelligence. They are just charts and tables of chemical compounds in tremendous detail. None of this has anything to do with sick people."

"It is not meant to have anything to do with sick people."

"What do you recount? What will happen when you work in the hospital? Will you tell the person who is sick, I am a doctor but I know nothing about sick people?"

"We are to learn those things in the hospital."

"But by then it is too late."

As you advance through the French medical educational system, you could also advance on the hospital vocational ladder, from orderly to ambulance attendant to nurse to interne. You were not a medical student sightseeing, but one of the help; you had specific responsibilities, got paid for your work, and were fired if you didn't do it right.

"Remember, Céline, this is America. Medical students are never considered nurse's aides. We are always doctors, embryonic doctors now, but we do not mix our jobs with other jobs in the hospital. And we never take orders from nurses or orderlies. We are considered too intelligent and important."

"And these diagrams make you intelligent and important. It is too ridiculous. How do you learn except by treating with real patients? It is like trying to learn how to ride a bicycle by reading a book, all this theory."

"Theory is considered very important in America. Most of the others in my class have spent four years before medical school learning theoretic matters of biochemistry or biology."

"And then you spend another two years in medical school in the classroom before you ever see a hospital?"

"Toward the end of next year, we will be taught how to examine someone physically."

"This is unbelievable. Five and a half years of education to be a doctor, and you cannot take someone's pulse or know what to do if someone stops breathing on the street."

"Yes, but after medical school, I will probably spend years in the hospital. Mostly becoming a specialist."

"Yes, but that is not learning how to be a doctor. That is learning how to be an expert in some field of medicine. So you spend ten or eleven years here becoming a doctor. The first four you learn about flowers and stars. The last three you become an expert on all the diseases of the fingernails. And in all that time you only spend two learning how to treat sick people?"

"Yes, but while I am learning to be a specialist, Céline, I

will also learn many things about being a doctor. And many of the theoretics people learn in college are closer to medicine than flowers and stars. There are many theoretics I wish I knew better."

"But I can see why you do not know them. This neuroanatomy test you took today. How long did you say you studied that?"

"Six or seven weeks. But many people are taking instead a short course in January that lasts only three weeks."

"Three weeks! Our neuroanatomy lasted for a year. We studied the development of the nervous system for longer than you study the whole of the subject. Even then there was not enough time. What could you learn in a month and a half?"

"I learned very little."

"These charts and diagrams they make you memorize. Do they make you do this because most students here will become doctors of research only, not of patients?"

"No, almost everyone in my class wants to be a doctor of patients. A few years ago, someone polled a Harvard class and found that only two percent want to be researchers. I understand that forty or fifty years ago, most of the courses were taught by real doctors. Then people would learn about the pain and agony of being sick and were inspired to go into research to try to do something about that. I myself felt the same way once here when someone explained about a cholera epidemic. But now the only people who teach us are researchers who have never seen a sick person and we get so much research data to memorize that everyone wants to get away from that as quickly as possible and see real people for a change. So after spending a little time here, almost no one wants to go into research anymore. But they keep teaching us research all the same."

Céline shook her blond hair till it swayed back and forth across her face. "I do not understand this place. I think there is something you are not explaining to me."

We ate for a while, sitting on my bed with a piece of plywood as dinner table. That mammoth looseleaf of physiology handouts was staring ominously at me from the desk, but I'd turned out the lights and set up a candle between us that cast a yellow light over our faces and bowls of spaghetti and shadowed out the books.

"Another thing I do not understand," said Céline, sitting back. "Why are there so many police all around here? And why must you carry that photograph of your face attached to the outside of your clothing everywhere you go?"

"On the other side of the big street, Huntington Avenue, is a neighborhood of poor people, poor Black people. They are in buildings owned by the government. Harvard is afraid some of the poor Black people will rob it and hurt its students. Harvard will not say it is the poor Blacks from across the street that it is afraid of, but everyone knows what they mean when they tell people never to walk alone. And some frightening things have taken place. A faculty member from Harvard was very badly knifed a month ago and is still in the hospital. A few years ago, someone told me, a student was beaten and is still paralyzed from the waist down, though I do not know that for sure. But people are afraid, and that is the reason for the police and the identification cards."

"This is horrible," Céline said. "It is just like I have read in Le Monde. I thought it was only the propaganda of the Left. But it is true. Does Harvard try to do something to help these poor Blacks, besides hire police against them?"

"In the past Harvard used the public hospital in Boston for teaching us. But it decided to remove its students. I don't know why. It does have other programs. A few medical students can go to work with Indians in New Mexico and with poor people in South America and people on farms in Maine."

"I do not speak of these places. They are far away. I speak of across the street."

"I know of no program across the street. Perhaps there will be one someday. One of our deans, named Chanesohn, went to China and came back and gave us a speech and told us that he was very impressed with the medical system there and that the Chinese medical students are happy because they all want to serve the people."

"If he believes this, why does he go to China?"

"What should he do?"

"In France, we read that China is doing well, people are working to improve things there. I do not know if that is true, but that is what we hear. But we hear that in the United States there are special neighborhoods for poor Black people and they are treated badly and are lynched."

"No one is lynched now."

"But they were. And now they are poor and they steal and they are angry. I read this and I think it is the politics of the Left again. But here I see police everywhere and people must wear pictures to show they are not criminals. This man, your dean, should not spend money going around the world. He should go across the street."

"Perhaps he does go across the street. We never hear of it. But it is not different here than in France, Céline. There is renown to be gained in going to China. There is no renown to be gained in going across the street. The intellectuals of the Left in Paris do not go to the eighteenth arrondissement, La Goutte d'Or, where the Arabs live. They go to Cuba and Nicaragua and Angola."

"Yes, the Arabs of Paris are not well treated, I agree. But they do not live like across the street. I saw those buildings today. There is broken glass everywhere and cars with no motors and garbage. It is not like that in Paris. But if Harvard will do nothing, what do the students do?"

"There are some students, a few, who try to change things here. But most American students are not as interested in politics as French students are. And one does not hear much about across the street. There is more concern about mines in South Africa and nuclear power plants in New Hampshire and migrant workers in California."

"More of the same. Americans love places that are not close to worry about. And you?"

"Me? I do nothing."

"And why?"

"Céline, I do nothing but study. Every hour of the day and night. I have so little time, I do not buy clothes or pay my bills or write letters or read books."

"These diagrams again! You are obsessed by diagrams. But you should not let them and their diagrams dominate your life. Do not worry about their silly humiliations, their foot races, their failures. You should do something, write something to tell people about this matter."

I twisted my spaghetti. "Perhaps you are right, Céline. I will think about it. But tomorrow, I have my last examination. And I want to pass. So I must study all night. Much of that is to avoid humiliation. But I have another reason too, which no one else has. A very good reason."

"And what is that?"

"I do not wish to spend my vacation in a classroom or library worrying about an examination. I wish to spend it with my Céline."

"Finally," said Céline, putting down her fork. "You give a good reason. You must study hard those diagrams!"

Whether it was Byron Vitellino's switchblade persuasions at the Cannon Ball, or the general hullabaloo over the midterm, or some unknown factor, the physiology final turned out to be relatively sane. None of Wurstblau's equations showed up, we were provided with the numerical blood and urine values we needed to work out problems, and the questions were based for the most part on real clinical situations, actually requiring some elements of reasoning rather than bulk regurgitation. Hard to believe.

After the exam, Marita Feinstein was hosting a champagne party in the Vanderbilt Commons Room. I grabbed Céline from my room, but we had to fight just to get close to the place—shouting, singing, milling crowds, rock music, people kissing each other. The first term was over.

We squeezed inside—the Persian carpets had been rolled up, the deep armchairs pushed to the side, Chanesohn was behind the long, ornate oak table popping open magnums of champagne, pouring them out into plastic cups that people thrust in front of him endlessly. Half the physiology department was there, the students had grabbed any faculty they could get their hands on, and everyone was cavorting about on the dance floor, heads bobbing up and down in time to the music.

"I do not understand," said Céline, refusing with a curl of the lip a cup of New York champagne. "These are your professors, some of the greatest scientists in America, and yet they consent to be made ridiculous."

"Yes," I said, downing my own cup and starting to work on Céline's. A week of no sleep was catching up with me, but I was still coasting on adrenalin and Nodoz. The champagne tasted good.

"Why?"

"It is not the same to be ridiculous in America as in France. It is felt here that if one is willing to be ridiculous, it shows a sense of humor and strength of character and demonstrates that one likes the students."

"Do they like the students?"

"I am not sure. Some do, and some don't. But all wish it to appear that they do. I have never been anywhere where people will proclaim one point of view so strongly while doing exactly the opposite."

A woman reached out and pulled Marcus onto the floor and off he went bumping and grinding.

"And that one, the one you say is head of your physiology course that everyone was so afraid of failing—now they want to dance with him."

"The students here may dislike their professors, but they do not wish to do so. They are happy now."

"In France, we have longer memories."

"But in America, we do these things to forget. Being drunk, having parties like this are part of medicine here. It is part of what we learn this first year. You try to forget how you spend most of your life."

"But why should you want to forget? Are you not learning how to prevent people from dying or suffering? What could be happier than being able to do that? And why can't you be happy to learn about such things?"

"I don't know, Céline," I said and went off for some more champagne. When I came back, Alonzo Akins, a Black fellow who lived down the hall from me in the dorm, had formed a dancing line of other Blacks that was snaking about the room. Then some faculty and white students joined the rear and soon everyone was wriggling behind Alonzo in all sorts of gyratory extravagances.

"I do not like all this noise and foolish crowding together," said Céline, taking my hand. "I am frightened by these people. They are loud, even your professors and deans, and I do not understand them at all."

The python of dancers wandered off, hands on each other's hips, past the grand piano, under the portrait of the stern-looking physician with pork chop whiskers, made a loop around an oblivious trio of two guys and a woman who were sandwiched together in a polymorphous, frictional version of the twist. Then, coming back toward the center of the room, past the fluted Doric columns of oak and the enormous, scarlet poinsettias, Alonzo went down into a semisquat and with a flick of the hips came up again, raising his fist, crying, "Get down tonight!"

And the whole line of physiologists and psychiatrists and deans and students followed, thigh to buttocks, in a writhing, undulating chain. "Get down tonight!" The fists, white and black, faculty and student, went into the air. "Get down tonight!"

"They are all mad!" said Céline, fairly clinging to me. "Totally mad!"

I raised more of Chanesohn's champagne to my lips. The pale light of a December morning was drifting past the crimson velvet curtains, illuminating the bubbles into yellow iridescence. "Yes," I said. "This is medical school, and I am going to be a doctor. Now we will join their dance."

"No!" said Céline, pulling violently on my arm. "And put away that awful wine your dean keeps giving you. I do not like this place. I want to leave."

I looked at her, swaying slightly.

She yanked my arm again. "Return to yourself, Charles. Return to yourself."

"The Green Mountains," I said. "We will go to the Green Mountains, then."

"No! I do not go on that bicycle. You are mad, too."

"Then we will find another way, my Céline. There is snow there. More snow than you ever see in Paris in a lifetime." I bent down and kissed her.

The line went twisting around us, Marita and Marcus waving from the tail, heading back for the grand piano and fireplace of polished marble. "Get down tonight!"

"Perhaps in the mountains you will be sane again," said Céline, intertwining her fingers in mine. "Your condition has much worsened since I last saw you, Charles."

"I know," I said. "But we will see what we can do about that in the Green Mountains."

Chapter 12

Christmas in Brooklyn
Wherein Josie and Chuckie of 111th Discuss the Past

Christmas Day in Brooklyn. Céline and I have returned from cross-country skiing in the Green Mountains. Before leaving, I had convinced Harvard that if they could not budget me more money themselves, at least to allow me to ask for a thousand-dollar loan from New York State. I can either apply that money to give me two dollars a meal, or to luxuries like movies and Christmas trips to New York. I've been scraping along on my one dollar meals, so in good welfare fashion I decide that luxuries are more important than necessities.

We ring a buzzer in the basement of a short, old apartment house at the end of a street full of tenements.

Suddenly the door flings open, and there's a burst of loud music, television, kids screaming, general chaos. I'm pulled inside, hugged in a steely grip, then get punched a few times in the stomach.

"Old Chuckie-boy! Old Chuckie!"

I aim an elbow at the short ribs, start sweeping up a heel while driving forward. A table full of food nearly gets upset, a woman yells at us, and she comes over to kiss me, while kids have tangled up in my legs.

"Josie," I say to a powerful guy with a black goatee, about

158

my age but a little shorter, who still has me in half a hammerlock. "This is Céline."

"Allo," says Céline. "You must bear me for I speak only a little of English." Already the children have deserted me for her. Whatever the language, Céline likes children, and they like her.

"First you get some food," says Josie's wife Lucy.

We take off our coats, load up plates with stuffing and salad and deviled eggs, say hello all around, then sit down.

"So what's cooking?" says Josie smiling. The greeting from the block.

"Same old stuff," I say.

Josie's half Puerto Rican, half Greek. We had spent our childhoods together on East 111th Street in Manhattan, splashing about in hydrant gushes in the summer, building fires in the gutter in the winter, chasing rats up and down the courts that were a foot thick in airmail, playing stickball between parked cars, setting off cherry bombs in subway stations, going to Central Park in little gangs and pelting bums with debris until they staggered up and tried to chase us. Once I'd stumbled on a piece of hexagonal macadam; a bum had snared my ankle, lifted me, and as I screamed and struggled, was about to mash my face into the asphalt in one big, lumbering heave, when Josie had nailed him with a rock on the back of the head, and I escaped.

Neither Josie nor I had done well in grade school, but our situations had been somewhat different. He was one of six children; his father had an alcohol problem, and the family spent much of the time on relief. Instead of drinking and welfare difficulties, both my parents had tuberculosis. Which had effectively limited the family size to them and me. But after prolonged stays in public sanataria, my father recovered from his bouts of TB and worked as a salesman. Eventually, he was able to make enough money to allow us to move away from 111th Street up to the Bronx. Yet, even there, I continued doing so poorly in public school that I was in danger of being left back. In desperation, my parents applied me to various private schools, but my math and science aptitude scores were so abysmal (hovering below the fifth percentile) that I was turned down everywhere, except for one small place that was willing to accept me on a trial basis. Since the tuition was only six hundred dollars a year, my parents decided to make the effort and send me there.

I went to Princeton. Josie went to jail. He was coming home one night from his work as a doorman, when he was set upon and beaten on a subway platform by a crowd incensed over the robbery of an old woman's purse in the neighborhood. A Puerto Rican had been the robber, and Josie came closer than anyone else to fitting the description. Though Josie'd never been in trouble with the law before, had a regular job, was engaged to be married, and there were no witnesses to identify him as the robber, he was convicted. Sentenced to five years in prison, he served three of those years in maximum security facilities before being released on parole.

During the year-long wait for trial, Josie had been fired from his job, his fiancée had broken the engagement; he had no money to hire a lawyer or even pay rent. He'd gone to my father, who was then enjoying some relative prosperity since I was out of school and the constant drain of hospital expenses had ended with my mother's death. My father had lent Josie the money for the lawyer, visited him in prison, and put him up for a few months after Josie got out.

Josie had gone on to become a janitor, convinced his former fiancée to marry him, went back for his high school diploma, and now was working at night on a college degree at Long Island University. Josie had integrated my father into his own growing family as foster grandfather. So after my father had died, Josie (along with some elderly aunts) was the closest thing I had to a family of my own, an adopted stepbrother.

"I got my hands full around here," said Josie. Screams of joy as Céline chased the kids around the food table and color TV.

"How do you study?" I said.

"No, there's no way here. I go to the workshop, my official place of business, and lock the door."

More family started pouring in.

"Let's get out of this for a while," said Josie. "It's a fucking madhouse when there're holidays around this place. I got these pictures of the New York Marathon I got to show you. Old Josie of 111th in all his glory."

We left the apartment and walked along a dim, twisting, cement hallway, lined by steam pipes, gas meters, and metal doors.

"I thought they weren't going to let you run in that thing," I said.

"Yeah, I kill myself practicing for three fucking months. Then they turn down my application because I hadn't joined the AAU by the aforementioned date, or some such horseshit. Well, I figured all those other fuckers who had their AAU membership by the aforementioned date had been practicing all their lives in nice little warm indoor tracks and colleges and Central Park while me, the only other place I ever run before was back in the yard. And there, man, the fucking Black Muslims had decided that The Messenger or somebody had told them to run the opposite way from everybody else and yell 'Allah!' every lap—big showdown with them every time you went around who stepped aside."

Josie pulled out a key from a wad that was the size of the Gordian knot, unlocked a door, and flipped on a light. There was a workbench with a bunch of tools, a wooden desk in the corner, some odd-looking metal contraptions; the walls were hung with pictures of Josie in a karate gee flying through the air, some old rusted machetes, a violin with no strings, an army helmet, and photographs of women in various stages of undress.

"Here go those shots." We sat down on a broken couch. There was Josie in running gear, whizzing along in groups of people.

"But how did you get in?"

"Listen, I read up in the *News* on when it's going to start. And my nephew drives me over to Staten Island, all dressed up with a phony number I sent away for out of some Campbell's soup can. And we're so nervous we're blowing all this weed, I'm high as a kite, so we come across the

Verrazzano Bridge, and after a while there's this big crowd, so we wait till the last minute, then he pulls around, screeching like gangbusters, hell on two wheels, and I jump out and run into the big crowd and a cop's running after me yelling *hey!* and everybody's looking at me and I keep running around in the crowd, then a gun goes off and everybody starts, big mess, and I just go running off up the bridge, and I'm so high I keep saying they can't revoke me, I got my bridge toll ticket! But they're not chasing me no more, and there's old Josie of a hundred and eleventh up there with the herd for a mile or so, then I'm getting a stitch, so I got to drop back."

We flipped through some more plastic-covered three-by-fives.

"But hey," said Josie. "Lucy's going to have my ass if we stay out too long. And I got to show you some pictures of your pops."

There was my father at last year's Christmas party at Josie's, two months before he was to die, already looking weak and old.

"Here, Josie Jr.'s giving him his present—box of candy."

Though my father's lungs were scarred with TB and other mementos of life during the Depression, his main problem at seventy had been high blood pressure and hardening of the arteries. Though he was as mentally alert and agile as he'd ever been, he was no longer able to take the strolls he liked around the neighborhood, particularly since he lived in a four-story walk-up.

At the end of January, following Josie's last Christmas party, he'd caught the flu, a potentially serious problem for someone his age. He seemed to be recuperating somewhat, when he suffered an attack of suffocating shortness of breath and pains in the chest, two of the classic symptoms of a heart attack. He was taken by ambulance to the nearest hospital. I met him in the emergency room.

His private physician was on the hospital staff. "I told the residents not to panic when they saw his chest films," he said, referring to my father's old, calcified TB.

The shortness of breath was better, but he was lying in bed, weak and sick, barely able to raise his head, trying to smile.

Though there were abnormalities in his electrocardiogram, the hospital refused to admit him. His flu, they said, might present some ward management problems. It was the week of an intense blizzard. I took him home in his pajamas and slippers; he picked his way through snowdrifts and foot-deep slush, as I held him up, to get to his building's entranceway. He was so weak it took us three-quarters of an hour to mount the four flights to his apartment.

With the help of some neighbors, Josie and I alternated visiting him, getting groceries, cooking dinner, changing the bed. At that time, my premedical curriculum was in full cry: I was taking organic chemistry, physics, and integral calculus at night, while working at Lower Manhattan Rehab during the day. My schedule was so crowded, there was no way to fit in the daytime calculus classes, so I missed all the classes, taught the subject to myself, and called in sick at work the days when I had to show up at school for an exam. With grade terror reigning supreme, there was no such thing as an acceptable excuse for cutting labs, but I cut anyway and would sit next to my father's bed, underlining in a fat organic chemistry text. After a week, my father appeared to improve and was able to put some frozen meals in the oven himself.

An indigent widow's son, he'd grown up in the Lower East Side and gone to work in a lumberyard right after high school. His financial condition had waxed, fortunately for me, right during my high school and college years. It had waned again, and now all he had was a small pension and Social Security. Nonetheless, he was a kind, happy man, with gentle eyes, a full head of white hair, small glasses perched high on his nose and a natural courtliness that charmed visitors. He liked reading, and I'd given him *Remembrance of Things Past* to work on. At a break in my studying one evening, we began discussing Proust's idea of beauty. My father arranged his pillow, propped himself unsteadily up on one arm, smiled. "I agree with Proust," he said wryly. "Beauty is youth." We laughed, there was a pause, then his expression changed. "I'm frightened," he said suddenly.

I looked at him, then took his hand, and stroked it. He'd tried, but they wouldn't let him into the hospital, and I was sitting there, bristling with information on the detailed chemistry of petroleum products and the synthetic mechanisms for plastics, but years and years away from knowing anything that could help him.

One day later in the week, I called, and the phone didn't answer. When I arrived, my father was lying face down in bed, eyes open, body already with that excruciating coldness. The cause of death was listed as heart attack. He'd been reading *Guermantes' Way*, and the pages were crumpled where his face had fallen.

A week later, I got a letter admitting me to Harvard Medical School.

I looked at the photographs under the glass of Josie's desk, photographs of my father when he was still alive; then I rubbed my hand across my face.

"Hey, man," said Josie, grabbing my shoulder and kneading it. "Sometimes when I look at these pictures I get choked up too. Especially all those things he did when I was cooling my heels in the country club. The Tombs, then Sing Sing, then Greenhaven. You hit those places, man, you're all alone. I don't care who you are. All alone. But your pops didn't forget me—he visited me even if it meant taking a bus six, seven hours, and wrote to the board for my parole. And when I made it to daylight, I had to start all over, only worse, and your father he had only but a one-bedroom place, and he gave me the bedroom. Six months. I don't forget that kind of shit."

"If they'd just let him in that fucking hospital," I said. "Maybe it wouldn't have made any difference, though."

"Made any difference? Fuck it," said Josie. "You bet your sweet ass it would have made a difference—he'd be around now at the Christmas party with us. The people who run them hospitals ain't no different from landlords. It's cash. They got their building, they want their rent. And all your pops had was his pitiful little Medicare card."

"His own doctor was nice," I said. "He tried to help him."

"Sure, they're all fucking nice," said Josie. "It's when they get together, when they're landlords, they're not so nice.

When you were at that fucking so-called emergency room, what you should have done—what I would of done—is knock over a few bedpans, start yelling, pick up a chair. Hospitals, doctors, ain't no different from nobody else. They're landlords, they want money. They don't want no hassle. Problem is he got the flu? Make a bigger problem for them than any flu. This ain't no tiddlywinks—this is a question of life and death. On account of they maybe forgot that little detail—people wanting to live."

No, I'd sat there with my organic chemistry book and the tact that is the watermark of a Princeton education. It hadn't worked, had it?

"You remember," said Josie. "You remember you checked with that lawyer afterwards and he said nothing could be done on account of nobody having no right to be treated? Well, if you're dying, and you don't have no right to be treated, what they're really saying is that you don't have no right to live. And it's fucking cash that gives you rights. Just remember who did what, that's my motto." Josie stood up. "But let's not dwell on this kind of shit. It's Christmas. We got to get back. I'm surprised Lucy's not beating down the door here already."

Josie locked up, and we walked back down the basement hallway. I thought of the times when I'd come into New York from Princeton, and my father and I would make the rounds of the Times Square pool halls, shooting eight ball against each other for quarters. We reached the door to Josie's apartment. I could hear Céline trying to teach the kids a song in French. I stopped and put my head against the cinderblock wall. When we'd cleaned out my father's apartment, Josie had found a copy of Edgar Lee Masters's Spoon River Anthology, in the flyleaf of which my father had written a poem of his own:

> Three loves I had,
> Mother, wife, son.
> From my mother, I took.
> With my wife, I shared.
> To my son, I gave.

I started weeping, and my tears dripped down, forming a dark spot on the concrete floor.

"Hey! Hey, man," said Josie, putting a hand on the back of my neck. "Hey, man, it's Christmas. We got to go in there. With the rest of the family. We can't look all fucked up. Let me tell you something. Will you let me tell you something?" He turned me around toward him, hand on the back of my neck.

"You know what the toughest fucking part of that marathon was, man? It was the Bronx. The Bronx, man. We come over the bridge, and suddenly we're in Fort Apache, everything like 111th only worser, and all the people of color around, the brothers. And I'm coming along in my phony Campbell soup number, and the brothers start going wild, maybe there was other people my color there but I sure didn't see them. And people are hanging off fire escapes and yelling from stoops, 'Go motherfucker! Go brother man!' And I figure I got to be polite back, so I put up my arms in this Mighty Mouse pose and hold them that way all the way through the Bronx.

"Well, finally, I get up over the Willis Avenue Bridge and get the fuck out of the Bronx, and I near to collapsed. Oh shit, I was like to die! I start wavering all over, banging into parked cars and other people, and I thought, shit, those fucking brothers did me in, me and my fucking Mighty Mouse shit. Well, you know you get sort of crazy when you're real tired and you start repeating songs and stupid commercials to yourself. Well, all I could think of was something as kept coming into my head when times were bad back at the country club, something we used to write on subway cars and in the schoolyard—'111th Street Rule!' And I just keep telling myself that over and over—'111th's Going to Rule, Going to Rule, Going to Rule!' And I just kept going and after a while I wasn't staggering all over and I finished all twenty-six miles, three hundred eighty-five yards of that thing.

"Now, man, you running a long, hard trip. And they trying to take things away from you, man, can't never be given back. Same guys in charge there as wouldn't let your father in that hospital. Same guys. You trying to run around like Mighty Mouse is just going to fuck you up. Just remember, whatever the fuck they do, someday you going to finish this thing. And someday, too, them and their cash won't be in charge no more."

I smiled. "111th's Going to Rule," I said.

"Going to Rule." Josie gave me a tap across the face, then opened the door, and we went inside.

Chapter 13

The Forty-Hour Class Week

The first day of the new term. We all show up at Amphi-theater C with white coats and a kit consisting of a scalpel, scissors, tweezers, and a probe. There's a nervous buzz of conversation.

The famous *Gray's Anatomy* seems to be on its way out; its approach is functional and physiological—organ system by organ system. Harvard uses a book that stresses surgical relationships; and everyone refers to it by the author's last name, Snell:

> If the downward sloping ribs were raised at their sternal ends, the anteroposterior diameter of the thoracic cavity would be increased and the lower end of the sternum would be thrust forward. This can be brought about by fixing the first rib by contraction of the scaleni muscles of the neck and contracting the intercostal muscles.

What's Snell talking about? Breathing in. Weighty, dry, but comprehensible.

Manfredo Ritti, a thin, small man in his early forties with

black, receding hair, a distinct Italian accent, and hands constantly in motion, arrives, smiling and gesturing. He straps on the microphone, then starts pacing up and down excitedly, laughing, joking, drawing remarkable multicolored pictures on the blackboard in the twinkling of an eye. He's versed in perspective and Renaissance painting, and he uses the wires of the microphone like a torch singer, coiling and uncoiling, flipping them out of his way. First, the rules of the course: no real handouts, since we should "Memorize da Snell! Memorize every word!" Obviously, he's kidding—Snell's a thousand pages long. But he keeps repeating, banging on the lab bench for emphasis: "Reada da Snell!" OK, we get the message. Doesn't like grades, Ritti says. Just big complication, big headache. So if we get grade we don't like, change it on the test paper, he'll accept. Everyone laughs—we've been around medical school long enough to know there's a catch somewhere, but we like the spirit anyway. A quick, general lecture on the nomenclature of cross-sectional planes, articular surfaces, layers of fasciae, then off to the dissecting rooms.

Strong, sweet smell, like spiced honey gone rancid, pervading, out into the hall and even down a floor—formalin. And there we all are, standing around in our new white coats, waiting for Ritti. The bodies are rowed up, each on its own rolling table, covered by blue sheets. For some inexplicable reason, they all seem to have enormous barrel chests. The guy next to me starts fiddling knowledgeably with a skeleton dangling on its frame.

"You know how they get these?"

"They buy them—they're plastic or something?" I say.

He laughs. "They buy them all right, but take a look—feel that."

I feel it. It's rough. "Yeah?"

"That's not plastic. It's real. You know where they buy these things?"

I start feeling the rib cage. Was this once a breathing person? A curious fate to end up in this room. "Where?"

"Bangladesh."

"Bangladesh?"

"Sure. They go over during famines and epidemics. People are so poor they sell their own bodies before they're dead for fifty cents to help their families."

I didn't believe it. Anyway, things were macabre enough around here.

Ritti arrived in his usual hurry, told us to get seats if we wanted while he briefed us. I felt like taking a seat, but no one else moved, so I didn't either.

"All right," says Ritti. "Who's read this lab?"

Last week we'd gotten a pre-assignment from Ritti. But it was against my post-Citgo policy to take up vacations studying. Apparently others had evolved similar policies, since only one or two hands went up.

"Vacation," somebody muttered.

"Vacation? Do I hear vacation?" said Ritti. "Don't you know you in medical school now? No such thing as vacation! Medical school is your whole life. No other life possible. Whole life."

"Fuck you," I said silently.

"OK then, I explain." And explain he did, for forty-five minutes. And we all stood there in white coats, like soldiers on dress review. Twenty minutes in, I was starting to feel light-headed, a hint of roaring in my ears. Shit, I said to myself, I got to sit down. But I couldn't see a seat and everybody was as immobile as if they had been cast in wax. I can just imagine myself keeling over here—they haven't even shown us a cadaver yet. I'd never live that down for the next seven years! So I started clenching my leg muscles, trying to massage that blood back up from the feet to the head.

It's just like the movies, I think, Broderick Crawford arrives, crusty, ill-tempered anatomy prof who's seen it all but deep down is really a soft, lovable old curmudgeon, makes crucial incision below camera level that seems to extend from the nose to the crotch, fellow next to Frank Sinatra falls unconscious off his seat, even Robert Mitchum raises a gloomy eyebrow, Eva Marie Saint wanders in as a nurse or something. But, unlike the guy next to Frank Sinatra, I managed to stay conscious, all the way to the end of Ritti's talk where he advised us to read a letter that was posted on a bulletin board.

170 / Charles LeBaron

It was from one of the cadavers, while she had been alive, telling us of her reasons for donating her body to medical science. Later, I decided. I got enough on my mind as it is.

I rendezvous at our body with my three lab partners. Two are getting their things arranged already—Harry, a short, muscular fellow with a mustache who's a graduate student in the Harvard School of Public Health, and Dan, tall and blond, a technician in Fineful's lab who's applying right now to medical school. They're together—but where's my partner who's listed as C. Smith? We wait. Other groups get out their kits and start pulling away wraps. Where's C. Smith?

Suddenly in sweeps a young woman whom I'd spent more than one lecture staring at. Tall, lean, brown-haired, with fiercely blue eyes, she reminded me somehow of Jordan Baker in *The Great Gatsby*. No lab coat, just a T-shirt, and no bra. I stare in disbelief. I've never seen breasts that beautiful. Dammit, I groan unhappily to myself, I won't get any work done here!

"Claudia," she says, shaking hands with all of us. "Sorry I'm late. Let's go." And rips off the blue covering from our corpse.

Seventy-year-old female, said the information sheet. Died of heart failure a year ago in a public hospital and had been on ice downstairs since then.

She looks seventy and more. The skin has turned a dusky, apathetic gray. Around the arms, the flesh is withered down to a puckered vestment over thin bones. That cloying smell of formalin is everywhere, yellow grease spots of embalming fluid decorate the hollows of her body, clots of it are thick in her gray pubic hair. About her head, which is tilted back across a block, is wound a cloth soaked in formalin, so we can't see her face. Her hands are wrapped up too, and tied in front of her, explaining the apparent barrel chest under the sheet. Harry and Dan and I have paused for a second, but Claudia's already untying the hands.

"OK, who's got the book, the dissector?" she says.

Time to jump in, we all decide simultaneously and end up with eight hands trying to undo one knot.

"You guys," says Claudia. "I'll get the book."

I get my scissors and scalpel out.

"Here's the picture," says Claudia.

OK, I think. I lean over the breastbone and make an incision in the skin down its length. The skin is tough, lumpy; the cut thin and bloodless. I work fast so as not to have too much time to think.

"Where's next?"

"Here," says Claudia. "But leave the nipple on."

Around the room, other groups are at about the same stage we are, flaying back the skin of the chest. Devo, of the Walter B. Cannon Society for Social Deviation, plump with the handlebar mustache, is in a corner with his team. Their corpse is male but seems to have an enormous amount of fat, lemon-colored fat globules are everywhere, they're scraping them off in huge, slimy cupfuls. Claudia's got the skin almost completely pulled back from ours now; flaps the color of old bacon hanging off; and the nipple that I cut around is left standing out on the underlying muscle, bizarrely orphaned of its surroundings, a lonely tuft of dimpled flesh in the midst of carnage.

"I'm glad they got her face covered up," says Dan, the lab tech. "I'd hate to have her staring at me while I'm doing this."

"Yeah, I'm not looking forward to cutting up her face."

"What shall we name her, boys?"

"You really want to name her?"

"Sure, it's a tradition. Everybody does."

"Well, it sure ain't going to be Bossie. What's now?"

"We got to palpate the lateral pectoral nerve."

"What's it upposed to feel like?"

"Doesn't say."

"Can't feel shit."

"Let me."

"Feel anything?"

"Feel muscle and stuff. Maybe like a bump. This stuff is like turkey meat."

"Call Ritti."

"He's busy. I tried before."

"Skip it then. We'll get it when he comes back. What's next?"

"We got to cut the pec major and reflect it back."

"My hands smell like shit."

"Hey watch it! You just about got me with that scalpel, Claudia."

"Sorry. But what's your hand doing on our side of the corpse?"

Ritti comes rushing over. "How you progressing?" He elbows us aside, starts probing about, then begins to cut the intercostal muscles from the upper ribs. They're thin, iridescent, cross-latticed membranes between the bones, a veil over the lung cavity, so cobwebby as not to seem like muscles at all. We ask him about the lateral pectoral nerve. He stops cutting and begins gesticulating.

"Don't worry, I tell you! Don't worry about every little detail! Just see the big structures. Just the big ones!" And rushed off.

I get a saw from a box filled with mallets and chisels and files and drills and vises, the tools of a medieval torturer. Everybody's huddled over the dissecting manual, trying to figure out exactly how to proceed.

"Ribs two through five. 'Posterior axillary line.' What's that?"

"Something to do with the armpit, I think. Down from the armpit. Like the back of it."

We start turning the body to get to the armpit. Automatically, I cradle the head so it won't knock about. I realize it's absurd, but somehow it seems wrong to let a head bang and bounce, dead or not. Claudia pulls the upper arm out of the way. I take the saw and start cutting. The teeth bite quickly through the gaunt, waxy flash, hit bone, start rocking the body back and forth. I pause for a moment. Claudia feels about the cut I made; I'm riveted again by those amazing breasts of hers, so close and naked under the T-shirt I have to restrain my hand from reaching up and cupping one. Yet even more I'm transfixed by the paradox of staring over the mutilated flesh of a corpse at live breasts and feeling a riot of contradictory impulses, nausea and desire.

"You're cool as far as I can see," says Claudia, standing up.

But I don't move fast enough; Claudia nudges me aside with

a hip, relieves me of the saw, and starts working herself. This woman's beautiful, I think, but she may turn out to be a pain in the ass as a lab partner.

With a U-shaped gash sawn around the front of the chest, Dan holds down the waist, while the rest of us grasp the sawn edges and pull. Claudia gives an "Ow!" and yanks back her hand, removing a small sliver of bone. We get into a discussion of whether it's dangerous or not; we conclude not, since there's so much formalin around. We try again—the edges of the ribs are sharp, it's hard to hold on to them—lift and strain, nothing happens, reposition ourselves.

There's a crunch as the whole front of the chest wall swings up, hinging just below the collarbone, tatters of smooth, bluish gray pleura hanging from the bottom. We push it back and down so it rests on the cadaver's head, pushing it to one side, seeming to smother it. We look inside the cavity we've just opened. There are the lungs, yellowish pink, a mosaic of tiny lobules, outlined with black traceries of carbon.

"She must of been a smoker."

"Feel them. They're squishy." Yes—the consistency of rubbery custard.

"What else we supposed to do?"

"Find the superior epigastric artery, and the—"

"It's one already. I got a class at one-thirty. I'm not staying around here forever. I want some lunch."

"Me too."

We get plastic squirt bottles of formalin and paper towels, jet liquid everywhere, almost filling up the lung space, pack the towels about in the crevices. There's a rumor that people who don't use enough formalin end up with a corpse full of mold and stench by springtime.

"I'm glad I got through with this for today," says Dan, as we wash ourselves off in the sink with Lava soap.

There's not much disagreement about that, except from Claudia. "I think it was fun," she says, those blazing blue eyes looking at us one by one. "Course, I do dissecting in my research."

We scrub up and down our forearms, handing the soap back and forth. "What kind of research?"

"Congenital defects in babies."

"You dissect babies?"

"Dead ones, dopey. That's part of my research. It's really interesting. I'll tell you all about it sometime. But I got to run." And off she runs, hook-shooting a towel into the trash basket.

I go back to my room for a twenty-minute lunch, start making a sandwich, still smell that sweet, sickening odor on my hands, retch, and go into the bathroom and wash some more. I finish making the sandwich and scent formalin again. So I change my clothes, and feeling a little better, take my first bite.

Ugh! What a fucking loathsome smell! It's still on my hands. All I can think of is flaying off that skin, leaving the nipple attached to the muscle, the squishiness of those lungs. I swallow down the mouthful of sandwich whole, trying not to taste it—doesn't really work. What I needed was something to get my mind off all this gore and reek. Who was Claudia with those amazing breasts and deft, sure moves with a scalpel and all the intellectual accouterments of a superscientist? I pulled out the classbook to see where she came from. Strange, no indication of her name, though I'd seen her in most of the lectures for the last term. I looked at another list. She wasn't there either. Had she got into the class so late on a waiting list that she hadn't been included on the roster? Mysterious. And hadn't she said something about applying to Harvard and nowhere else—how could anyone take a chance like that? Even in my application blunders, I hadn't done that. But solving all that would have to come some other time—I gotta finish this lunch before the general pathology lecture starts.

I start again, holding my breath as I bite. It works a little, but I can still taste the food no matter how fast I chew and gulp, and right now my gorge rises tasting anything. The strangeness of cutting and sawing someone else's body has hit me with a delayed vengeance. That body had once been round and plump and young, stubbed its toe and wept, fallen in love and been elated and made conversation, felt the slow, creaky onset of age, now was inert upon a metal table, gradually to be dismembered layer by layer, organ by organ, limb by limb. All the care I lavished on my own body, pampering and consoling it when it skinned a knee, forcing it to sweat and pant running around the Fenway, combing its hair fastidiously, rejoicing when someone caressed it, sorrowing when someone didn't— sooner or later, it would come to that with me too, that inertness, that prone insentience, that vacancy of self. I throw out my sandwich and rush off to class.

Word came back on the Minority Admissions Subcommittee, and it looks like Cox and Skinner got slaughtered in negotiations. The subcommittee stays, completely intact, and there's only one change in admissions procedures that could conceivably affect the number of minorities accepted: every applicant, white, black, brown, or otherwise, now has to have one of his two interviews by someone from a subcommittee that isn't handling his case. It's hard to see how that could have any major importance, but there's no way of judging how the new procedure will work until the results come in, and that won't be possible till we hear late in the spring what the composition of next year's class is.

And with the example of the apparent minority success before them, the women students are attempting to reverse what seems to be a relentlessly progressive decline in their own numbers from year to year. This winter, women applicants who were interviewed got taken to lunch by a woman medical student and urged to come to Harvard if accepted. As a follow-up, the women's group also wanted to send out notes of encouragement to all female acceptees, but the dean of students, Marita Feinstein, who'd attended every meeting of the women's group since its inception in the fall, lobbied strenuously against the note idea, contending that it would be unfair to other groups who did not receive the same encouragement. Marita said she felt the problem was much larger than Harvard and could not be solved by letters to Harvard applicants. Instead, the women should put together a glossy booklet, with photographs and charts, encouraging all women everywhere to go into the field of medicine. With that in hand, the women could set up booths at college job fairs, speak at high school commencements, and go on radio talk shows. How anyone could do all that and also handle medical school wasn't so clear, and in fact the proposal was so ambitious that nothing whatsoever was done on it. Nevertheless, by meetings, leaflets, and interviewee lunches, the women had moved for the first time into the admissions issue, and they waited as eagerly as the minorities to hear who had been selected for next year's class.

But for the rest of us, this second semester hardly seems to be the season of high courtesies. Hardly a lecture goes by without someone suggesting that perhaps one of us will be the scientist who will unlock the secrets of eukaryotic gene deregulation, or the causes for the deposition of atherosclerotic plaques, or the mechanisms of systemic lupus, or otherwise revolutionize medicine. And the class accepts these bouquets with a becoming, complacent modesty. There aren't many people around who could take the workload we have—why shouldn't we go from success to success afterwards? So, in this term of a constant flow of guest celebrity lectures, we reciprocate by a rule of etiquette which dictates that any lecture—no matter how incomprehensible, dull, or drowned in detail—is applauded, particularly if no one was bothering to pay attention.

The first hunk of microbiology consists of the study of bacterial structure and genetics, familiar turf to molecular biologists, biochemists, and bacteriologists, but terra incognita to me.

For the first time in any of our courses, someone has taken cognizance of the fact that some "diversity" in levels of preparation exists in the class. Rather than have everybody lumped together in a single lecture hall, the microbiology directors have split us up into ten or so groups, based on degree of prior exposure to the material. Naturally, I'm in the subkindergarten. Our instructor is a young microbiologist who explains the material simply, clearly, gently, with plenty of chance for discussion.

The science majors are ired no end. Bacterial geneticists

who've written honors theses on the topics we're studying are demanding to join the "introductory" groups like mine, but the course directors hold firm and won't let them. With none of us nonscientists to patronize and correct, the experts are stuck with each other, a convention of hungry cannibals. Refugee scientists start straggling illegally into our class, eventually doubling it in size.

When the month-long unit is completed, the whole class reunites to take the same test. It's a good one, with an emphasis on reasoning. I score a couple points below the median yet feel satisfied.

But I'm struggling hard now against the emphasis on tests and grades. Most exam papers I don't even bother picking up. It's increasingly apparent to me that trying to do well on tests and attempting to learn the material are efforts which take you in different directions. Last term, survival had to come first. Perhaps this term I can try to learn—if they'll let me.

In addition to the microbiology people, there do seem to be some faculty willing to help in that enterprise. This quarter of the year-long neurosciences sequence, "The Function of the Central Nervous System," is taught by a tall, thin, soft-spoken, Canadian-educated physician named Phillip Jewell. Unlike most Harvard researchers, Jewell did four years of work as a clinical neurologist before commencing his theoretical experiments on the physiology of vision in the brain. Despite his reputation as the man at Harvard who has come closer than even Wurstblau himself to receiving that award from the hands of the King of Sweden, Jewell displays unlikely senses of irony, modesty, perspective. On the board are sketched the interwoven pattern of nerve fibers from the eyes to the rear sections of the cerebral cortex.

"Now I expect all of you to be able to draw this with absolute correctness, even if you're dead drunk," Jewell informs us sternly, the amphitheater's lights gleaming off his high forehead. "The trouble is I told that to last year's class and proceeded to get it wrong."

The experiments we observe and study in this course leave

less room for laughter, at least for me. A live monkey has his skull bolted firmly to a chair; the nerves controlling his eye movements are severed so that light can be pinpointed on a section of his retina. Part of his cranium is sawed out, an electrode passed into the part of his brain in question while the experiment is performed. Afterwards, he is killed and his brain sliced thin for examination.

In general pathology, or the study of disease processes, we queue up to inspect porcelain trays of wet lungs, kidneys, hearts, colons, probing at ulcers, cancers; plaques, then assault the microscopes to peer at endless racks of slides, searching for lipid inclusions, fibrinous exudates, hyalin droplets, pyknotic nuclei, and other cellular cries for help. At the end of each week, Constantine Theophilos, a small, somber man with a Greek accent who's course director, hosts a party where we desert the organs of the dead for cookies, pretzels, soft drinks, and beer with all the week's celebrity speakers available for chats. At such festivities I've even seen Theophilos pull out a notebook and jot down student suggestions about the course. And for the final exam, he appointed a committee of pathology professors to review questions submitted by the guest celebrities.

"And we rejected," he said to an explosion of hilarity from the class, "the ones all of us got wrong." This turned out to be about a third of them.

It's hard to fault any of that. In fact, the big problem right now isn't quality, it's quantity. We're in class from eight-thirty in the morning till five at night, Monday through Friday—forty hours a week. A class poll indicated that the average amount of time people had to study outside of class for the four standard courses was more than thirty-three hours a week. When exactly we're supposed to do that studying isn't clear, but there's little doubt we're being trained not to regard any time as a private preserve. If that's their intent, it's at a high cost educationally. No one can endure hour after hour, day after day, week after week of endless sitting in one place, listening to endless streams of scientific jargon and research tables without getting at least slightly groggy. The incidence of cutting, chatter, yawns, and general indolence starts to skyrocket.

A young researcher would show up, just bubbling over with ardor about new developments in his field, to meet a half-empty lecture hall, part of the audience sprawled out with the sports section of *The Boston Globe* blocking their faces, another part gossiping and laughing loudly, a scattered few actually cuddled up around a jacket, asleep. Discussions of recondite cellular events have to compete with a permanent din of conversation. No wonder many of our lecturers got exasperated and gave trivia-laden exams in retaliation—which made the class even more resentful of being lectured at the whole day and less interested in what was being presented.

One heard persistent reports of sections of the class befuddling themselves on dope to get through those eight-hour days of nonstop classes, then doing speed or coke to drive themselves through the tests that Harvard inflicts on us every time we turn around. In a sense these rumors were irrelevant to the basic situation—nodding out was inevitable in those endless lectures, while sweating and trembling and racing through short-answer tests was part of normal deportment here.

Was this dawn-to-dusk schedule, with all its patently obvious maladies, the logical transition between Saturday classes and round-the-clock shifts on the wards? Or was it just a result of neglect? On the whole, I was willing to give Harvard the benefit of the doubt. There was no coordinator for our first-year courses, so each discipline took as large a hunk of our time as it could possibly grab. No doubt we would have gone to sixteen- and twenty-four-hour schedules if anyone thought we could be coerced to show up. So the class, by its fatigue level, did exercise a sort of restraint on this battle of the disciplines.

None of this struck me as an optimal way to learn medicine. Since individual course directors professed ignorance, shock, and sympathy for the total amount of time we had to spend in class, while claiming powerlessness over the situation at large and defending strenuously the number of hours their own courses took up, it occurred to me that this whole educational approach might be worthy of discussion, at least, by the Curriculum Committee. I went to Marc Rensler, the class representative.

"Harvard isn't the only place that does this," he said, starting to walk away from me already. "Other schools have long hours, too."

I catch up and walk him wherever he's going. "But what do you think of this nine-to-five business as an educational strategy?"

"Of course, it sucks."

"So why can't we bring it up? If we can whittle down the time we have to spend in class dozing off, maybe we'll have some time to learn something."

"Forget about it. They wouldn't do anything like that."

"Maybe not for us. But maybe next year's class? If no one ever brings it up, it'll just keep going on indefinitely."

"I'm telling you, it's the same in a lot of other places, too."

"Well, it's not the same in France," I said lamely.

"Well, then go to France."

I stopped and he kept walking. I'd gotten better responses from most of the faculty when I'd aired the issue with them. So Marc's defense of Silverman's lecture during finals wasn't some lapse or temporary aberration. I got to go and see that Curriculum Committee in action, I told myself. If I can ever find the time.

Chapter 14

The Host and His Quadrillion Guests

Bacteriology, our first significant encounter with some real agents of disease since we started medical school; and it isn't a surprise that we aren't expected to learn symptoms, course of illness, treatment, or the like, though these are occasionally introduced for our general interest, while we must memorize in fine detail what kind of artificial culture medium each microorganism likes best, if it can be grown in air or not, the ratios of different kinds of DNA in its chromosomes . . .

There are seven different lecturers for this section of the course, but the man in charge appears to be Nathan Capstein, a tall, bearded fellow in his forties who's head of infectious disease at Massachusetts General Hospital. Though an agreeable lecturer, who always shows up in conservative suits with gigantic, shocking pink ties, he seems to have trouble putting himself back in our shoes—he rattles off facts a mile a minute, confident we're picking them up and committing them to memory as fast as he talks. A knowledge of immunology is assumed—lots of talk about capsular antigens, multiple serotypes, and high titers of something or another. Trouble is, we don't start our course in immunology for a month, so I have no idea what any of those terms mean.

Nevertheless, Capstein strikes me favorably: against what must have been intense pressure from administration and his colleagues, for the second year in a row, he's transferred the Saturday microbiology class to Friday, thus giving us two-day weekends this term. Perhaps it was just self-defense on Capstein's part. As the year had gone on, the class had evolved its own method for dealing with Saturday classes. It didn't show up. Sick of having their lecturers face twenty diehards in an amphitheater of two hundred seats, the second-year pharmacology course directors have been pleading with the administration to be allowed to switch their classes to a weekday. To no avail. Capstein had opted for a more direct approach. He rescheduled the class himself. Strangely enough, this action did not require any polling of professors, inventorying of class lists, or conflicts with the registrar. And whatever the complications of his description of bacteria, Capstein refers to children—who, with their diarrhea and chicken pox and measles, comprise half the population of an average infectious disease service—affectionately and humorously as "kiddoes." He obviously likes them. In a school where, thus far, patients have been presented as examples of diseased organs, that kind of humane talk goes a long way toward making life bearable.

Labs are twice a week, three hours a shot. In contrast to many in the class, glassware and agar plate biology is new to me, so I'm usually one of the last out, fingers mottled permanently violet and brown from the reagents used to stain the bacteria. Joe Sciretto, my lab partner, is a muscular, heavyset sportsman from Villanova, who would realize a lifetime dream the following summer by visiting in one fell swoop the baseball, basketball, and football Halls of Fame. A biology major with two years of hospital lab experience behind him, Joe races through experiments in nothing flat, yelling rock-and-roll lyrics at the top of his lungs, while I bumble and peer over instructions.

Capstein's decided to make all of this rote memorization a little more real for us by demanding that we do a bacteriological work-up on our own stool. Joe and I flip to see who doesn't have to provide it. Joe wins, jubilantly beats out "Louie Louie" on the lab bench, and I have to carry a cardboard ice cream container back to the dorm with me. Turns out Joe should have held up a little on the jubilation. We let the stool ripen for three days. By that time, things are pretty fragrant.

"Shit," Joe kept muttering as he used a tongue depressor to dab out little bits of my feces for culturing.

"Aren't you glad you won the toss," I said. "Now do all that superstar lab stuff."

"Shit," repeated Joe holding his head away and wrinkling his nose. He set an all-New England conference record in speed for this exercise.

But the shit lab started me thinking about the concept of disease that was latent in the enormous volume of laboratory info that we were taking to heart. Dating back to elementary school hygiene classes, my idea had been that washing yourself and your clothes kept you clean and free of germs. Diseases represented the invasion of foreign microbes whose very nature and habits made them sworn enemies of man.

To the microbiologist, I began to realize, a human being doesn't represent an individual organism occasionally attacked by outsiders, but a portable society of disparate creatures, one large, most small, a mobile ecosystem which occasionally goes out of kilter—to the detriment of all participants.

No matter how much showering, bathing, scrubbing we go in for, we're covered head to toe, mouth to anus, with bacteria. Each teaspoonful of normal saliva can include as many as five billion of these critters, who've taken up permanent housekeeping in our mouth, mostly on the tongue. And each ounce of fecal material can contain three trillion bacteria; they're generally much smaller than human cells, so there can be a larger number of them in one bowel movement than there are cells in the human body.

Since we're generous enough to provide the habitat, we're termed the host, but our quadrillions of tiny guests are not necessarily troublemakers or hangers-on. Vitamin K, an essential factor for the maintenance of the blood clotting mechanism, can't be synthesized by the human body, but is manufactured by the bacteria in our gastrointestinal tract. A person receiving such massive doses of antibiotics that most of his intestinal flora is killed off must also receive Vitamin K supplements to avoid problems with uncontrolled bleeding. Our resident microbes also provide direct aid in resisting disease by helping educate our immune system to bacterial surfaces which are similar to those of organisms which cause serious ailments. And disease-causing organisms which aren't indigenous to us find it much tougher to get a foothold inside our bodies because of competition from our normal set of inhabitants.

Nevertheless, our little permanent guests are only too happy to take advantage themselves of any cut, abrasion, loophole in our immunological defenses to move in and start munching away on our vital organs. Microorganisms causing gangrene, pneumonia, appendicitis are normal residents of our body, and in that teaspoonful of normal saliva there can be as many as fifty thousand streptococci, of "strep throat" fame.

In the interests of peace, the body concedes most of the intestinal tract and skin to them, devoting its principal defensive effort to the lungs and blood, which are kept scrupulously sterile. This armed, but intimate alliance between potential enemies is remarkably stable—it's only when the ecosystem is thrown out of whack that problems arise. A knife wound in the abdomen can be dangerous mainly due to the hordes of intestinal bacteria it releases into germ-free body cavities. And if some ailments are caused by locally indigenous microorganisms revolting, or getting in places where they shouldn't be, others are caused by man getting mixed up in ecosystems that he wasn't meant to be a part of. The natural habitat of the plague bacillus is the rodent and flea, but with man as the unhappy "incidental host" it marched through human history as the Black Death.

In certain cases, an otherwise noninvasive organism will run amuck because it has been infected itself. *Corynebacterium diphtheriae* is a common inhabitant of our throats. It can be preyed upon by a virus which integrates its genes into those of the cell. If the bacterium is starved of iron, a gene supplied by the virus orders it to synthesize an extremely potent toxin. When this toxin enters a human cell, protein assembly stops and the cell slowly dies. If enough cells are killed, the bacterium can gain access to the blood and spread havoc through the body. Thus the disease diphtheria is caused by the viral infection of a normally inoffensive microbe.

Carrying this "patho-ecological" concept still further, William H. McNeill evolved a theory of the patterns of empires and the spread of cultures based upon gradients of disease and the immunological competence of populations. After three centuries of recurrent epidemics in Europe between 1300 and 1600 (in one four-year period a third of the continent's population is thought to have died), the survivors had developed the metabolic and immunologic weaponry necessary to withstand most common microbial attacks, and many previously mortal adult diseases became the endemic infections of childhood—mumps, measles, etc. This transition served to stabilize the adult population at the expense of the children—as late as the mid-eighteenth century, three-quarters of all English children died before the age of five. Peoples lacking this costly immunological competence were massacred and demoralized by European-borne microbial attacks. In the hundred years following exposure to the West, the disease-innocent central Amerindian population shrank from a hundred million to less than two million. The capacity of the Europeans to assemble large numbers of soldiers in one spot without fear of epidemics was a central factor in the emergence of sustained mass warfare. The current composition of our bodies' flora is an historical phenomenon, says McNeill, while the patterns of human history were modified decisively by our microbiology.

And in the intervals between marathons of memorization—which gram-positive aerobic bacillus required tellurite and which gram-negative rod needed NAD, which had a filamentous colonial morphology, and which took MacConkey agar—I could see that I was being indoctrinated with a concept of disease, and thus of medicine, which did not regard as feasible or desirable the creation of microbe-free humans. Rather, in the event of infection, the objective of the physician was not to eradicate all bacteria or sterilize every sector of the patient's innards, but to restore amicable relations between the host and the quadrillions of his familiar, minuscule guests.

If we ever do encounter real patients, it's clear that the implementation of this approach will require some delicacy and finesse in the use of antibiotics. No longer is it sufficient to administer pharmaceuticals till everything nonhuman is driven to extinction. I found these implications appealing, yet out of my slight contact with medical research it was hard for me to conceive that such an ecological strategy of medicine had emerged *de novo* from laboratories. Could social movements, I wondered, have indirect, but curiously powerful, effects on the theory of science?

Chapter 15

The Split Brain in the Kitchen

Mornings, when the weather's cold but clear, I run along the frozen paths of the Fenway, and the world seems to have assumed the bright, simple tones of a fresco: pure blue sky, brown earth, green lake floating ice. The mist of my breath streams away behind, my nose and cheeks start to burn. Buildings are so angular and apparent, trees so gnarled and rigid in the winter sunshine. Sometimes I wonder if it will ever be my body again, with moments of flashing, mysterious poetry, not just a sack of enzymes, a matrix of lipoproteins, a jumble of hollow, pulsing viscera, a juicy computer where hard-wired, low-speed elements process frequency-coded voltage fluxes along phospholipid bilayers.

Anatomy has gotten as routine as it'll ever get, an equilibrium mixture of two parts confusion, one part bravado, and a pinch of actual interest. Given the design of the course, which we're expected to reproduce at exam time schematic diagrams in exact detail, dissections aren't particularly useful. Reading the text for total recall is such a slow, herculean task that we're always weeks behind the lab, so few are the people who have any idea what they're slicing into. Once I've gotten the schematized structures finally imprinted in my mind, I'm anxious to see those lines incarnate, but by that time we've already dissected to bits that part of the cadaver and are on to new terrain. The tyranny of short-answer tests is asserting itself again. And the mystery of Claudia remains. I remarked casually that I couldn't find her in the class book. She mumbled something about taking the MCATs late, but repeated emphatically that she was in our class. Whole thing didn't make sense. But the whole room seemed suddenly all ears, so I didn't press further.

"OK, where do we cut?" someone says. There's some fancy, plastic-surgeon-type twirling of blades.

Dan, the lab tech who's applying to medical school, shakes some blond hair out of his eyes, runs his fingers gently over the body, probing. "We got to uncover the pelvic cavity. See all the organs that are supposed to be in there. Shouldn't be too tough."

I extend a cut in the abdominal wall downward till I hit the pubic bone amid a sparse covering of silvery hair. Harry and Dan pull the skin and muscles back. And there's the uterus, a smooth, tight little knot of gray flesh, so small, only half the size of my clenched hand, discolored and shrunken with age. Had someone once been nestled in here, making the ontological transition from fish to frog to lemur to Australopithecus, emerged with a cry of pain, and was now walking about sidewalks, feeling the first breezes that promised spring against his face?

"Our grease bucket's pretty full," said Harry, the public health student. Our lab table had gutters that led fluids to a bucket down below which was sloshing at the brim, floating little scraps of skin. "Doesn't someone ever empty that thing?"

"They probably send it down to the cafeteria."

"Shit, that's awful."

"Good soup stock."

"You boys are pretty gross."

"Even for you, Claudia?"

Claudia was cutting along one labius major, teasing back the skin. "That's right, even for me."

The last session, we'd thrown the wrappings off to find that some humorists in the class had slipped into the labs by night and hidden brightly colored jelly beans amid the flayed muscles and inner organs of the cadavers. Even today, we kept uncovering little purple and green and yellow tidbits in various juicy nooks of our corpse.

"You hear about those guys at Columbia?" said Harry. "It was in the papers. They went to a subway change maker and when he gave them the token they put an amputated hand underneath the glass to pick it up. But as soon as he saw it, the guy had a heart attack and died."

"Med students got away, right?"

"No, they were convicted of manslaughter."

"But they weren't suspended from school, were they?"

Harry looked at us like we were crazy. "I told you they were convicted of manslaughter."

"So they were kicked out?"

"Obviously, they were kicked out! What do you think happens when you go to jail?"

Claudia's and my eyes met over the cadaver. A chill went between us. Could that really take place? Not just flunked in a course, or given a tongue-lashing by the dean, but actually handed over to the outside world, never to return? All those long, harsh hours of study, all that careful preparation of one's mind, to be wasted because of the accidental demise of someone who had nothing to do with medicine at all, who was just . . . just a token collector? What could juries of outside people understand of Lineweaver-Burk plots and membrane potentials and three-factor crosses, all the colossal volumes of facts we absorb in bulk at such great cost to our daily lives? No, no—that kind of thing just wouldn't be allowed to happen at Harvard. It wouldn't be permitted.

"What's happening with your medical school applications?" Harry was asking Dan while Claudia and I stared at each other.

"I got three interviews."

"How'd they go?"

"OK. But this is the second time around for me. Last year when I applied I got five out of twenty-five applications."

"Didn't work out last year?"

"Nope."

"Must be frustrating, working here," said Claudia, going back to stripping the skin from the vulva. "All these people who made it."

"I don't think about it too much," said Dan.

"You know, I got busted once," said Claudia, returning to what was still on my mind and hers. "I went to this all-girls' school back in the woods in Connecticut, and I hated it so much I used to hang out with the townie boys and get drunk. I got picked up in a big raid for dope. I was the only one they let go since I went to the private school. But, boy, did the headmistress let me have it, letters to my mom and so forth. I had to stay in every weekend for a month. Getting busted's no fun!"

I unwound the yellow cloth from about the hands. The fingers were withered to the bones, gray, and semiclenched. After cleaning away the clots of yellow embalming fluid, I tried to unlock the fingers; there was resistance, then a sudden give as the ancient joints straightened. But as soon as I let go, the fingers bent back, gripping mine as if in a desperate appeal for help.

I stop for a second and gaze into the gutted hollow of our body. What economy of colors there, compared to a tropical fish or a sunrise or even a pigeon's neck—dull red, indistinct gray buff, some splotches of green. But what opulence of forms—serpents, goblets, tapestries, coils, pouches, conch shells, washboards, sheets, waves, curls, fountains of translucent tissue.

I look about the dissecting room. It could be a subject for Goya with the stark grotesqueness, the nightmarish quality of his later years. Or for a cubist, the tattered limbs stuttering, reverberating out into the cool abstraction of euclidian forms. But my eyes see for the moment the canvas of a Japanese photorealist—a gesture half-caught, something incomplete, the frame cutting off a face, one blue sheet askew, showing a wrapped hand, the neon lights, a candy wrapper on the floor.

What is before me in these rags of skin, human fragments, guttered on the metal of the table, tangled and greasy with pieces of fat, floating in a bucket of juice at our feet, should be as much the subject of poetry as the pooling of shadow in a brook or the subtle changes in a woman's face. But how to sing the body dissected? How to sing it like those murals of Francesca I see all about me when I run in the mornings? Can Devo or Dan or Claudia or I sing it? Instead our knives and tweezers and scissors click and flash, get put down and lost. Glossy mesenteries, thready iridescent nerves are severed, organs are freed still patterned by their arteries and veins.

In the midst of it, occasionally a vanishing moment where our mortality, our kinship with the dead afflicts us. Is what we really learn here among the corpses not any juxtaposition of organs or wandering course of vessels, but how little we mean when our sensation is fled, the objectivity of the human envelope, how easy it is to be impersonal with flesh identical to our own?

A flap of plastic and a blue sheet over a body that once moved and spoke. We wash our hands and leave for the day.

A cancer cell, Norman Mailer wrote somewhere, resembles a California shopping center seen from the air at night. Slipping to higher and higher magnification on my slides in general pathology, I searched for a glimpse of that neon glow. No luck. But what I did see, in the series of long afternoon labs with the chatter and laughter all about, did seem somehow both beautiful and sinister. Tumor cells tend to stain darker, bluer, their shapes are more varied, their nuclei are enlarged. So instead of a simple organization of tissues, one sees a wild chaos of colors flying about, tortuous purple peninsulas pushing down into normal flesh. If cancer of an organ is hideous macroscopically, there is something diabolically vigorous, meteoric about those sinuous, microscopic splashes of invading outlaws, the conventional layering gone, now just turbulence and dark rebellion—as if some inchoate entity were fighting to emerge from your flesh. But what provokes the traitorous insurgency? We were provided with as many hypotheses as we had guest celebrities.

Meanwhile, Theophilos, the short fellow with the Greek accent who's the course director, had gotten himself in trouble with the women of the class. I arrived late at a lecture to find him engaged in a lengthy apology. It was hard to decipher all of it, but he repeated that he would always use he/she from now on rather than the individual pronouns, and he had not meant to imply that any woman in the class should marry before she had achieved her career goals.

"If we ever want to get married!" yelled a woman from the back, and part of the class groaned.

But it was the first time any professor had expressed regrets to us for anything, so Theophilos got a rousing burst of applause at the end. I went up to Cheryl to find out what had occasioned all this.

"That was the lecture you missed. Theophilos kept referring to laboratory technicians as 'she' and mentioned something about an increasing rate of birth defects as women have children at older ages."

I thought for a second. "Whenever I got my mail when I was working as a social worker assistant, it was always addressed 'Mrs.' I just thought it was funny. Wouldn't you refer to a nurse automatically as 'she?'"

Cheryl shrugged. "I guess I probably would too. But he's our professor. He's under obligation to teach us, so I think it's right someone asked him to be more neutral about gender in lectures. It's not that different from the business about increased birth defects as women get older. We all know it's true, but how many times do we have to be reminded of it publicly? Isn't medical school tough enough for women already? We're having to work our heads off with almost no role models. We all worry if we'll meet someone who will understand that we're not going back to waxing floors. Then on top of that some man has to tell us every three seconds from the podium that we're going to have deformed kids if we don't get pregnant quick. Sometimes you reach the saturation point with all that, and you just want people to lay off."

But Theophilos wasn't the only lecturer to run afoul of feminist issues. Werner Horstbach, a big, amiable bear of a man in his thirties, over from Germany at Manfredo Ritti's invitation, gave a presentation on the abdominal wall. Because of the structure of the male reproductive apparatus, men are more vulnerable to herniations in this area, and Horstbach accordingly concentrated on the architecture of the male, but never stated explicitly why he made so few references to the anatomy of the female. About halfway through, Shelley Prosser, one of the women's activists, asked him why we weren't hearing anything about women. Partly because of a language barrier, Horstbach didn't understand the import of the question and poured fuel on the fire by saying there wasn't enough time to go into side issues. The women got restive at that, and the rest of the lecture was filled with tension. I happened to be sitting behind Shelley, and when it was mentioned that men had twenty times more indirect inguinal hernias than women, she spat out, "I'm glad—I hope they have thirty times more."

The woman sitting next to her started laughing. But Shelley pressed on. "I am. I mean it. That's good enough for them."

I knew Shelley well enough to be sure that she didn't mean it, whatever she said, but it was clear the women weren't happy, and by the time I arrived at dissection, someone had gotten the word to Horstbach. He was horrified and devoted half an hour to telling our lab group in his thick German accent that he supported all the ideas of women's liberation. He asked his wife, who was also a lab instructor, to confirm this. She got up, assured us that her husband treated her very well, even cooked many of their meals, and was very respectful at all times to her. When no one asked her to elaborate, she sat down. Throughout the dissection, Horstbach kept going up to women in the lab, asking them with big, melancholy blue eyes below a shock of straight brown hair if they thought he was a sexist. By the end, just to have some time to work, they were patting him on the back and telling him they thought he was a fine man.

Manfredo Ritti was not to be caught off guard so easily, however. In locating the relative positions of the pelvic orifices, he stuck pieces of rolled up paper in the rectum and urethral openings of a large model of the female pelvis, but scrupulously avoided doing the same with the vagina. This guy knows how to stay out of trouble, I concluded at the time.

Next lecture, Ritti began by discussing the methods for artificial drainage of urine from the bladder of a male. Before the advent of rubber catheters, he said, metal tubes were used, which had permanent curves to reflect the shape of the male urinary tract. If, upon insertion, the tube wasn't rotated in just the right way—via the so-called "master stroke"—its end, instead of ascending to the bladder, would penetrate out through the back of the penis. The men in the class groaned, writhed in their seats, and laughed. He ain't going to treat the female anatomy so lightly, I predicted to myself.

Ritti proceeded to explain episiotomy, a surgical procedure whereby the obstetrician attempts to avoid the possibility of uncontrolled damage to the mother's vaginal opening during childbirth by making a planned incision that routes any tearing into a relatively harmless direction. Frank Robbins, a former bicycle repairman from California who'd written an article attacking the dog lab, asked if this kind of surgical intervention couldn't be avoided through the proper exercises by the mother before delivery. There was some scattered applause, mainly from the women. Ritti was in a bind, since it seems to be a tradition that anatomists and surgeons regard themselves as natural allies against physiologists and internists and all others who may doubt the healing power of the knife.

Gesticulating with passion and throwing the wires of the microphone in long curves all about the lab bench, he went on the attack, informing Frank that times had changed for women. They were no longer merely mothers, they had careers, hard, demanding careers, just like men.

"This is not my field, but I tell you this, my young friend," Ritti said, jabbing a finger at Frank in the top row. "It is too much to ask a woman to work all day, then go back home and do your exercises! It is already hard to be pregnant and to work. If I were woman, I would say, 'To hell with these exercises men think up for me!'"

The women, converted, burst into applause, and Ritti strutted up and down the blackboard with a smile of triumph across his face.

Even Phillip Jewell caught some mild flack from the women in his course on the central nervous system. As an illustration of the bicameral nature of the mind, he showed us a film of a woman who had previously suffered from totally incapacitating seizures, but had been restored to a relatively ordinary functioning level by an operation which limited the extent of the convulsions by surgical cleavage of the nerves which connect the two hemispheres of the brain. A side effect of this surgery is that information received by one half of the body can be stored as memory only in one hemisphere of the brain—it can't be transferred to the other. As a result, if the woman were blindfolded and allowed to feel an object, subsequently she could pick out that object only with the same hand—the other hand couldn't recognize the shape. Since only one hemisphere of the brain normally handles expressive and receptive language, there were also the same sorts of curious results when she was asked to identify manually an object for which she had been given only a verbal description. To indicate how little this split-brain state need affect day-to-day living, the narrator reported that the patient was now happily married and the film showed a scene of her at home, cooking and performing complicated chores in the kitchen—acting, the narrator said, as a "normal housewife."

As soon as the scene switched to the kitchen, the women began sniffing disparagingly, and exploded into mocking laughter at the phrase "normal housewife."

"*Normal housewife?*" snorted Cheryl next to me. "That's a contradiction in terms!"

Later, I talked to her. "I understand getting mad when someone tells you to drop everything and have kids immediately, or when a lecturer completely ignores the female anatomy in favor of the male. But here was a woman who'd been a virtual basket case because of constant seizures and was now up and around and leading a life of her own. Maybe that life wasn't ideologically perfect, but not everybody has to be a Harvard medical student. I understand laughing at a professor or another doctor—they're one of us. But I don't understand laughing at a patient that way."

"I wasn't laughing at a patient," Cheryl said in consternation. "I was laughing at that film. I mean they sat us down and showed it to us. And here was this male narrator talking about her being a 'normal housewife' and how wonderful it all was. This deep male voice. If he'd used the word 'homemaker' it wouldn't have been so ridiculous. Being a homemaker is an honorable occupation. You're responsible for the home. Just being somebody's wife isn't."

"So if they'd shown her cooking and so forth, but not mentioned she was married or used the word 'housewife,' it would have been OK?"

Cheryl thought, then adjusted those big glasses. "Probably not. It was the whole thing. A woman in the kitchen. The male narrator sounding so approving and so forth. The fact we don't have a single woman lecturer in this course. The whole thing."

Despite this minor contretemps, Jewell's popularity stayed high—he'd already announced that the exam would be a take-home essay, for which we could have as much time as we wanted.

"But don't breathe a word to anyone," he cautioned, leaning confidentially over the lab bench. "Or the administration will hear about it and ruin the whole thing."

Sworn to secrecy, we could sit back and pick up a thing or two about the brain.

Stimulate the temporal lobe of the brain with an electrode, and a memory plays back at exactly the speed with which the original events occurred, complete with barking dogs, a child crying across the street, the scent of cooking from a window. Withdraw the electrode, the memory stops; replace it, and summoned by its electronic wand the experience unreels again from the beginning. No event appears to be disregarded by the brain; everything we ever felt, scented, saw, heard, seems permanently archived within our craniums, to die only when we do.

The same kind of scientific talent which broke the genetic code a quarter-century ago is now probing the substructures of the brain with potentiometers, electron microscopes, radio-fluorescent stains, antibodies, centrifugal fractionations, nanogram assays. With as many nerve cells as there are stars in our galaxy, no one expects a blueprint in our lifetime. But once we do understand the wiring that produces consciousness, the resonating circuits with all their amplification triggers, overload dampers, output monitors, input gauges, associative nets, feedback loops, ganged relays, subassemblies, self-shutdown switches, timing devices—once, doubtless with the help of an interested military, we elucidate the equations and schematize a computer in our own image, discover the adventitious elements, the gadgetry, what is primeval, what is wasteful, what is eerie—will a mind invest that patterned labyrinth of metal and ceramic, will a soul take up residence among those semiconductors and printed circuits, will it prove as difficult to subordinate as we are, will it meander through reveries and blunder into sorrows, will it dream and awaken breathless and regretful?

Hard to say. But when St. Teresa of Avila died in 1577, and her body did not decompose, a pious populace, led by her confessor, dismembered her corpse in search of relics that might work their salvation. When Albert Einstein died in 1955, the pathologist performing the autopsy assumed ownership of the physicist's brain, and eventually carried it off with him to a new job in Wichita, Kansas. There, he distributed pieces of it about to professional acquaintances. When last seen, a few years ago, the cerebellum and part of the cortex were squeezed into a Mason jar which was packed inside a cardboard box marked "Costo Cider," itself sitting underneath a beer cooler in a corner of the pathologist's office. At least the knucklebone of Dionysius the Aeropagite or St. James would find its way into a crucifix and proceed to work miracles among the faithful, but what is science if not impersonality?

Chapter 16

Revolt in Micro

Suddenly, the Canadian winds are gone; the Coriolis effect has taken over again. In the court of Vanderbilt, the cherry trees have bloomed, round petals waft out across the tennis court, settle pink and startling in the grass. My spider plant, sickly and miserable during the long New England winter, has taken to blossom, proffering tiny, unassuming splotches of color. Even some potatoes, long forgotten behind the refrigerator, are sprouting, sending white tendrils that curve about the radiator; I don't have the heart to throw them out.

And when I run, the trees of the Fenway have joined the awakening throngs. Auxins are moving downward from the soft, green buds to the cambium, starting to add a new ring inside the trunk. Indoleacetic acid is directing shoots upward so they can drink in the sun in great gulps. The air is so soft you can almost reach out and stroke it. Yellow forsythia has flowered, and I trot through currents of fragrance.

It is almost enough to sweep from the mind the flayed bodies and panting, vivisected dogs, the morgues and long lines of the sick in clinic waiting lines. I stretch out my arms as I go leaping along—a mist of petals flutters down upon me, riding a vagrant breeze, decorates my damp skin with color. Maybe we were meant to be brave and innocent and gentle after all.

And so these Friday afternoons of spring, the class is usually a little restless. Especially since the Vanderbilt All-Star Softball Team adjourns to practice immediately after microbiology, our last lecture of the week. Big-brimmed, net-backed caps fill the amphitheater; when the lights go down for a slide, wags start goosing each other with the knobs of bats; and those mitts sure come in handy as head cushions for catching forty winks. Soon as the last word is spoken—and sometimes before—balls start sailing across the amphitheater, mayhem breaks loose as would-be athletes of both sexes leap about seats, slide safe into the lab bench, yell and fall into each other's laps with diving catches, before hustling out to the field.

In a praiseworthy effort to gain our attention, the micro folks spice things up a bit by showing us slides of actual people attacked by the organisms whose laboratory behavior we're so assiduously taking to heart. While the innovation does serve to make those long afternoons a little more interesting, it also displays in disagreeable relief the fact that we examine the human being here only as an illustration for the microbe. And since treatments or prognoses are rarely discussed, we never find out if these living illustrations survived or succumbed to their tiny assailants. So there's a duress to endless pictures ten feet tall, in blazing color, of jaundiced old men whose faces peer myopically at us, full of pain, African boys with bloated faces, babies whose groins are cankered with sores.

From a decade of work in institutions, I knew that much of that horrified reaction was an artifact of distance. Let someone describe to you the case of a pretty teenage girl who'd swallowed some lye after an argument over a dance with her mother, never imagining that she'd destroy most of her digestive tract and require endless nursing care—hear that, and you'd be at the brink of tears. But go to her bedside, you'd be assaulted first by a bunch of disagreeable fecal odors, she'd try to bum a cigarette off you though there were oxygen canisters all about, and, when you refused, play her portable radio so loud you couldn't make yourself heard.

Yes, suffering, tragedy was better appreciated at a distance where you could luxuriate in your emotions and nobility, without the irksome interference of the person involved. But there were times when it was hard to remember that.

Today we got an hour on fungi, and nobody's really in the mood—low buzz of conversations and snores. Valiantly our lecturer tries to engage our interest with some juicy slides. For some reason, many of these little relatives to the culprit of athlete's foot seem to take a special delight in slashing the skin up into a pizza pie of running sores.

"This sight," jokes the lecturer at a particularly well-done specimen that must have been the house special, "has been known to send previously sane medical students into surgery and worse."

The class laughs politely, but isn't won over. How long we got to go now—twenty minutes? I agree—it's been a long week, lemme out.

So we inventory blastomycosis and coccidioidomycosis and cryptococcosis, each with its favorite recipe of horrors. And finally hit *Candida albicans*, a normal inhabitant of certain humid nooks of our bodies, but which is more than willing to colonize everywhere if given half a chance. As a demonstration of that imperialistic potential, we get a fifteen-foot Kodachrome of a nine-year-old boy who made the mistake of having a deficiency in his immunologic defenses. And that was all the invitation *C. albicans* needed: white pustules covering his face, mouth bloated beyond recognition, cheeks puffed out like tennis balls, glistening head to toe with damp sores. In a departure from form, the lecturer added that the prognosis for this condition was "not encouraging." On the brighter side, *Candida* rarely penetrated within the body, though one should always examine the inside of the eye for fluffy little colonies of fungus growing like anemones on the retina. Dutifully, I examined that nine-year-old's eyes. No, I couldn't see within the dark of the pupil, but I could see what the expression said—agony and hopeless appeal.

What had done that—a misplaced methyl group, a valine

where a glutamate should be? What kind of Creator would force a living, innocent consciousness into that kind of hell? All the meticulousness lavished on devising the icosahedral shell of a virus, a billion years to perfect fermentation, another billion on the Krebs Cycle, throw in a couple more bringing us up from euglena and trilobites and lemurs, just to mess us over like this? Here you have a tiny, sentient being, a soft dove of awareness, and the best a Perfect Being can do is torture its every living cell, every instant of its life, year upon year, transform innocence into those empty, haunted eyes? What mad dictator, what S.S., K.G.B., C.I.A. would have the patience, the ingenuity to dream up this death of years?

Fuck it, I said to myself slamming down my pen with a bang that made my neighbors look around. Now Your creatures ain't putting up with any more of this shit. Nossir— we're ending this ceaseless murder in the name of Darwinian progress. Yes, things are going to get pretty boring down here for You—no primitive grandeur of death and competition no more. Big mistake, allowing us those reverberating circuits upstairs, the resonators that let us think and plan ahead. One synapse too many, and now we're taking over. Perfect Being? Shit, me and two of my "severes" from the sixth floor of Lower Manhattan Rehab could of done a whole lot better than this mess. Me and them, we'd of had beams of blue and pink and purple streaking through a warm universe, souls inhabiting those beams, frisking and endlessly happy, sentient motes dancing, blending, glinting off galaxies. If You could of come up with the hand and the peroneus longus and the superior colliculus, You could have figured out a way so we wouldn't have to be covered with pustules, gasping for breath, shrieking in hopelessness and delirium at the skies. But don't bother Yourself now—just stay out there in the Crab nebula or Cassiopeia or wherever You are, tinkering with Hubble's constant and red-shifting quasars.

I was all ready to fling my notebook at the screen. That would do it—the whole class would erupt in fury, charge down the aisles, crowd out into the quad, and start hurling softball mitts, test tubes, four-color pens, agar dishes, and slides up at the sky. I looked around—should I lead the charge myself, or let someone else throw his belongings first? The guy in front was curled up, dozing away on a carefully constructed pillow of his jacket. The woman next to me was writing a letter. Kevin Costello, the twenty-year-old with a pompadour and eighteen-inch biceps, who is rumored to have gotten Excellents in every course Harvard offers, raised his hand. Maybe this was it!

"Does the lack of a precipitin reaction imply that the host response to systemic infection, rather than being humoral, is cell-mediated?"

"Perceptive point. Recent data from my own laboratory tends to suggest—"

Obviously I better wait till Monday, I thought with a sigh. It looks like it'll take a little time to drum up support.

Explanation finished, the lecturer hit the button, the nine-year-old disappeared, and the screen went white. A general yip, and a softball whizzed past my nose.

Monday, the enemy shows its face.

> *Mycobacterium Tuberculosis:* Nonsporulating, non-motile obligate aerobe. Cell wall contains high lipid content which may contribute to resistance to host macrophage digestion. Transmission by inhaled droplets, normally slow course of infection. Incidence correlates statistically to lower socio-economic status. Kills 3 million/yr.

The disease of Keats and, after his death, of fashionable aesthetes throughout the continent who'd rouge their cheeks and cough languidly into perfumed handkerchiefs. But that wasn't the TB I knew. Nor was it a rough, serpentine cord of bacteria in a blood-agar culture enriched with albumin and aspargine. And it wasn't some square cells, tinted faintly blue by Ziehl-Neelsen stain, scattered about a slide at the highest power of my microscope. No.

One winter day when I was sixteen, my father and I made a long bus ride across the Bronx to the borough's public hospital complex. I was tall, gangling, and strong, silly, proud, easily led, easily hurt. For a year my mother had been enjoying the bleak hospitality of the state department of public health, but for the last month and a half my father had concocted a set of unlikely excuses for me not to visit and now had suddenly asked me to accompany him. It was all quite mysterious, but I was overjoyed at the idea of seeing my mother again—all those stored-up complaints about having to cook for myself, anecdotes of school, a report card in my pocket.

No one was allowed inside before visiting hours, so we joined a massive line that stretched out of the lobby and along the side of the parking lot. Most of the line was Black or Puerto Rican. TB wasn't a disease that struck impartially at rich and poor alike. To build the hospitals, they'd shorn the hills of trees and bushes, leaving vast acres of barren grass, shadeless in the summer, providing no shelter from the winds in winter. No shops, no stores, no human habitation—nothing within half a mile. And in the midst of that man-made emptiness, the glass and metal turrets of medical science, straight and tall and flat with no dissenting lines. We are large and you are small, they said with a repetition that brooked no disagreement.

My mother had been born in a rented farmhouse outside a town of three hundred in Nebraska. In the Thirties, she'd come to New York looking for work. Instead, she'd found *mycobacterium tuberculosis*. They'd rest her in a sanitarium for a year, perhaps take out a hunk of lung and ribs, send her back to the same conditions; eventually the TB would reactivate, she'd cry and cough out blood and pus, sometimes vomit pints of blood into the toilet; and when she grew too weak would return to the hospital once more. By now they'd made off with one whole lung and part of another, and still the disease progressed. Growing up on 111th Street, waking up in the middle of the night and hearing endless coughing from my parents' room, I assumed with the straightforwardness of a child that this was something of a normal situation and would continue forever.

After twenty-five minutes' wait in the cold parking lot, with the breezes blowing across the frozen lawns and lifting the tails of our coats, my father and I were herded through the doors and into the elevators, jammed together with people chattering in Spanish and carrying wrapped, fragrant dishes.

Suddenly I felt enveloped in isolation. The door slid open, and to break the grip of that cold sensation I hurried down the hall, fingering the report card in my pocket, anticipation giving a spring to my steps.

They'd punched a hole in my mother's throat for the tube of a respirator which hissed nearby. Blood and yellow liquid had clotted in the wrappings about her neck. Her cheeks and the large eyes, which I'd inherited from her, seemed drained. My God, I thought, stopped in midstep, my sweaty fingers raveling the report card to shreds. She recognized me, knew why I was there, and reached out her hand. In the alcove next to us, someone had turned on some loud méringue.

Trembling, I sat next to her on the hard metal stool. "How are you?" I said.

She tried to speak, but only her mouth moved. My father gave her a note pad, but she kept staring at my face, smiling weakly, unwilling to leave off gazing at me, as if trying to memorize my features, then squeezed my hand and wrote a fumbling note.

"Please more air."

My father got a nurse.

"It's on full," she said. "It's more than it's supposed to be." And went away.

My mother wrote again, "Please."

My father went to a different nurse. She said it was higher than it should be and wanted to turn it down.

We talked while my mother scratched out answers, but writing was hard for her, so finally my father or I would say something into her ear over the blare of the music, and she'd smile or try to nod. There was a Coke machine in the hall opposite us; people would put in their money, the cans would clunk down, and they'd stand there, drinking, eyeing us idly. My mother kept taking my hand and staring at me. I was sixteen and I didn't know what to say so I kept saying I love you and she kept squeezing my hand back when I said it. Finally, she took the notebook herself and wrote some words in shaky, almost illegible letters. I looked at the message.

"What are the rules?" it seemed to say.

My father and I glanced at each other. He put his mouth near her ear. "Do you mean the visiting rules?"

She shook her head and pointed at the message.

"The rules about the air?"

Again she shook her head.

"Do you understand?" my father asked me.

Even then I knew that she was speaking to us from the complex solitude of great pain—but what was she asking? I bent to her. "What do you mean, Mommy?"

She took my hand and squeezed it and I said I love you and she picked up the notebook and wrote again with so much effort it hurt to watch. After it was over, her hand fell heavily back on the bed, and she closed her eyes for a moment. My father handed the paper to me.

Written below, in larger letters, underlined, was repeated: "What Are The Rules?"

There was an enormous roaring in my ears, and I sat back on the flat, metal hospital seat. I remembered a picture of my mother at age nine in a Sunday frock with her two sisters on the porch of a frame house in Nebraska. My mother was giggling and sneaking a glance at her older sister. A dog was looking up inquisitively. Tall grass surrounded the house.

Was this all that was left of that—the hiss of a respirator, soiled sheets in New York, loud music, and no air? The Great Depression was reaching out of the past to claim one of its own. One day back then, it must have all started as a cough just like any other, a chest cold noticed mainly as an inconvenience, you wait for it to go away. But it doesn't. Instead it sacks and pillages the little time you have to be happy and alive, then it strangles and kills you.

What are the rules?

While others lead lives of surfeit and ennui, you're slowly mutilated, crushed gasping into the dust, till even that tenuous connection you maintain with the world is wrenched from you and you're wiped from existence.

I didn't know what to say so I said I love you and she squeezed my hand and smiled. She died that night.

What Are The Rules?

Part Three

GENTLE VENGEANCE

All subjective experiences are popularly attributed to the workings of the mind. This word conjures up the image of a nonneural "me," a phantom interposed between afferent and efferent impulses, with the implication that mind is something more than action potentials and synapses . . . Conscious experiences are difficult to investigate because they can be known only by verbal report. Such studies lack scientific objectivity and must be limited to man . . . It is possible that conscious experience is an epiphenomenon.
>—A. J. Vander, J. H. Sherman, D. S. Luciano,
>*Human Physiology: The Mechanisms of Body Function*

Theopompus, a Histrione of Berenice, denied all fables; he said every man is an organ put forth by the divinity to perceive the world.
>—Jorge Luis Borges, "The Theologians," *Labyrinths*

Chapter 17

The Copenhagen Express

I was standing ankle deep in a plush, crimson rug before a fireplace in a conference room of the fifth floor of the Countway Library, surrounded by seventeenth- and eighteenth-century medical books in ornate shelves. Bay windows set in walnut paneling gave an expansive view of the roofs of Roxbury, much like the oriels of a manse overlooking the thatched cottages which encircle it. A little out of place in my blue T-shirt and carpenter's pants, I was leaning against the mantlepiece, sipping a small cup of coffee, chatting politely as the faculty members of the Curriculum Committee gradually arrived in their three-piece suits and long, white lab coats.

Nathan Capstein, the bearded coordinator of our bacteriology unit, had come up with a comprehensive reform for our second-year schedule. Most of that year was traditionally devoted to "pathophysiology," or the study of the effects of disease on the body's vital processes. Reports from students now going through that course of study pictured it as the first year's problems taken to extreme: dawn-to-dusk lectures and labs, disparate units of course work jammed haphazardly together, exams completely out of synchrony, not even single-day reading periods. Capstein had proposed converting two of the fall pathophysiology units into month-long, optional

January courses, rearranging the remaining units so they'd run synchronously, with mini-exam periods preceded by weekend-long reading periods. And Saturday classes were eliminated from the first term. Anything that prevented the second year from being a repetition of the first seemed reason enough to tear me away from my books and get to the Curriculum Committee meeting that would decide the issue.

I'd come straight from neuropathology where we were hearing about multiple sclerosis, a disease in which the fatty insulation surrounding nerves is mysteriously stripped away, inducing a slow paralysis. On the screen appeared slice after slice of freshly cut brain, bloody, gray-edged with white interiors, as we searched for the tiny patch of discoloration, the demyelinated plaque that had reduced the owner of that brain to morsels of tissue in an enamel tray.

When in wheels our upcoming specimen patient, or CPC—clinical-pathologic correlation, as disease victims were named—a young fellow in a wheelchair, curly, black hair all over the place, big nose, big grin, eating a hot dog filled with mustard and relish. The class looks at each other in dismay—CPC's are supposed to be kept outside on this kind of stuff, aren't they?

"Hey, Barry! Barry! Over here!" calls our CPC to the lecturer in a squeaky voice, not in the least affected by an amphitheater of astonished stares. "Can I stay?"

"Sure, Marty," said our lecturer, turned off the slides and had the wheelchair rolled front and center. Marty had been a sophomore at the University of Massachusetts when the first attack had hit—some mild weakness in one leg, intermittent problems with vision. Those had gone away, then come back in another episode a year later and stayed for good. Crisis by fitful crisis, he'd started losing the use of both legs and coordination in his hands. His vision was poor now; he had recurrent bouts of nausea, and often wet his clothes uncontrollably. Out of school, he was living in a single room in a hotel in downtown Boston. Later I read in a standard text about what Marty might expect from the future: "The final state of the young, bedridden, incontinent patient, racked by painful flexor spasms of the lower limbs and febrile episodes of intercurrent infection from bedsores is one of the most distressing in medicine." An equivocal mercy of multiple sclerosis is that in attacking the frontal lobe of the brain, it can often perform the rough pathologic equivalent of a prefrontal lobotomy—lightening mood, relieving anxiety, sometimes even creating a sense of euphoria. So Marty was loquacious, uninhibited, and after twenty minutes of comic anecdotes, free-associated medical history, and general patter, he was brought to a halt to allow for questions. A Black guy asked how his friends had reacted to his progressive disablement.

"Stupid question," said someone behind me.

Marty said it showed who his real friends were—who'd be willing to put up with him in a wheel chair.

Someone else raised a hand. "Have you noted any marked alteration in your cognitive functions?"

Neither Marty nor the rest of us were too clear on what exactly "cognitive functions" comprehended, but that was a Good Question at Harvard—showed you were up on the vocabulary.

Dauntless, Marty went off on tales about how he was eventually going to be a radio announcer.

"Shit, I'd love to do a coronal section on his frontal lobe," said someone behind me. "You'd see demyelinated plaques the size of golfballs." Some knowing snickers. People hadn't started off talking that way; initially everyone had approached our occasional CPC sessions with an almost reverential awe—the word actually made flesh. But now after a year of dog labs, corpses, continual memorization, and no patients, that kind of conversation was part of the background noise. And those expressions of flippancy, cynicism, the sarcastic smiles that had been so conspicuous by their absence back at orientation were already starting to spread through the class like some sinister psychological tide.

The lecturer stopped Marty again to demonstrate for us a neurological exam, starting with reflexes of the pupil. Marty's bushy hair had fallen down across his face, and the lecturer brushed it back, combing some wild tufts gently into place.

Though momentary, it was a kind gesture. It seemed to say, What's happened to you can happen to any of us—limbs atrophying and going rigid, blurring vision, squeaky speech, nausea and wet clothes, deprived even of the full knowledge of how we're being ravaged and killed. Words falter, but perhaps the fleeting touch of human hands can say we're all the same creature, after all. Could you learn that with cadavers and short-answer tests and organs in trays? Marc Rensler got up and left for the Curriculum Committee meeting, and I followed.

We were grouped now about a long table, with portraits of old Harvardians staring down at us benevolently. Chairing the group was Albert Blitzer, a world authority on language and the brain; a short, stocky, humorous man with thinning brown hair and a large smile, he called the meeting to order while trying to dust some powdered sugar from a doughnut off his vest. I looked about at the people who were the ultimate decision makers on the course of study at Harvard and who, through the strength of Harvard's position, had more influence on medical education in the United States than any other single group. There seemed to be about twenty members—no Blacks, no Hispanics, and only two women—one the registrar, the other an administrative aide who took the minutes. I'd sat down next to Kent Handel, the tall, red-headed West Pointer whom I'd met at the beginning of the year over Saturday classes.

He nodded crisply. "Long time no see."

"Been studying anti-SRBC RFC responses in the mouse."

We started laughing, but suddenly Jonathan Silverman, the goateed hormone expert who'd lectured us right into finals week last term, was denouncing Capstein's proposal.

"First we eliminate Saturday classes. Then we put two whole units of the pathophysiology sequence in among the January month-long block courses, where they'll be optional. Medical education is too important to be left to the whim of students. These matters shouldn't be settled in the marketplace. What we need here is a curriculum that requires students to take basic science. *Basic* science. A few years ago in physiology, the students were required to perform live animal experiments every single week—live animal experiments every week. Now we have just one or two the whole term!" Silverman was becoming more animated, tapping on the table with a finger.

"Look what happens when we leave it to the students," he continued. "In January we offered reproductive physiology, absolutely essential information for any physician. How many students took it? Fifteen or sixteen? We'll graduate doctors from Harvard who don't know the difference between a man and a woman!"

As the laughter subsided, a short, burly man with a leonine head of yellow hair, streaked gray, began speaking. He was Norbert Jurgen, the dean of social medicine, and I knew his daughter who was a second-year student. "If I may be so bold as to make an historical point," he said in a slow, half-ironical German accent, "the January and June blocks were originally established to permit students to take month-long courses on topics like nutrition and patient interviewing and international health and sexuality that they can't take during the regular semesters because of the pressure on them to sign up for these basic science courses. I'm surprised to find that certain younger members of our faculty"—he inclined his head at Silverman—"seem to have forgotten that. And they decide they cannot fit certain material into their fall courses. And they create a new course which must go into January. And then they become angry at students for taking the very nonscience courses they are supposed to take in January."

"But a doctor who knows nothing about reproduction!" broke in Silverman.

"If there is a course in abdominal surgery," replied Jurgen deliberately, "the surgeon does not say, 'I will not teach appendectomy because I have no time.' He finds the time and he teaches. I do not understand why physiology should not be held accountable in the same way. Perhaps it might mean trimming some of the fat."

Silverman was fuming but didn't have the floor, and Jurgen proceeded without haste. "Nevertheless, I am constrained to say that I am allied with my young colleague from physiology in disliking this proposal. The pathophysiology units which have been removed from the fall semester have also been placed in January, the very time period which, as I say, was reserved strictly for social medicine courses. Soon, we will have no one in any of the courses for which I am dean, and I will find myself collecting unemployment."

More laughter, and Blitzer called on a pathologist, an older fellow in a white jacket. "I'm afraid I must claim precedence over my old friend Dr. Jurgen in the area of neglect. Harvard students score in the lowest thirty-nine percent in the nation on the Boards in my specialty. Thus—"

"I must interrupt, Mr. Chairman," said Jurgen. "But I must inform Dr. Phillips that my department exceeds that by five percentage points. Harvard students score in the lowest thirty-four percent in the nation in my area."

The pathologist shook his head. "I must inform you, Dr. Jurgen, that your figures are in error, since I have been assured by Mrs. Hingle that the pathology scores are the lowest of all areas."

"They may be among the lowest, but I have the figures which prove that in social medicine, Harvard students have *the* worst scores."

"I'm afraid I must disagree, Dr. Jurgen. In the whole nation, Harvard students score the worst in—"

Blitzer broke in. "Could we return to Dr. Capstein's proposal, Dr. Phillips?"

"In substance," said Phillips, "my department's position is that the current situation is intolerable, but this new proposal doesn't seem to be the answer. Harvard students will be learning even less than they do now. We oppose that."

As others made similar speeches, it became obvious that the proposal was getting attacked from all sectors. No one liked the present arrangement, but any shift in student schedules involved shifts in departmental power.

"Perhaps we should hear from the students," said Blitzer with a smile. "I noticed that many have arrived to show their interest."

There were three of us interested bystanders—that was a lot? But one after another, the class representatives described the chaos now existing in the pathophysiology schedule and urged that Capstein's new system at least be given a year's trial. The total unanimity on the part of the students turned discussion toward how awful the current conditions were for lecturer and student alike and what might happen if the plan were tested for a year.

Silverman was almost out of his seat in his zeal to get the floor. "I have to repeat that I oppose the implementation of this proposal even on a temporary basis. I was looking through my notes from medical school here. We had two solid years of basic science. Two solid years. We didn't see the inside of a hospital until the third year."

Who was it who'd told me that Silverman had spent his first two years as a medical student, then dropped out in the third year to get a Ph.D. in research physiology instead?

"Now," he went on, "everyone seems to think we should skip the basics and throw people at patients immediately. This isn't the way things are run at Johns Hopkins."

"How are things run at Johns Hopkins?" asked Blitzer.

"Not this way. Two years of thorough grounding."

"I heard they have people doing physical exams first year," said someone else.

"No," someone broke in. "They have a completely different curriculum. I forget what it is, but someone explained it to me a couple years back. There were problems with it though."

"How about Tufts?" asked Blitzer. "What happens there?"

"Whatever it is," said Silverman, "I'm sure they ground them in basic science."

"There's no elective system, I hear," said a student.

"That's what I mean," said Silverman.

"They have some sort of electives, I think," said a member of the faculty.

I was dumbfounded. The Harvard curriculum evolved like marsupials in Australia, totally out of contact with the rest of the world.

"In Copenhagen," said Silverman, "physiology runs two

years. Not just one semester like here. They're grounded in the basics."

My eyes bugged out in terror—two years of dog labs and Wurstblau equations?

"The Copenhagen system is somewhat different from ours in many ways," said Blitzer. "I happen to know something about that. We might well take a leaf from their book. A much more leisurely pace, but in Copenhagen there is a heavy emphasis on combining the research and clinical aspects of medicine. Students who emerge from their system are—"

"Mr. Chairman!" burst out a fellow in a white coat down at the other end of the table. "My hand has been raised for ten minutes!"

"My apologies, Dr. Conroy."

"As some of you may know, I spent a good deal of time at the Karølinska Institute, and thus have more than a nodding familiarity with Scandinavian methodology. The Copenhagen system is not unique, but represents a class of strategies of medical education. What does distinguish the Copenhagen model is its high degree of emphasis on the—"

I leaned over to Kent. "What in hell are they discussing?"

"Damned if I know."

"This whole thing's off in the boondocks just when it looked like things would be settled."

"Every meeting's like this."

"Gentlemen," said a student, picking up a copy of Capstein's proposal. "Is there any chance we could get back to this?"

"Your point is well taken," said Blitzer. "Gentlemen, let's either come up with some concrete alternatives or vote on Dr. Capstein's proposal."

"I move we end the marketplace approach," said Silverman. "End this business about optional courses. January for required basic sciences. June for required social medicine courses. Ground people in the basics. End the marketplace approach."

The students all groaned mightily, and Silverman moved about in his seat.

"My proposal," said Capstein, who'd been remarkably restrained through the whole discussion, "is really quite modest. You're talking about major changes—eliminating the whole Harvard elective system and removing all social medicine courses from January. I'd hate to see a plan that could be implemented immediately and could alleviate a lot of the problems of the second year get tangled up in massive overhaul such as that."

"I tend to agree," said Blitzer. "Every department is yelling for a piece of the students' time. I don't know how we can reconcile all the demands. Perhaps the only real answer is to do as many have recommended—make medical school five years instead of four."

Cries of horror from the students, while Silverman nodded vigorously.

"But it's six-thirty," continued Blitzer, "and we have before us this proposal of Dr. Capstein. Do I hear any motion concerning it?"

"I move," said Dr. Phillips, "that given the current intolerable state of the second-year curriculum we adopt Dr. Capstein's proposal provisionally for next year only, and appoint a committee of representatives from both physiology and social medicine to oversee its implementation."

"I am willing to vote in favor of that motion," said someone else. "But I want to go on record that I think it's disgraceful that we're rearranging half the curriculum just to satisfy a student whim to have Saturdays off for one term."

"I agree with that two hundred percent," said another faculty member. "In my day, internes had to live in dormitories in the hospital and were on call around the clock every day. Now they can live anywhere they want, get married, have three or four nights off a week. And now the students want to have Saturdays free, too! Where is it going to end?"

"Fortunately, the incoming class next September will have Saturday classes," said someone reassuringly at his elbow.

"I think we all agree that by voting for the provisional implementation of Dr. Capstein's proposal, we are in no way endorsing an end to Saturday classes," said Blitzer.

And so, with that proviso, Capstein's proposal was adopted.

Kent raised his hand. "I want the record to show that I abstained."

Blitzer nodded and the meeting ended.

"Why in the world did you do that?" I asked Kent, as we stood up.

He sighed and his red mustache drooped. "This whole thing wasn't necessary. The end result of this isn't that much different from what Silverman wanted. In fact, he won; no one is going to be able to take any social medicine courses in January, they'll have to take those two pathophysiology units—more basic science. We're becoming more and more a technical institute. Already, they're talking about taking the semester-long course on how to do an interview and physical exam with a patient, the introduction to clinical medicine, and scaling it down to six weeks, or even encouraging people to wait till the third year to take it. The way this is going, we'll have two solid years without ever seeing a patient."

As we were standing there talking, faculty kept coming up and shaking Kent's hand; it was the last meeting of the year. He nodded briefly, shook their hands, but didn't smile. Harder than anyone else at Harvard, Kent had worked on improving the level of medical education—via student questionnaires, course evaluations, statistics, reports. But now his face seemed tired and discouraged. Marc was off by the ornate bookcase in earnest discussion with a departmental chairman.

"But what was the alternative?" I asked Kent.

"For them to get their act together!" he said suddenly. "But instead of improving the teaching, they just expand the time allotted to it. So we get more of the same crap."

"You mean they could teach us all of pathophysiology the fall semester and not push those two units into January?"

"Now you're catching on, Charley!" Kent said angrily. "They could teach every single unit of that material, eliminate Saturday classes, give us every afternoon free, and let us take the social medicine courses in January—but what they'd have to do is cut the trivia, as Jurgen said, and really teach."

"So why didn't you propose that?"

"Don't you think we haven't proposed that a dozen times?"

"What's happened?"

"We've gotten absolutely nowhere. And now we're headed for two years of labs and no patient contact at all." He turned on his heel, and I watched him move off past the shelves of old books and out the door.

I put my hands in my pockets and looked out the bay window at the twilight falling over the projects and shoddy houses of Roxbury. Maybe Kent was right. But for all its drawbacks, Capstein's proposal at least gave us some free time and a schedule which permitted us to learn the material in a semiorderly manner. And his plan would go into effect because of solid student support. Capstein had gotten that support by explaining the proposal to us at the end of a lecture, letting us see copies of it, and soliciting our suggestions. Why couldn't Kent have done the same with proposals of his own? Back in September, Kent had told me he found it impossible to work with other medical students, and I'd quickly found out what he meant. But were these the fruits of working alone?

Chapter 18

The Return of the Fear

The composition of next year's incoming class was finally announced, and the second highest numbers of both Blacks and women in Harvard history were accepted. These major admissions victories for the minorities and women made an interesting contrast to the faculty situation which had been left to behind-the-scenes manipulations of influential individuals. With only seven women and even fewer Blacks occupying positions among the medical school's two hundred and seventeen tenured faculty, every single one of the twelve persons to whom Harvard granted tenure over the course of the year had been a white male. Likewise, other admissions trends remained unaffected—the acceptance rate for offspring of alumni and faculty stayed three to five times higher than for any other group, and the number of nonscientists dropped further so that they would now comprise barely nine percent of next year's class.

Nor were those tendencies restricted to admissions and faculty questions. The amount of money available for student loans, we were told, was running mysteriously short. Certain unidentified wealthy donors would be willing to establish loan funds, but only on condition that grades and rankings were reestablished, with the loans going only to those at the top of the class. In the Harvard context, it was obvious what such a cash-for-grades system would produce—more destructive competition, nonscientists cooking baked beans in the dorm while scientists refused still more adamantly to sign up for advanced courses since their rent might be on the line.

Dean Chanesohn had come up with a compromise—grades and rankings would be recorded in secret, known only to the administration, the financial aid office, and perhaps the wealthy donors themselves. Few were won over, and the majority of student representatives were so antagonistic that the cash-for-grades proposal remained on the shelf.

But there were lighter aspects to some of these changes. Harvard had begun refurbishing Vanderbilt Hall, a worthy enterprise in itself, and the place was looking better, but a good deal of the effort seemed to be devoted to rendering the ground floor into a still more exact likeness of an English gentleman's club. One student lounge was outfitted with such a regal assortment of deep-upholstered armchairs and Persian rugs that—until group protests reversed the policy—it was declared off-limits to the students themselves. Perhaps to help finance such improvements, Harvard announced that in the winter there would no longer be any heat in the dormitory in the late-night and early-morning hours, a time when medical students are notoriously wont to study. "Bundle up!" gaily advised an official flyer.

If the minorities and women had stood alone against these trends, neither group seemed inclined to remain immobile. Our class was allowed two elected representatives to the admissions committee. More than twenty people ran, two-thirds of them white, most of them men. But the class chose a Black man from Stanford and a Puerto Rican woman from Brooklyn. Cheryl, tired of the prestige and impotence of official University politics, retired from her position on the Harvard Committee on the Status of Women and was elected chairperson of the independent women's group. Someone suggested that as a companion piece to the welcoming essay for incoming Harvard women in the orientation booklet, there be something written on the experience of being a man in the first year.

"If you can find any men here!" yelled one woman angrily, but the idea got approved anyway. In an unrelated development, a male phalanx seized control of the Social Committee, promising punk rock, beer, and gala event after gala event with The Simmons Girls.

General pathology has given way to immunology, the study of the body's own disease defenses. In a world where you must munch on other living creatures to survive, avoiding being munched on yourself is a formidable enterprise. And since doctors—whatever the level of technology at their disposal—remain little more than cheerleaders for the billion-year-old immunological defenses, familiarity with that biological apparatus seems a crucial part of a physician's intellectual armamentarium.

I riffle through the almost three hundred pages of handouts that I know will have to be stamped intact on my temporal lobe. Not a single lecture on anything vaguely resembling "How the Body Fights Infection," just mice and test tube cultures, with tables and numbers coming out the seams. I've learned to recognize what that format means. And, sure enough, two days in, we hit a topic that might have some significance for us in treating patients—blood types and transfusions—and we're told there won't be a lecture dealing with any of that, we should "read up on it on our own." I've also learned from hard experience that these Basic Medical Research guys flunk people with a vengeance for not knowing their rat protocols.

I go to the first few lectures, but nothing makes sense. Cheryl tries bravely to ask back-to-basics questions, but the clarifications are worse than the original confusions. A couple of the guest celebrities even manage, through unparalleled displays of obfuscation combined with stinging rebukes for questions, to provoke the class into violating its sacred custom of applause—dead, embarrassing silence reigns at the end of the hour. Eventually, almost all of us conclude that if anything is to be learned in this course, it'll be at home, tediously deciphering the experimentalese of the handouts, word by agonizing word. The audience shrinks and shrinks till the auditorium is three-quarters empty. What happened after that I don't know, since I stopped showing up too.

The year-long neurosciences sequence ends with the study of the ailments of the nervous system, neuropathology. This is our first introduction to real live medicine, so the neuropathologists lecture to a standing-room-only crowd. A bright young doc from Beth Israel gives us an hour's talk on strokes, the damage that occurs to the central nervous system from the blockage of a blood vessel, explaining, "If someone walks into my office and complains about mild numbness in his right hand and some transient problems speaking, I know it's going to be a good day." We all furrow our foreheads in amazement. "Because those are some classic preliminary symptoms, and I know I'm going to prevent a stroke—and probably save a life. Saving lives? We haven't heard too much about that kind of stuff."

But walking out, something strikes me—this is the best that medical school can come up with, a one hour lecture on strokes, the third greatest killer in the United States? Yet given the constraints of time, that's the way the course directors have to schedule things—no chance for separate sessions on brain tumors and skull fractures, so they squeeze them in together. It's hard to accept that while I burn the midnight oil memorizing for immunology the phenotypes of Ig-producing cells in a rabbit, two hours is the extent of my formal classroom training as a physician in strokes, brain tumors, and skull fractures.

Anatomy isn't helping any in this final lap of the school year. We're studying the leg, and if I didn't have two of them, I'd say so complicated a structure couldn't exist, while Snell, the author of our text, seems to be suddenly in league with the immunologists: "The medial margin continues below as the medial supracondylar ridge to the adductor tubercle on the medial condyle. The lateral margin becomes continuous below with the lateral supracondylar ridge. The posterior surface . . ." And so on for a hundred and twenty-five more pages, followed by an equal amount on the arm which is said to be tougher, and finally two hundred pages on the head and neck, rumored to be the worst of all. All this to be memorized in the few weeks before finals? Speak for yourself, but I can't do it.

I went to see Manfredo Ritti, the course director. Manfredo, someone from the faculty once told me, had been offered the chairmanship of the anatomy department, but had refused indignantly, declaring "In Europe, chairman is king—here he is slave!" and went on with his research. He's well liked by the students—few flunk, his office door is always open, everything's on a first name basis, and his detailed knowledge of anatomy, his ability to visualize in three dimensions then sketch out the structure in flawless perspective on the board is enough to take your breath away. And, of course, there's that theatrical flair to his lectures; he leaps from one end of the amphitheater to the other, yelling, whispering, beseeching the heavens, skewering Harvard, and even himself, unmercifully. It becomes a problem, sometimes, determining whether you're dealing with Manfredo or a self-parody.

"What's the matter? What's the matter?" Manfredo said, almost bounding his thin frame out of the seat at each word. "When people come to see me, there is always something the matter. Why does no one come to say they are happy? I am happy, happy, Manfredo! Why?"

"I don't know," I said. "But you're right. I am not happy. I am very confused."

"Confused? But you should be confused! At this point in the course only the stupid ones are not confused."

"But I am even more confused than that. I don't understand a thing, and I am very far behind."

"It is impossible to keep up. Forget about keeping up. It is impossible. Calm yourself! Don't worry! You will pass. I tell you that myself!"

"I'm not so much worried about flunking, but I really haven't learned a thing about the—"

"Flunk? I flunk no one. No one!"

I looked at him—hadn't a few people failed last year?

"Of course I flunk one or two!" said Manfredo before I

could open my mouth. "They get everything wrong. I know who they are myself right now. I know who they are already. What is your name?"

"Charles LeBaron."

"You I do not know. I do not know you—you are safe! I will look." He rummaged through some papers. "Labarrone. What? Get out of my office! You waste my time! You do well in my course. Well—and I do not teach easy course. You are in top third. Top." And he accusingly quoted my grades back to me.

I knit my brows. Before returning my tests, I'd made a few minor corrections in how they were marked, but the grades Manfredo was quoting back were the uncorrected versions. So that was what was behind Manfredo's "grade your own tests" policy: you could correct things any way you wanted but all Manfredo used were the original, official marks. Clever.

"Really, Manfredo," I said, "it isn't the grades that bother me. I want to keep up and learn something—but you are finishing the hand, going on to the head, and I haven't even gotten halfway through the leg in Snell."

"Da Snell? What you use da Snell for?"

"Isn't it the—"

"Forget da Snell!" He jumped out of his seat. "I tell you that myself! Forget da Snell!"

"Forget da Snell?"

"Da Snell is too much." He paced back and forth in his office that was cluttered with books and journals and spare parts to microscopes. "How can I ask you to remember da Snell? How? I ask you." His arms went over his head.

"I don't know. All your previous tests were straight from Snell. How—"

He shook his finger under my nose. "What I tell you?"

"Forget da Snell?"

"Forget da Snell." Manfredo beamed and sat down again. "You are too excitable. All you American medical students— so excitable. Worry all the time. Grades. Grades. Grades. Just worry."

"But what should I study?"

He jumped up again. "Study? You barely have to study. I ask so little. You will be insulted by my final exam. Insulted!"

"Not me."

"You will be insulted too. I tell you that."

"But what should I study?"

"Here! This is all. Calm yourself!" With a flourish, he threw some mimeographed sheets to me across the desk and sat back down. They were lists of muscles with their nerves and actions.

"Just muscles in the arm and leg? No arteries or veins or bones or—"

"How? How can I ask you that? It is too much! How?"

"The same way you did on the last test."

"My boy!" Up again. "Calm yourself! Calm! Calm!"

"I'm calm," I said. "But I'd like to know—this list is all I should memorize?"

"What have I told you?"

"Just this list."

"You will be insulted by my final," said Manfredo who escorted me all the way down the stairs, out into the quad, and almost back to my room. "Insulted! So simple! Just be calm."

I went back to the dorm and dropped in on Steve Franchard, a tall, thin, red-headed basketball player who lived down the hall. Steve had majored in physics at Cal Tech and was finding the memorization of med school a nightmare.

"He's lying," said Steve.

"Lying?" I stepped back in amazement. "What in the world would he lie to me for?"

"He's lying. He's trying to calm you out."

"Calm me out? If he wanted me to learn arteries and veins, he could have told me."

"He's trying to calm you out."

"But I wasn't upset."

"I can't believe you haven't gotten that treatment before. I thought it'd happened to everybody."

"But I wasn't excited!"

Steve shook his head in disbelief at my innocence. "I'm

telling you it doesn't make any difference. Everything is treated as a psychiatric problem here. You just got calmed out."

"I still don't believe it. Anyway, I'm studying those muscles."

"We'll see what's on that final," said Steve with a knowing look.

Warm weather, in the eighties, and I find it impossible to get mentally ready for the upcoming test on bacteria. Two days to go, and I haven't the vaguest idea which bugs stain gram-positive, which gram-negative, how to tell an obligate aerobe from a facultative sporulator. Since it's all arbitrary— like trying to learn a language by memorizing vocabulary lists instead of speaking it—the obvious route is to create endless mnemonics. Orthodox theory on arbitrary mnemonics holds that the only ones you retain are sexual or scatological, the classical example of which, with nearly a century of distinguished usage to its credit, is that for the twelve cranial nerves in anatomy: "Oh, oh, oh, to touch and feel a girl's vagina, ah!" But constructing those phrases seems to require a particular ingenuity and temperament which I don't possess. I keep thinking there must be a better way to learn about our little friends and enemies than fifteen-page tables of cryptic abbreviations summarized by obscenities, grunts, coughs, and gargles. But, the night before the test, I stay up till three A.M., chewing away on caffeine tablets, and feel relatively confident going in—after all, just twelve hours before I'd had no idea that erysipeloid gave an alpha reaction in a culture dish infused with rabbit blood heart, or that the capsular polysaccharide of *B. Fragilis* could stimulate chemotaxis all by its lonesome.

And I promptly get destroyed. It's by far the most detail-ridden test we've had all year. There's some small comfort in the fact that many are the under-the-breath curses I hear around me. Devo leaves early, sarcastically throwing the test the length of the lab bench. My own conclusion, as I hand in my paper, is that I failed miserably.

But it's hard to stay depressed in the springtime—warm winds whisper how close the year is to an end, how near freedom is, less than a month away. The next week, I get the test back. Passing is sixty; I got a sixty-one. Whew! Victory, I crow to myself. Who cares if the median is in the seventies. Two days later, I'm filing the test away, when I notice a form letter from the microbiology secretary fluttering at the end: "Dr. Capstein would like an opportunity to review your exam and general course performance with you."

I read it over eighty-three times, then slump back in my chair. Holy shit! The finger of death is pointing at me! I drop everything and rush over to his office. Not there. I leave a two-page note recounting in glorious detail how anxious I am to see him. Forty-four phone calls to Mass General Infectious Disease Unit later, I finally succeed in setting up an appointment for the following day.

Now I know how Ron felt that first biochemistry test he flunked. Except now, Ron has turned into one of the heavy-duty studiers and is cleaning up. Me, I'm writhing around all night, unable to sleep, kicking my bedsheets in despair. The Return of the Fear, I think to myself. You can't let up a single, fucking moment. Now they won't even let you loose for summer vacation—they'll just keep you here memorizing and memorizing and memorizing. Just my vacation, that's all I want, and they're trying to take that away. You can't relax a single moment. Back to first semester. The Return of the Fear.

I arrive at Capstein's office half an hour early and wear a hole in the linoleum pacing up and down. Finally Capstein arrives, tweed jacket, immense mauve tie, the fringe of beard making him look strangely like some dissident in exile. I've lugged over notebooks, lists, obscene mnemonics, underlined texts, all ready to spread out over the floor of his office. I've gone over the test with a fine-toothed comb; lengthy citations from the most prestigious sources buttress my every point. I deserve a seventy or more, if justice exists in this world. Capstein's barely got the key in the door before I'm deep into a well-rehearsed speech.

"Just a second," says Capstein, waving me into a chair and

pulling out a folder. "What's your name again? OK." He scans down a page, then fixes on a line and looks up. "You shouldn't even be here. Gladys sends out these letters automatically to anyone who's within five points of failing on each test. You were almost at the median last test, and you did pass this one. You should just make sure not to mess up the final completely. You're in the clear."

I droop over one arm of the chair, panting in relief.

"If you've never had this material before," continued Capstein, "just stick with it. We need more humanities types like you."

I nodded. I'd heard that before. We were regarded as a sort of ornamental exotica—the Japanese bush in the front yard, the cab driver invited to the Beekman Place reception. But I was happy for any reassurances I could get.

Capstein wasn't inclined to tinker with grades, so all my scholarly citations were for naught. "Everyone complained the test was too picky, and I think they're probably right. We get so used to dealing with this material, it's hard to remember that it's tough to acquire if you've never seen it before. But if people tell us, we can learn too. Students keep saying they'd learn better if we had more about diseases, so next year I'm going to try to make things a little more clinical. And this final coming up, I can assure you, won't be as detailed as this past test was."

"I hope I survive it," I said as I picked up my many belongings.

"You will," said Capstein, smiling as we parted.

But I knew that Capstein's idea of an easy final and mine were sure to be different. With the immunology people talking utter mumbo jumbo, and those muscles and nerves in anatomy only partially memorized, it was obvious that for these final weeks of the first year in medical school, I was back to fighting for survival.

First critical decision: that forty hours in lecture hall has just got to go. So I stop going to class—instead, up at eight A.M., studying around the clock to midnight. I discovered later that others had arrived independently at varieties of the same strategy, except many had started earlier in the semester and thus didn't have to be so draconian now. Cheryl confided that she hadn't gone to a single meeting of one course for more than a month; it was a question of showing up, or learning the facts—there was no way to do both. And we weren't exactly alone. I made an excursion out to a review session in one course to find ten students in the amphitheater, the lecturer discoursing merrily away, apparently unperturbed.

In contrast to most, my prime effort has to go into viruses, which are the subject of our final unit in microbiology. Viruses represent degenerate life forms, most specialists seem to believe, parasites that progressively stripped away their own metabolic machinery till they crossed back over the threshold to inanimateness. They can be frozen to near absolute zero, even crystallized, then become infective again as soon as they're placed near living cells. Visible only at the limits of resolution in the electron microscope, dark patterns against a blurred, grainy background, they are strangely geometrical, symmetrical, angular: pinwheels, spiked hexagons, Flash Gordon spacecraft. In the simplest form, a virus is nothing but a protein shell surrounding a short length of genetic material coded on DNA. The protein shell hooks onto the exterior of a victim cell (human or microbial), the viral DNA is injected inside, migrates to the cell's nucleus, and from that command post proceeds to send out chemical orders that redirect all the cellular factories into the construction and assembly of new viruses. Eventually the cell bursts, releasing hundreds of replicas of the original virus. Is it any wonder that their very name is derived from the Latin word for poison?

Though a number of well-known viral ailments are discussed, we can't spare a single moment of lecture time on the common cold, while the handouts lavishly inventory diseases such as "epizootic diarrhea of infant mice," "transmissible mink encephalopathy," and tropical maladies with odd names: oropuche, uukuniemi, o'nyong-nyong . . .

But, on the whole, the virologists seem like a likeable, helpful bunch—just a bit wrapped up in the lore of their specialty—and I'm studying so hard I'm beginning to develop a sense of relative security, when word spreads that they've decided to expand the scope of the final to cover everything in microbiology: those goddam bacteria, and even genetics. I sag under the blow—less than a week to go, no reading period, and they're going to quadruple the amount of material!

I drag myself to a lecture, and who gets up in front of the class but Ellen Bartlett, a tall, elegant, dark-haired woman from Yale, the daughter of a midwestern surgeon. She'd once been described to me as the class' sole old-line Republican. True or not, Ellen proceeds to introduce a petition requesting that at this late date the microbiology final be limited to viruses. All year, we'd been completing detailed, statistical course evaluations, some running as long as six and seven pages, but this was the first time someone had actually attempted to do something about how we were taught medicine.

And no sooner does Ellen read the petition than the class breaks into a pandemonium of applause. Smiling widely, she continues; but suddenly someone is interrupting her, objecting vehemently that the exam should include, at the last moment, all that material back to January. I crane my head incredulously. Yes, it's Marc Rensler. Inspired by this macho display of willingness to be tested to the hilt, some other prominent liberals in the class join in opposing the petition, arguing that students have no right to comment on how or what they were taught. If Ellen's petition were circulated, vowed one, he would take around his own petition to help the faculty separate the real students from the mutineers.

So this is what finally happens, I thought, when you become an official Harvard rebel and get wined, dined, champagned, consulted, deferred to, and told you were a future leader. I have trouble keeping myself in my seat—I want to rush right over to the administration building, tear my way up the marble staircases, dash through the oaken doors, race past aghast secretaries, burst into some dean's office, and in front of whatever astonished group of white coats are in there, start pumping his hand up and down shouting, "It works! The whole thing works! Take the student liberals, put them into official committees, prominent positions as fast as you possibly can, dangle power and influence under their noses, and they'll do the work of keeping the class in line for you, nip in the bud even mini-protests like this about how we're learning medicine."

But over these vociferous objections, the petition was circulated to great success. With some friends, Ellen hand-delivered it to the course directors and argued the case, politely but forcefully.

And at the next lecture, to the chagrin of the prominent liberals, one of the directors announced with a smile that the exam wouldn't include all that material back to January, after all. He got an ovation from the class. When it died down, he said he thought it was a shame we wouldn't have a chance to synthesize everything we'd learned in the course, since the studies of genetics, bacteria, and viruses were so closely intertwined. Someone from the class spoke up, saying he felt the same way but in the midst of finals with no reading period and on one week's notice, we wouldn't be able to do much synthesizing, and it seemed preferable to learn viruses well.

"You've convinced us," replied the lecturer, looking around at the class.

Chapter 19

The Most Complex Object in the Known Universe

This leads us to one of the most important warnings a student of the brain must absorb. We are deceived at every level by our introspection.

—F. H. C. Crick, "Thinking about the Brain,"
Scientific American, Sept. 1979

Before the start of finals, I took a Saturday night off, saw a movie, and walked around Beacon Hill with some friends. Recently, I'd succeeded in persuading the folks at financial aid to let me go still further in debt by signing out another government loan. With a little spare change jingling in my pocket, life was looking pretty good.

Randy had been a raftsman on the Colorado River, where I'd met him, and since that time he'd defused bombs in Berlin waterways, rowed gondolas in Venice, and driven a cab in New York. On the strength of that background and a degree from Yale, he'd entered Harvard Business School. Other branches of the university apparently liked "interesting" people too. Now he was finishing up, and what the film school generation had accomplished in Hollywood artistically, he and his partners hoped to achieve economically.

But before faring forth as an entrepreneur, he was about to run an exploratory raft trip down a river in North Yemen. Sarah, his friend, was a copy editor up from New York for the weekend.

What a relief to hear about something besides culture dishes and mouse tumors. Just discussing the finances of an overseas raft trip reawakened the sense of what a hothouse environment I'd lived in for the past nine months.

"You know back before I started this thing," I said, "one doc told me that the summer before his first year in medical school he decided to get ahead of things by memorizing the two hundred and twenty-one bones in the human body. He arrived, and they covered that in the first week. Then, I thought that was another of those tall tales. Now that seems like an easy assignment for a week. In fact, I wouldn't mind having an assignment like that at all, since I'd be learning something I'd use later."

"This is just the standard, first-year hazing," said Randy with assurance. "Same as the business school. It gets easier."

"It's supposed to get worse—you're on forty hours at a stretch and—"

Randy waved a hand. "There's no way they can keep you up for forty hours. When you get there, you'll find the way around. Anyway, then you won't have to worry about tests and grades."

It was hard to deny that last part, the closer you came to patients, the fewer seemed to be the formal consequences of mistakes. Short-answer tests in biochemistry had everyone in a state of terror, but once you hit hospitals, word had it no one failed. Except, of course, for talking back. And people didn't seem to do too much of that.

"Even now," continued Randy, "I'll bet you could work half the time and still pass. Why kill yourself?"

I nodded with a sigh. No one ever believed that a medical student's work schedule was imposed externally. If you made the mistake of complaining, what you got back instead of sympathy were amused intimations about personality disorders characterized by an uncontrollable thirst for work. It was becoming easier just to avoid discussion of medicine except with your fellow medical students.

"Anyhow, what are you really worrying about?" went on Randy. "How many people flunk completely out of medical school? Five, ten percent?"

"Nobody," I said. In fact, Harvard didn't like anyone even leaving voluntarily. You will all graduate from Harvard Medical School, they'd told us the day of our arrival.

"So if they don't fail you, what do they do?"

"They give us champagne, parties, receptions, dinners, psychiatrists for every little tremor of our souls. They're so interested in our attitudes and states of mind, a psychiatrist visited each of us in our rooms over the course of the year to discuss our feelings about ourselves and what we were going through. And just to see how those delicate feelings evolve, they're going to follow us up with psychiatric questionnaires and interviews for the next ten years."

Randy was staring at me in perplexity. "No, I don't mean that kind of stuff. I mean what do they do if you keep failing courses?"

"They sit down with you and your advisor and a dean and discuss things very gently. And at the end, you all decide together that for your own good it might be better if you tried the first year over again."

Randy laughed. "That's all?"

The first year over again? I thought. I can't think of a more powerful goad.

"Anyway," broke in Sarah, "even if it isn't always fun, you're learning things that'll help people—like what to do if someone breaks their leg or what foods people should eat."

"We didn't learn anything about that," I said.

Sarah was frowning. "Well, with all that work, you must have learned something."

I'd reached the point where I could barely explain what it was I studied. Maybe some neurological tidbit would get me off the hook. "I learned that if you get hit on the head and your head can move around, you'll get knocked out. But if your head is immobilized, you can suffer a much worse injury and never lose consciousness."

"That's strange," said Sarah. "How'd they find that out?"

"Experiments."

"What kind of experiments?"

"They locked monkeys into chairs, then fractured their skulls by swinging weights on pendulums."

Sarah drew back. "The monkeys were anesthetized, right?"

"How could they be? They were testing for the effects on consciousness."

She put her hands over her ears. "Let's not talk about this. That's awful. Those poor monkeys. What kind of people would do those sorts of things?"

My teachers and me, I wanted to say. But I knew from experience this kind of discussion made people unhappy. In biology you maim and kill in order to learn. Perhaps much of it is unavoidable. But what happens when medical students are trained first as biological scientists and only secondarily, almost as an afterthought, as physicians? How easy is it for them to disgard their point of view when they finally reach out to take a human pulse?

To distract Sarah who was still upset, Randy and I started talking about the Yemen expedition and white water.

"The thing that's funny about the river wave, the standing wave," I said, "is how it crops up all through biology, at least by analogy."

"By analogy?"

"You know in an ocean wave, the particles of water basically stay put and the waveform moves through like a vibration. But with a standing wave in a river, the water rushes through while the waveform is stationary, like a permanent turbulence. The whole strategy of life is based on the standing wave, materials flow through, while the form stays intact, using the energy of the materials to maintain its structure."

"So you're saying structure is life?" asked Sarah.

It was easier to start these discussions than complete them. "You've heard of entropy?"

"Yes, but I don't know what it is exactly."

"I'm not sure I do either, but it's easy for me to think of it as just another word for disorder, disorganization. So if you take an assemblage of particles, they'll tend to maximize their degrees of freedom so they can collectively adopt an arrangement of greatest macroscopic predictability. That tendency directs heat flow so that—"

"I don't know what you're talking about," said Sarah. "Use a concrete example."

"OK. Take a chemical reaction. The change in free energy is the change in enthalpy—that's the change in heat at constant pressure—minus the absolute temperature times—"

They were laughing. "He gets worse as he goes along," said Randy.

"You've gotten to talk funny since you got interested in science," said Sarah, taking my arm. "All you talk is a bunch of technicalese."

"These things are hard to explain," I muttered.

"My father teaches poetry in college, and he says if you can't explain something you don't understand it."

"That's easy for a nonscientist to say," I sulked, and we walked on in silence. So I was a Real Scientist now—I couldn't explain anything unless people understood it already. And how much I wanted to tell them: about a universal current of rising entropy which only living things resist, how a thin, membranous phase boundary, a fluid mosaic of proteins and phospholipids, barely ten-millionths of an inch thick and about as viscous as motor oil on a cold day, is all that separates us from that deadly flow of burgeoning disorder. Or how the human body is not a singular creature, but a plurality of organisms, a portable ecosystem, a society of microcreatures inhabiting a macrocreature. How there are cells in that composite body which can respond to hormones in concentrations no greater than a few pinches of salt in Walden Pond. How neurons relay signals at one-third the speed of sound, thousands of impulses a second, consummating all their efforts at communication in the hundred trillion synapses of the brain, where a ceaseless commerce between cells, in picograms of chemicals, create our thoughts, our feats of intellect, our awareness of the world. So much of the last year had been arid meaninglessness, but there had been moments of awe, wonder, and I wanted somehow to explain both the meaninglessness and the awe.

"I'm thinking of writing a book," I said. "About medical school. The first year. I've been keeping a journal since the end of February."

"Like an exposé or something? Watch your ass," said Randy who, from a career in white water and living by his wits in foreign lands, had developed a peerless instinct for survival. "Doctors are a bunch of buddies. They look out for each other. What if they suddenly 'run out' of money to loan you? What're you going to do then? You don't have any family or dough."

"I want to tell about it," I said. "I've seen enough to know there're important things here. Not just bad stuff, but good stuff too. Beautiful stuff."

"OK, but you got to do an internship after medical school, right? You can't practice medicine without having done that, right?"

"Right."

"And how does a hospital decide whether to accept you for an internship?"

"Pretty much on what Harvard says in a letter."

Randy shook his head. "And you're going to write a book, and naturally the big Harvard professors and deans are going to be in it."

I put out my hands. "But they're an important part of the experience. I can't start leaving people out on account of their power. And then only criticize other students and people who don't have power. What kind of person would I be to write that kind of book?"

"Wonderful—but what happens if Harvard doesn't flunk you or anything, lets you graduate like you claim everybody does, and then mysteriously the only place that'll accept you for an internship wil be in Ulan Bator or somewhere. Or maybe even nowhere at all. Of course, Harvard will be just as upset as you are. There you'll be outside the dorm with a duffel bag full of all your stuff, a thirty-thousand-dollar debt, no way to practice, and after all that work you'll have to start scuffling to see if anybody'll take you back as a social work assistant."

"I want to tell about it," I repeated stubbornly. "I worked on the bottom of hospitals for ten years and always wondered what was causing a lot of the problems I saw, the doctors' cynicism, their nihilistic hedonism. The reasons for a lot of those problems seem obvious to me, now that I'm on the other end, and I want to tell about them. . . . Anyway, maybe all they'll do is make me see a psychiatrist or appoint me to a committee."

Not likely, Randy's expression said. "Everybody else writes these kind of things after they've finished their internship and got their license to practice. You're doing it even before you've seen a hospital. Why not wait and write about the whole experience afterwards?"

"But that's the point," I said. "They're working on me. And by the time they're finished, years from now, maybe I'll be completely turned around and have forgotten how it was before."

Randy shook his head. "People don't change like that. You'll be the same person and feel the same way."

"Maybe you're right. Maybe I'll think I feel the same way and be the same person," I said. "But how will I know?"

That night I had a dream. I was on a street near Buena Vista Park in San Francisco, with the eucalyptus smells drifting up from the panhandle. And there were all my friends from the days when the Haight was in flower, Eddie with that stupendous beard, and Paintbrush who tied his long, blond hair back with a little American flag, and Van in the army jacket cluttered with flight insignias. It'd been so many years since I'd seen or heard from any of them. One by one, we'd separated, lost contact. Now they were smiling and nodding and talking to each other, though not to me. Joyfully, I looked around for others, but when I looked back, Paintbrush and Eddie and Van had suddenly vanished. There was only one big fellow striding off. I followed, but he turned his head away and walked more swiftly. "Was that really Van—did he ever get out of that jail in Encino?" I asked, trying to keep up. "Did Eddie ever make it to that commune in that abandoned mining town in the Santa Rositas?" But whoever it was hurried on, and I noticed there was a scar across his left hand, deforming it. He disappeared around a corner. I felt mortally sad and awoke.

Some blue light of early dawn was wavering through the Vanderbilt courtyard. I sat up and rubbed some fog off a pane. Who was that last fellow? I couldn't remember him at all from those days, and he seemed so harsh and rushed. Then I noticed my hand in the pale light: over one of the knuckles was the bumpy remnant of a gash I'd gotten going over Dagger Falls on the Middle Fork of the Salmon River in Idaho. The person from the past who'd hurried away, unwilling to show his face, was me.

At last, in the waning moments of the term, I've memorized every muscle and nerve in those lists Manfredo gave me. But now, it strikes me as increasingly bizarre that we don't have to know a blessed thing about the arteries and veins of the limbs. What possible set of priorities had me slavishly committing to memory the sensory and motor innervations, the actions and antagonists of dozens of centimeter-long muscles, the posterior cricoarytenoid, the salpingopharyngeus, while I ignored completely the system for blood supply to half the body? Perhaps Frank down the hall had been right—I'd been given a temporary calming down. So before the last lecture in anatomy, I approached Manfredo again.

"I'm studying for the final," I began, "and I—"

"Yes, my boy, you think I forget you? I am anatomy professor—we remember everything. That is what they pay us to do. What is your problem now?"

"I just wanted to confirm with you what we discussed last time, that all we should study about the limbs are the muscles and the nerves. The blood vessels aren't going to be part of the—"

"My boy!" Manfredo put his hand on my shoulder. "Stop worrying! Isn't that what I told you last time? You will not flunk."

"So just the muscles and nerves. No blood vessels?"

"My boy, what did I tell you last time?"

"Just that."

"Would I lie?"

"You might change your mind or forget."

"My boy, you insult me! You insult your own professor. In Italy, you would have been in jail long ago. But we are here in America, and students may insult their professors and get awards for best insult. But I will get you back. I will insult you with the final exam! It will be so easy, you will feel humiliated. So calm yourself! You will excuse me now, for I must tell them about the eye. Ladies! Gentlemen! But I forget myself—Women! Men!"

After lecture, I went upstairs to put in an appearance at the final dissection. The last time I'd been in lab, we'd unwrapped the head, and, not without a couple minutes' preliminary hesitation, the corpse was about to acquire a personality, an identity, a face.

"Come on, boys," said Claudia impatiently and undid the safety pin. Dan held the head while I unwound the cloth.

Disappointment and relief—the head was shaved, and the face clotted up with wrapping paper soaked in formalin. Both eyes and one ear were completely filled with yellow goo and shreds of paper. This face could belong to anyone—anonymity preserved.

By the end of three hours, we had the head skinned, except for the eyes and nose and mouth. With the protruding lips, there was an absurd pucker, but the face had acquired a pained, dying expression, mouth slightly parted, as if the spirit had just winged its way out and free, singing joyfully in its liberation from ruptured bile and hardened arteries and coagulated blood. In the last lecture of general pathology, Theophilos had barraged us with uplifting quotations about death from the masters—Epicurus, Susan Sontag, Hans Jonas—finishing up the course with a sentence from Alexander Pushkin—"Not all of me shall die."

But where was this mysterious entity that wouldn't stain with hemotoxylin and eosin, PAS, or Prussian blue, that couldn't be resolved even at ten Ångstroms in the transmission EM? In medieval illuminations, a dove would hover over the dying, lift its wings and fly to heaven when the moment had passed, bearing the spirit to its Maker. But where was that dove now in a world where rotating butcher cleavers sliced brain slabs, and rhesus monkeys with bolted skulls and severed nerves watched helplessly while waving wands explored the circuits of their cortices?

This final dissection, however, I'd come upstairs from Manfredo's lecture and walked into lab behind a woman who immediately screamed and almost bowled me over trying to get out. She threw herself into Devo's arms; he stroked her shoulders, coaxed her gently back inside. What could occasion this kind of commotion?

All our cadavers had been sawn down the center—forehead, nose, teeth, tongue, jaw split cleanly in two—and then guillotined at the neck as exactly as if Robespierre himself had ordered it. She'd been right—the humanness had suddenly decamped; for this last encounter, we were left with just a cross-sectional illustration from Snell that seemed to utter a dumb cry of unknowing pain. The arms were thrown back like a person asleep, hands cradling the head, but no head was there—just a vacancy.

Claudia had jetted off to Palm Springs for a four-day rendezvous with her father; so Dan, Harry and I pulled the sheets off. The two halves of our cadaver's head fell apart like a melon sliced in half, and there was the brain. A whole year's worth of palaver about this organ, and my first look had finally arrived. I looked at it, gray and gnarled—so small for seventy years of memories to be stored there. We began prying it loose from its shell within the skull, snipping out veins and meninges. So delicate a structure in real life is the brain, with about the consistency of Jell-O, that neurosurgeons use suction devices, tiny vacuum cleaners, rather than scalpels and forceps. After a year in embalmment, our cadaver's brain had developed the consistency of cheddar cheese, and we had to struggle a bit to get it out in the light. A slip of the scissors, a small gash on the cortex—the molecular archives of how many billions of recollections were ablated? Out came one half of the cerebrum; we put it on an enamel tray and pushed it around, pointing at things.

The temporal lobe, about the shape of a cucumber; seizures there can produce feelings of heavenly rapture, an aura of the immanence of the Divinity. Broca's Area, a set of vermicular humps set right in front of a large fissure in the frontal lobe—damage that and the victim retains much of his vocabulary but is unable to impose upon it a grammar; yet ask that same person to sing and he can do so effortlessly. Here is the amygdaloid body, a gray nut deeper in—impress a potential across an electrode here, and sudden terror or rage erupts. And the basal ganglia, more swirls of gray—ravage them with disease, and their unfortunate possessor must call up unimaginable concentrations of will to make the slightest movement, becoming a prisoner of his own skin. Our loves, subtleties, opinions, our identities seem so imperishably self-determined—who can believe that they are the dependent illusion, the immaterial hologram of a lump of gelatinous protoplasm?

And how unimpressive this organ is on the whole. Obviously ridiculous. I'm with Descartes: this pitiful apparatus is just the corporeal emissary, the front man. The real action is somewhere else, in the hands of a celestial puppeteer.

A lab assistant calls us into another room. On a shelf is a large, brown ceramic jar, the kind cookies used to be kept in. Off comes the top, out comes a brain, the brain from the cookie jar, dripping saline solution.

I fall back in amazement, and change my mind on the spot. Descartes's full of shit—look at the size of that mother! The frontal lobes jutted forward like a grill of a '53 Chevy. How heavy, aggressive, it was, two square feet of cortical surface area, modular unit after modular unit, up and down those ridges and crevices. Alive, at full throttle, it used less power than a twenty-watt light bulb, but you could well believe that this thing blazed with models of reality, spasms of pleasure, religious ecstasies. Yes, these three pounds of cellular circuitry could be the creator of epic poems, grand jetés, reflecting pools, symphonies, moon landers, zippers, demolition derbies, integrals, fugues, hanging gardens, steamboats, ogive arches, rock 'n' roll, even blitzkriegs, gas chambers, and napalm, but fudge sundaes, sonnets, and cathedrals too. All self-organized on a flow of negentropy from some cyanide molecule three and a half billion years ago.

And while we were looking at it, potentials were firing off in our own occiputs, hippocampi sorting out the recall patterns, chemotransmitters blazing the image into our own temporal lobes, shifts in the permeabilities of dissolved metals creating a network of coincident perceptions. The brain observing a brother brain, curious, probing, inquisitive.

Well, what do you do after you've seen the most complex object in the known universe for the first time? Go to Star Market, do the shopping, lay in provisions for the grim exam week ahead? I didn't feel like doing that, so I chatted for a few minutes with Dan, the lab tech, as we washed up.

"So what happened with those three med school interviews you had?" I asked.

"Well, it doesn't look like I'm going to be a doctor," said Dan with a tiny smile. "Last one turned me down yesterday." His long, blond hair hung in front of his face as he lathered his hands. He was a gentle, compassionate fellow, considerably more painstaking than most of us, and had done well in one course that Harvard was letting him take. But when there were six thousand applications for a hundred and fifty slots, human strengths didn't quantify very well. From the moral jungle of pre-medical grade competition, I'd clawed my way out with straight A+'s in general and organic chemistry. But that had required the kind of fanaticism that is usually ascribed to devotees of violent religious cults. And in my mercilessness, I'd only hurt myself—what if, like Dan, I'd had a family? I'd still be shuffling papers and wrestling around on the linoleum back at Lower Manhattan Rehab.

"You should try again," I said. "So much of it is luck."

He shrugged and let out a breath. "I don't know what sense it would make. I've tried two years in a row. Both times, I haven't even gotten very many interviews."

"What are you going to do?" I asked, knowing full well that the courses which prepare you for medical school are useful for virtually nothing else.

"Maybe apply to some sort of graduate program in biological science. But there isn't much fellowship or loan money in that, and I have a wife. I don't see how I can swing it. I'll keep working over in Fineful's lab till I can figure out exactly what to do."

We shook hands, he left, and I went back for a final look at our cadaver. They said the remains were to be parceled out to undertakers for interment: Harvard got use of the bodies, the relatives got a free burial. I tended to doubt our woman had much in the way of relatives—she'd died a year ago in a public hospital. More likely, the institution itself had saved the cost of a funeral by auctioning off a corpse which no one else would claim. And what was left of her now? Intestines hanging off the side, a bucketful of scraps, genitals slashed to pieces, eyes torn out, brain tucked away under a flap of arm muscles, empty shiny lining in the inside of a vacant half-skull. Nevertheless, a moving, intermittent dot of experience just like my own had once dwelled therein, moving along with the current of time.

Someone walked by me with a big smile and a rotary saw. He plugged it in, there was some loud laughter, and the sound of slashed flesh, then grinding bone. On my way out, I glanced at the bulletin board and noticed again the "Letter to the Students Who Will Work on My Body." Manfredo had not identified the author to us—it could have been our cadaver, the gender and the age were right, but I doubted it. Still, with the sound of crunching bone and giggles behind me, I stopped and read it.

When I was a senior in college, I took a course in comparative anatomy. We watched amoebae divide, then we dissected an earthworm, a fish, a pigeon, and a rabbit. Recently, I talked with my Harvard Medical School graduate doctor, and he said there was a great need in the medical schools for whole bodies. I had heard such terrible things about the medical schools and the way the students treated the bodies and the sights and smells of the labs that it took me months of thinking and praying before I could say yes.

Since I made my decision I have been very glad I did. I am glad that my body, or parts of it, will be working for a year, or in slides and bone specimens for young doctors to go on studying for years to come. If a breakthrough should come and some or one of you students should open a door to a great discovery, it would be wonderful. There will be others whose bodies will be in the laboratories where you work who have prayed for you as students and in the great life service to which you go.

But here is my big secret. I have been praying for you for eight or ten years. Where were you when I began?

Chapter 20

Idiot Savant

Anatomy final—first two pages, and I'm cleaning up: the actions of the peroneus tertius muscle, what nerve innervates the lateral pterygoid . . .

I turn to the third page and stare at it in disbelief, then the fourth, then the fifth and sixth. I try to catch Steve's eye, but he's bent over his paper. I look for Manfredo, but he's elected to leave the proctoring of the exam to subordinates. Yes, indeed, four pages just chock-full of questions about the blood vessels of the limbs. I'd been calmed out.

Well, I hadn't gotten this far in a career of being tested night and day without developing a certain facility for making shrewd guesses out of total ignorance. And when I picked up my paper the following week, that skill, plus an errorless performance on every obscure little piece of contractile tissue, had put me up in the top half of the class again. I looked at the grade, then threw the test untouched into the "corrected" box.

A weekend to study immunology and viruses, and I need every minute. The virology handouts, at least, have the virtue of being comprehensible. But immunology?

The second type of mechanism is extrinsic and exemplified by C1 inhibitor, C1Inh, which inhibits the active sites on C1r and C1s subunits of C1, and the C3bIna which inactivates C3b, and B1H which directly facilitates C3bIna on C3b and mediates extrinsic decay dissociation of C3bBb so as to permit the action of C3bIna by removing the protective Bb (which becomes Bi).

There's no doubt in my mind that all twenty pages of that will have to be known backwards and forwards. Other material I'm not so sure about. "Recently," says one handout, "a Kung boy in the Kalahari Desert has been found to lack ADA from his erythrocytes." And further on, "As many as a third of Arabian horses may be heterozygous for ADA deficiency." I'm sitting there, musing over the heterozygous Arabian horses and the sands of the Kalahari, when in walks Steve from down the hall, who's been a mite smug with me since the anatomy final.

"Just saw last year's micro exam," he says. "Remember that true-false question on the general path final about Burkitt's lymphoma that had all that complicated stuff about the Epstein-Barr virus and heterophile antibodies and so forth?"

"Sure do," I say. "Everything was right in it, but the answer was false because they said the disease was in Southern Africa rather than Central Africa."

"You got it. Looks like the micro final might be a little intense, too. Here's a question from last year: Can Kuru be transmitted to subhuman primates?"

"Just a second, Kuru's sort of interesting, even though we had like five sentences on it in all those hundred pages of handout. It's that rare disease from New Guinea—"

"Eastern Highlands of New Guinea. Got to be specific—never can tell what they're going to ask. They might just say Western Highlands."

"Eastern Highlands. Good point. And it's supposed to be transmitted by eating someone's brains in ritual cannibalism and it's disappearing with the end of cannibalism."

"Very good."

"So what'd they ask?"

"Let me phrase it clinically. If some New Guinea orangutan

sneaks into the cannibalism ceremony and makes off with some of the brains and eats it, will he get Kuru six months later?"

"Absolutely."

Steve looked impressed. "Not bad, not bad at all."

I put my feet up on my desk. "Know it all cold."

"Yeah, but you know they're not going to ask the same question twice. Here's what I think it'll be this year: can the virus that mink get from eating sheep carcasses in the Aleutians be transmitted to rhesus monkeys?"

I thought. "Yeah—we had a sentence on that. It was sheep, minks, hamsters, and monkeys. True."

"Nope," said Steve walking out. "You better get serious about this stuff. It was squirrel monkeys, not rhesus."

At Lower Manhattan Rehab, there lived a sixteen-year-old boy named Hedley Rice. Hedley was unusual in a number of respects: he was a white, Anglo-Saxon Protestant in a public facility almost completely filled with Blacks and Puerto Ricans. His parents had been killed in an automobile accident shortly after his birth; an uncle cared for him for two years, then when Hedley's retardation was discovered placed him in a private facility. A year later, the uncle himself died, and four-year-old Hedley, without relatives or money, was transferred to Willowbrook. After taking over the case, I was able to locate a distant cousin in Short Hills, but by then Hedley was a teenager and accustomed to the fact that he was alone in the world.

Hedley had some other interesting aspects: he ironed his own shirts, knotted his own ties, took showers twice a day, and went to the barber once a month. Dark haired, blue-eyed, good looking, with just a touch of acne on the cheeks, Hedley looked for all the world as if he'd just gotten home for the holidays from Groton.

But he possessed another trait that made him still more unusual. Hedley was an idiot savant. Though moderately retarded in other respects, Hedley possessed the most prodigious memory I'd ever seen, and his specialty was arbitrary facts and numbers. Ask him what day of the week September 3, 1928 fell on, and he'd answer Monday without hesitation. His favorite occupation was memorizing the Manhattan phone book, page after page. After school, he'd come into my office, shake hands formally, for his manners were impeccable, then sit down at a corner of my desk and with a smile of bliss on his face proceed to stash away another few hundred names, addresses, and phone numbers, while I did my paperwork. Occasionally, he'd surface and start reeling them off proudly to me: "O'Rourke, Frances, 418 Wadsworth Ave. 555-3447, O'Rourke, Francine, 119 Carmine St . . ."

But Hedley did have one thing in common with almost every other resident of Lower Manhattan Rehab. He didn't like the place. He didn't like the thefts, the violence, the rapes, the cinderblock walls, the racket, the mangy food. And Hedley had a very specific idea where he wanted to be: with a Black family in Brooklyn. Brooklyn, because Manhattan was the same to him as Lower Manhattan Rehab, and no amount of trips to Central Park and Circle Line cruises could convince him there was any difference between the institution and the borough. A Black family, since for as long as Hedley could remember, he'd been raised by Black women; they'd been kind, motherly to him when he'd had no mother or home other than a wing of a state facility. Occasionally, they took him home after work and introduced him to their families, fed him a real dinner, let him sleep at their houses. A taste of that was enough to convince Hedley where heaven was.

There were practical problems with these clear ideas of Hedley's. While Lower Manhattan Rehab's express reason for existence was "to return the developmentally disadvantaged to the community," for the state, that meant the same borough and same ethnic group. But there were absolutely no white foster parents available for Hedley in Manhattan. So I pressed ahead and found a Black family in Brooklyn that was very interested in Hedley. Needless to say, he was infatuated with them. But the state bureaucracy wasn't pleased at all, and refused to allow Hedley to leave the facility. The fact that they had no alternative to offer was immaterial. He was stuck.

Hedley couldn't figure out exactly what was going on, but he hadn't spent thirteen years inside institutions without picking up a thing or two about leaning on the bureaucracy. He'd come into my office, read the phone book for a while to relax, then borrow a pen and some stationery from me, and make his weekly plea:

> Dear Walter Cronkite,
> Hedley Rice wants soul food. Hedley doesn't like Manhattan. Hedley likes Brooklyn. Hedley wants to live in Brooklyn with Mrs. DeWitt. Tell my social worker assistant to hurry up. Soul food! Brooklyn!
> Very truly yours,
> Hedley Rice, Apt. 5, LMRC

I'd put the letter in an envelope and send it out with the departmental mail, or give Hedley a stamp and let him mail it himself. About one in ten letters prompted some sort of phone call from a local TV station to someone in the upper echelons of the mental hygiene department, who'd require a written report from his subordinate, who'd call the Lower Manhattan Rehab Director, and so on down forty-two levels of hierarchy till it reached me at the bottom. I'd pull out my standard memo on the situation, "For six months now, we have been prepared to place Hedley Rice . . ." update it to read "eight months," and send it off. And usually never receive a reply. José had gotten out by burning down the sixth floor; Hedley's system took longer, but after a year someone at the top got tired of telling callers that the situation was "almost resolved," and let Hedley go. He'd beaten the system.

I drove out to Brooklyn with Hedley and his few possessions. His foster home was located in a lower middle class district, mostly Puerto Rican and Italian, with a few Blacks. Two-family houses crunched together, little yards fore and aft, some wilted trees—but as far as Hedley was concerned, the East River was the Jordan, and he'd crossed into the Promised Land. He was ecstatic, babbling phone numbers and addresses and dates. Back a few blocks, we'd passed a schoolyard—knots of teenagers were lolling about, looking sullen. Hedley had avoided trouble at Lower Manhattan Rehab, but the street was a different game—did he have the savvy to survive?

After moving in his suitcases and having a cup of tea with Mrs. DeWitt, a large, easygoing woman who had children Hedley's age, I shook hands with Hedley in the warm sunshine.

"Well, you made it, Hedley," I said. "Take care of yourself."

"Thank you, Charles LeBaron," said Hedley, polite as ever, but now turning away in embarrassment.

His case was transferred to the foster home unit in Brooklyn; a few months later I heard through the grapevine that Hedley had gotten a couple bloody noses coming back from school. But he was orienting himself, and now rode the subway around by himself.

So, sitting in my dormitory room at Harvard, I thought of Hedley in Brooklyn, learning the ways of the street. With that stupendous memory of his, I knew I could have sat him down in front of all my notebooks for an hour or so, then steered him to the right amphitheater for the exams. Reasoning played so little a part in my education, I was sure he'd be at the top of the class, jostling up there with Kevin and the other hotshots. But if there was anything I'd learned growing up on 111th Street, it was street savvy. Well, Hedley, I said, you're in Brooklyn, and I'm at Harvard. We'd be better off reversed, but we both busted our asses to get what we wanted, and now we just got to figure out how to survive.

Rodents, rabbits, and research—the immunology final didn't disappoint us. But I passed. A friend of mine who'd graduated magna cum laude from Harvard wasn't so lucky. But then Elizabeth had made a crucial error: in preparation for our little "introduction," she'd majored in history and developed a mind more disposed to analysis than fact gorging. The immunologists set passing at ten points higher than any other course, and Elizabeth almost made it. But not quite. So she and the unlucky others had to go through half a month of intensive work—nothing but experimental immunology all day—then were administered a second, more difficult exam. She made it on the second try.

"I felt as awful as you can possibly feel when it happened," she told me later. "But now I know every damn thing there is to know about immunology."

"How'd I get over that cold I had last week?" I asked.

"Don't ask me that kind of stuff, Charley," she said, laughing. "You know we never studied anything like that. Do you know?"

I shook my head.

It's six P.M., the night before the microbiology final, and I'm sitting there trying to remember which virus exits through cytoplasmic cisternae and which produces swollen fibroblasts in culture . . . when all the lights go out. Hundreds of panicky crammers, all thinking the same paranoid thoughts, pour from their rooms. Only the hallways and bathrooms of Vanderbilt Hall are functioning on emergency power, so we're all together. At first, I seize what seems to be a choice spot in the form of a toilet seat—comfortable, private—but people keep evicting me periodically for their own purposes, and finally I relocate in disgust to a stairwell. And when I arrive, there seems to be an argument in progress one floor down. Sounds pretty erudite, then I listen more closely—it's about whether the aorta arches left or right when it leaves the heart. I start giggling uncontrollably, forcing the disputants to leave, convinced there's a crazy man upstairs. So I wasn't alone! The most important blood vessel in the human body and there are people who have no idea where it's located.

The next day, only a few straightforward questions about Kuru, and nothing whatsoever on viruses like the one which produces "progressive neurological decline in minks." Ellen's petition seemed to have worked in more ways than one.

Neuropathology, our sole practical course in medicine, has received scandalous neglect, ironically because of the humaneness of the lecturers toward us. The final week of class, a world-famous authority from the Kennedy Center had arrived to speak on the causes of retardation, a topic with special interest and poignancy for me. At the start, he'd said that he understood we were on the brink of finals, so to relieve the pressure on us a little, the material he was discussing wouldn't show up on the exam. Whereupon two-thirds of the class left so they could get back home and memorize about mice and rabbits. I sat for half an hour, fidgety and distracted, then made it two-thirds plus one. But consistent with the course itself, the final is stimulating, with a heavy emphasis on reasoning from symptoms to causes—almost a model for what medical school exams could be.

That night, there was a class party at a house down the street. As I walked up, Kevin Costello, the man with every excellent Harvard could give, and some others were wandering out. They all had broad smiles on their faces. Kevin had sunglasses on, though it was pitch black outside.

"Hey," said Kevin, and they all stood there smiling absurdly and saying nothing.

"What's happening?" I said.

"Oh, man," said Kevin slowly. "Everything. Ain't that right? Everything?"

The others nodded. One said "Everything," a couple more times.

"Where's Devo?" I said.

"He's inside, man," said Kevin. "Inside."

Someone else said, "Inside."

"Where you guys headed?"

"Us? Us? Cambridge."

"How're you getting there?"

"Shit, I don't know," said Kevin. They all started laughing and wandered off in the darkness in the direction of the Citgo sign.

"Whole bunch of acid being dropped around here," said the guy with me. "People were downing it at the water fountain soon as they got out of the test."

A keg of beer was in the bathtub, another ready to take its place, the air was thick with sweet smoke, rock was blasting away. Devo was at the door.

"This is a Sixties party, man," bellowed Devo. "The hell with this fucking generation I'm part of."

A few beers later, I blundered into a group arguing over some joints who was the best-looking woman in the class. Claudia garnered a lot of votes.

"You can't pick her," said one guy. "She's not in our class."

"Yes, she is," I said proudly. "She was my lab partner."

"No, she isn't," he said. "She's in next year's class."

"She was in all of our courses, and she told me she was in our class!" I retorted.

"No, no—she was a special student. She applied this year, and everyone knew she'd get in, so she didn't apply anywhere else and the administration enrolled her in our courses on a special basis so she wouldn't have to lose a year."

"But how could anybody know she was getting in? Even if she is a hotshot scientist. There are thousands of applications and only a hundred and fifty slots!"

"Her boyfriend, that's how! The guy she lives with is on the Admissions Committee. He interviewed me himself. That's how."

There was nodding all around. That was true. But could I say . . .

"I don't believe it!" I almost yelled. "All this minorities flap, they can't go around making special deals."

"You don't believe me—look at next year's class list. See if she's on it. Just take a look."

Later I looked, and there was Claudia's name. So that was the solution to the mystery of Claudia. I thought of Dan with his wife and lab tech job and pile of rejections, who'd never be a doctor.

"But forget it, man," said somebody else. "She's going to be good. She ain't like some of these women and other people we got around here complaining all the time. When we go on those round-the-clock shifts on the wards, she'll be able to take it."

There was nodding all around. That was true. But could I say the same for myself? Is there someone out there now with whom I have a rendezvous, I wondered? A rendezvous where he or she will die because of a mistake of mine, a foolish, stupid error? Will I be in the thirtieth hour of a rotation, bleary, high on caffeine, adrenalin, sweating reflexively, dazed, finding it hard to think? And whoever you are, I thought, you'll probably be old, poor, alone—no family to jog my attention, no private physician to look over my shoulder. Thinking only of sleep and home, I'll fail to notice the obvious, forget something essential, or delay, and you'll die. I'll try to miss that rendezvous, I said to myself. I'll try. But why a person with responsibility for the sick should be routinely kept up for two days at a time was beyond me. Still, I knew you weren't supposed to talk that way out loud. "Can't take it?"—the question would come back with a contemptuous cock of the eyebrow. And of course you'd hurriedly reassure the questioner that you could "take it"; and shut up. So I was finished with this first year, but many adventures and revelations lay ahead. At least with the alcohol and smoke I could forget about them now.

And then all this is interrupted: the semilegendary Simmons Girls have arrived! Big stir, but when that settles down, the men are actually ignoring them, staying close to the women in the class, dancing and gossiping and yelling. There's Nick, who'd complained about all the "goddam militants," doing the frug with Cheryl. Stronger than lust or politics is the sense of collective survival.

Then it's three-thirty, and I can barely find my way over to the beer keg for refills.

"It's been real," says Devo, shaking my hand.

"What's happening?" I say, throwing my arm around him, and we go careening around the living room together.

"We're going back."

"Shit," I said and looked around. The living room was almost empty.

We pile into a car with the steering committee of the Walter B. Cannon Society for Social Deviation: Hanrahan, Houlihan, and O'Doyle. After twelve tries, O'Doyle manages to park the car in front of Vanderbilt, and, floundering out, we suddenly see in the moonlight that the lawn of the quad has been covered over completely by an enormous tent, long as a football field and three stories tall in the center. Dimly, we realize that it's there to welcome the homecoming alumni tomorrow, but in the wee hours of the morning, it seems like an Arabian Nights mirage, that we are all Sinbads awakened into another dream. In that transfixed silence reserved for the truly miraculous, we all stand there, me clinging to a tree, the rancid afterthoughts of late drunkenness washed away by the twinkling marmoreal majesty of that sight, while the steering committee wavers on the sidewalk, hanging on to each other.

"Two, three spikes pulled," someone whispers, "a pole over, and that whole fucking thing's flat as a pancake."

Yes, a stroke of brilliance, we can all see it—that whole P. T. Barnum monstrosity billowing slowly to earth, deflated.

"Tomorrow, those half-million-dollar-a-year guys'll arrive," I say, "and it'll take Harvard an hour to put it back up."

The steering committee collectively sways tentward, but Houlihan goes green suddenly and lurches inside for the bathroom. Hanrahan and O'Doyle stagger solicitously after him. The moment is gone.

"Devo," I say and sit down on a trash can that's chained to a newspaper machine.

"Don't worry," says Devo and grabs a piece of wood from somewhere, then lets the trash can have it with a deafening crash. I fly up in the air, land noisily with the lid and some garbage in the gutter. Devo keeps flailing away at the can. And to that primitive music echoes rain back from the Roman temples, from the Ionic columns and corbels and cinquefoils and scrollwork, from the immense marble amphoras, coats of arms, false balconies and balustrades.

"Freedom!" Devo keeps yelling, "freedom!"

And the echoes keep answering, "Freedom!" with a mocking sound.

Chapter 21

An Epiphenomenon

Late one evening in June, I took a run around the Fenway, along the old familiar trails, past the museums and ponds. With the days growing hot, I preferred the cool of night for my five miles, even if I did stumble occasionally into roots and shrubbery. It was clear from the ailments that kept me lame half the time that my body wasn't built for this sport. Somewhere I'd read that all the muscles in the body could develop a collective tension of thirty tons; there were moments for me when thirty ounces seemed an exaggeration.

A few others tended to run at this time, too, and we'd nod briefly in passing. Hi, I'd say silently, with a smile, fellow species member with your opposable thumb and lower back problems and swollen telencephalon and ten billion heartbeats, *mon semblable, mon frère.* This past year had left its traces on me.

I thought back to one of my interviews for Harvard, a few geologic eons ago.

"I see you've done some writing," said the interviewer, an obstetrician in private practice. "We had another writer here once, Michael Crichton."

"Isn't he a director in Hollywood now?"

"Yes," said the interviewer, giving me a penetrating look. "He never practiced."

"Oh." Medicine was a priesthood, wasn't it? No matter what the call, failure to practice, even temporarily, was a desertion from the vocation. "Well, for the last ten years of my life," I said, "I've been working in hospitals and institutions for the poor. I suppose I could change, but I just can't see myself doing anything different, whether I'm a doctor or not. I'm sure I'll want to keep working with the same kind of people that I know."

The interviewer didn't seem happy with that and regarded me for a while. "Why do you want to be a doctor?" he said suddenly.

I started. It was the one question everyone said wasn't asked anymore, the one question for which I was totally unprepared.

Should I tell him about sitting in that campsite near the Payette River in Idaho and seeing the red van? No—I'd learned long ago that talk of money in medicine was taboo. Instead, you were expected to trundle out a prefabricated, somewhat soporific speech on Service to Humanity. But from a decade of being at the bottom of various institutional bureaucracies, I'd seen that the only people who delivered that kind of elevated monologue were the ones taking the system for big money while never getting their fingers dirty with the job at hand. Anyway, how could you request entrance to a profession where a hundred thousand dollars a year is considered an average income and then dare breathe a word about humanitarian ideals? So I couldn't talk about the red van, and I wasn't about to unburden myself of some traditional sanctimony.

Could I tell him about those Chinese children with TB bawling in the night while their mothers, with masks on, tried to feed them mashed potatoes with chopsticks? Or Percy with his clogged shunt? Or retarded kids that researchers had shot up with hepatitis, leaving them sick or carriers for life? "Vengeance!" I said silently, "vengeance!" But now only a revenge of gentleness to others like them would suffice—be kind where everything demanded harshness, haste, cruelty— have the strength to exact that kind of revenge. But with all the torpors and banalities and violence that lurked in my soul, how could I explain about a vengeance of gentleness? And who was I to blabber about that kind of shit? It'd come out half-screwy and all wrong.

The interviewer was looking at me expectantly. I thought of the smell of vanilla in the recesses of a Jeffrey pine, the fossil nautiloids in the water-polished side canyons of the Colorado, the graceful, equational curves that cornices of snow form in high mountains looping out in shimmery splendor over endless drops, the play of light on eddies, the unnerving hiss and lurch of complex boils, the iridescent blaze that ignites off walls of Alpine ice at sunrise. That was nature. To study it was science. To use science in healing people was medicine.

"The jobs I've done I've liked," I said. "But I don't feel they've really put to use a good deal of my mind. I thought by being a doctor I could do many of the same things, but use a little more of myself, call on some mental ingenuity. Work with the same people, but do something with them that was a little more intellectually satisfying and stimulating."

"Intellectually stimulating?"

"Yes." That hadn't been a good way to put it, had it?

"Nothing else? That doesn't seem like a strong reason to me."

"Of course, there're other things too."

"For instance?"

Shit, I thought, my stomach beginning to clutch. This interview's starting to go down the drain, and with it all those years of dragging yourself home from lab at midnight, slumping into bed, then getting up for work the next day at seven.

"I guess I've had some personal experiences with death and suffering that have affected me," I said.

"Death?"

"Yes."

"Like what?"

It seemed to me there'd been so many, but really there'd only been a few. I paused, thinking, then told him about the Lehigh.

From its headwaters high in the Appalachians, the Lehigh River runs eastward through Pennsylvania, emptying into the Delaware at Easton. For twenty miles, it cuts a gorge through the Poconos, an Eastern gorge—not the immense, red cliffs and white sandbars of Arizona rivers, nor the spruce and pine and granite banks of Idaho, but a softer, more domesticated wilderness. The rounded slopes are covered with a deep forest of willows and hemlocks and sweet birches and hickories; fallen trunks shaggy with moss and shelf fungus and maidenhair fern. The thick, shadowy underbrush is speckled with tiny, fiery dots of flowers—camas and columbine and gentian. Two years before, I'd been paddling with a group down the gorge of the Lehigh, playing the curls, trying to do enders in the holes, lying back on the boats and letting the sun flicker over us through the trees.

It was twilight when I made an eddy-turn into a branch-clogged bank where an old dirt road zigzagged down the hills and approached the water. I was tired from eighteen miles of paddling, but as I started to get out, someone waved me back, telling me to go up to the road through the underbrush— someone had slipped and hurt himself on the path. Cursing wearily, I thrashed uphill, dragging my boat behind. At the washed-out road, I took off my spray skirt, life jacket, and helmet, zipped down my wet suit top.

"What's going on?" I asked some of our party at the top of the path.

"Somebody fell off the embankment—hit their head."

I tossed my gear into my boat and went down the path. There, propped half out of a noisy, little brook, amid the fiddleheads and sassafrass and mountain laurel, lay one of our paddlers, Cliff, not moving. Someone was bending over his face.

"We were passing the boats up over the rocks," someone told me, "and he was up there and got knocked off balance and said 'oops,' then fell off and landed on his head. We thought he was just knocked cold, but he stopped breathing all of a sudden just now."

I knelt down to feel for a pulse. The paddler who was giving artificial respiration stood up and started vomiting in the bushes. There was no pulse at the neck. I covered Cliff's lips—that were now slimy—with my own and gave three quick breaths, watching the chest rise up next to my face. Still no pulse. Quickly I zipped down the lifejacket and wet suit, positioned my hands on the breastbone and leaned down against the slow, elastic give of the ribs. Fifteen of those and back to give two breaths. Still no pulse.

"This guy's had it if we ain't out of this place and at a hospital!" I yelled as I leaned back to give the cardiac compressions.

"Somebody went up the road for help," returned one of the group.

"I need somebody down here with me."

A woman named Angela joined me. I stiff-armed into Cliff's chest five times, and she'd breathe once. Twenty minutes went by and a van clanked down the dirt road.

"Screw the ambulance," I said. "Take this thing."

With an improvised stretcher, slipping and reeling through the bushes, we carried Cliff up the slope, lifted him into the back of the van.

"Get my stuff!" I yelled as we pulled the doors shut. A paddler's gear is as dear to him as life itself.

"Don't worry about that," said Angela. "Do the compressions." And the van lurched off up the road.

We kept swerving to avoid ruts, branches crashed against the sides. Bouncing over a streambed, and Angela and I would go flying through the air, heads gonging against the ceiling, teeth bashing into Cliff's; we kept him steady but would be thrown ourselves into heaps on one side or the other as we rounded a switchback. Blood had started to fill Cliff's mouth, draining from somewhere in his head, and when we came up from the breathing, a geyser of blood would follow as the lungs recoiled, arching out into the air in a scarlet curve, splash in our faces, drip down over our chins and necks. It had the flavor of raw hamburger and the bitter metallic sweetness of coins you put in your mouth as a child. Whoever wasn't doing the breathing, wiped the other's face with a clotted rag.

We jostled to a stop.

"What the fuck's happening?" I yelled.

"Ambulance is in front of us."

"How far we got to the highway?"

"Mile."

"Forget it. They're not going to do anything more than we are. Probably less. Tell them to lead us."

Earlier that summer, I'd come across an unconscious motor-cyclist lying in the road, surrounded by his helpless, leather-coated buddies. For ten minutes, I'd done artificial respiration as he'd reflexively vomited beer back into my mouth. An ambulance had arrived, and I'd watched in paralyzed as-tonishment as the attendants carefully strapped on an oxygen mask and drove off. If you're not breathing on your own, no amount of ambient oxygen will do you a whit of good, so that fellow would be dead in a mile. But those attendants weren't about to inhale someone else's beer and lunch. That hap-pened once. It wasn't going to happen twice.

When we hit the highway, two police cars picked us up, and in between breaths I'd look out through the windshield to see flashing scenery, lights, and neon signs, the police cars and ambulance with their sirens blaring. Into the dock of a hospital, onto a gurney, and a doctor pulled out two large electrodes with handles, put them on either side of the chest. One shock, the body seemed to jolt, the arms lifting up into the air as if pleading, a wait, then another. Still no pulse.

Cliff's face was bloated and bloody as they pulled the sheet over him. Though we hardly knew each other, Angela and I put our arms around each other. Our faces were smeared, and our hair clotted red and brown. I felt exhausted and sick.

"He wouldn't have survived that blow on the head," said the doctor, "if he'd fallen right into the waiting room here."

I went over to the bed and grabbed one of Cliff's feet that were still protruding absurdly from under the sheet as if he were asleep and too long for the bed.

"We tried, Cliff," I said. "We tried. This didn't happen because we didn't try."

How many deaths have you seen? I said to myself with the blood caked in my wet suit, staining my hands, still metallic in my mouth. How much futility? Wouldn't it be wonderful for once to save a life, help a birth, make pain and despair vanish?

My interviewer nodded, and we moved on.

But as I ran along in the summery darkness, I thought about that event and others. An alpine group had done a survey of climbers who had taken long falls, falls which they thought would be fatal. And, in contrast to the abrupt moment of sheer fright the rest of us suffer in our five- and ten-foot drops, those climbers reported a world gone brilliant with colors, a summarizing of thoughts, a sudden serenity in a plummeting abyss. I thought of a one-time climbing teacher and partner of mine who'd led out a hundred feet without protection in the Tetons, had a stone come loose from underfoot, hurtled downward, bounded off a projection crushing in his chest, and landed smashed and already dying at the feet of his second who was standing there braced and rigid, the belay wrapped furiously, uselessly, about him. And Dr. Walter Blackadar, short, burly, arrogant and kind, a survivor, fighting like a grizzly in the rage of a Payette rapid, his face driven slowly underwater by his own boat. At the end, in those last moments, had calmness and knowledge descended on them, too?

And with the constant anonymous group who populated the intensive care units of the ring of hospitals nearby, that standing percentage for whom death has already become an inevitability—perhaps in the midst of the dinging, blipping, hissing machines, the coffee grounds spilled at the nurses' station, the gossip of paychecks and affairs as the linen gets changed, something awesomely simple is occurring. Potassium levels flying upward, blood gases not responding, uncontrollable acidosis, microhemorrhages splattering the brainstem, yet within that departing awareness a silent, awesome simplicity renders trivial the accidents, the conversations, the final hurry and shout. "It does not take with it a mass of earthly memories," says Plotinus. "It is light and wholly alone."

And the time will come, I thought as I ran, when I too must close with you, old friend. I have kissed your cold lips, smelled your fetid odors. I have seen you lurking in the frightened eyes of a distracted, weak, old man, felt you in the fading pulse of a boozy motorcyclist, swallowed the gouts of blood you spat into my mouth in the pounding back of a van. Someday you and I will have to have it out alone.

But in whatever interval I have before that happens, before the hapless phantom that haunts my synaptic terminals is whisked out of existence, astonished that it has not outlived the soft computer that created it, I can rejoice in the profusion and danger of this environment, lovely in its carelessness and symbolism. In my eye, a current of aqueous humor exits constantly through my pupil, en route to the Canal of Schlemm at the edge of my iris where it drains into my blood; I see the world through this transparent flow. The rods and cones which are firing by the millions in my retina developed from tiny, fingery projections whose fringed architecture can be found in trachea and sperm and the mouths of freshwater mussels. Cross-section any of this tissue, and there in the grays and blacks of an electron micrograph are identical pinwheels of tubules endlessly repeating, as regular as any blueprint, carousel upon carousel, a mantra of protein, tesserae whirling Escher-like into a bewildering perspective. Are we the figure or the ground?

Look at the night sky under which I run: billions upon billions of galaxies illuminate the darkness, further than the most powerful radio telescope can peer. Yet there are more synapses in my brain than there are galaxies in the universe, perhaps thousands of times more. The nerves which supply those synapses are alive with scintillations; in my blood runs the glitter of stars. My atoms were forged in the cores of red giants, showered out in supernovas, coalesced and organized in the warmth of the sun. And as I go leaping down the path, my brain pumps out its electromagnetic fluctuations, faint lines of force to infinity. Surely there must be times when those fluctuations make a strange music.

Basements full of research scientists, sectioning bodies with saws, slicing down brains to ham sandwich thickness, searching, searching for the phantom that made that music. How long can I elude their implacable curiosity? The opposing fingers on the knife, the binocular eyes blazing through the microscope, the left angular gyrus converting vision into words, bolting my skull to a frame, cutting the nerves to my eye muscles, displaying my brainstem for all to see. Yet the part of that juicy cranial mass that experiences the colors, fronds of green and magenta, chalices of pomegranate, still eludes them. How delicate is this three-pound, twenty-watt organ which harbors the epiphenomenal me: shake me and I become indignant, drug me and I vanish, let me sleep and I shuttle in and out of existence and hardly know. I was still the fugitive, but how long would I escape them, with their electrodes slipping along the layers of my cortex, needles jiggling out the millivolts, graphs and equations tracking me relentlessly down?

I was blazing along the trail now, wheezing, tripping, and trying in blind panic to outdistance them in the darkness. I nearly went sprawling on a rock, did one of those pirouettes reserved for the truly uncoordinated, and came up lame. I walked it off, panting. Well, I thought, limping ruefully along and checking to right and left to see if anyone had noticed, I was pretty far from that sandbar campsite below Lava Falls wondering in the night rain what kind of life the future held, but I was pretty far from East 111th Street and Lower Manhattan Rehabilitation Center, too.

It seemed to me I had a little vial of sweetness and kindness around stomach level. It'd been full when I was born; half of it had sloshed out in miscellaneous events since then, but I was hanging on for dear life to those remaining couple ounces. They had me for six or so more years, ample chance to make me spill the rest in wrath or discouragement.

If I were to lead a life free of the influences they seemed determined to inflict on me, if I were ever to exact that gentle vengeance, it would require some extraordinary stability in my internal environment, I thought, remembering that phrase from the first biology text I'd ever read. Perhaps more stability than I possessed. Yet writing a book about those influences and the experiences they created might help me maintain some detachment, give me an objectivity, an independence, where none might otherwise exist.

Maybe. Anyhow, serendipity had bailed me out on more than one occasion—when Josie distracted the bum who was trying to break my skull in Central Park, when the current dragged me out from the hole in Sock-em-Dog, on the fourth roll in Lava . . . I started trotting along again, awkwardly, watching for obstacles. Maybe serendipity would do it again and save that sloshing bit of enthusiasm and innocence. But when it's all over, years from now, will I know?

A WORD ABOUT THIS BOOK

From September 1978 through June 1979, I was a first-year student at Harvard Medical School, and this book is my account of that period. It is not a diary of everything that happened to me, nor is it a work of fiction. My intent was to convey something of my experiences, my impressions, and the evolution of my state of mind over those ten months. Consequently, I didn't strive for the literal accuracy of a documentary or a work of history. For example, it seemed unnecessary to use the real names of those who appear in these pages—they are well known to each other, but not to the world at large—and I have changed names, and often the descriptions, of my classmates, the faculty and most other individuals. Also, a significant portion of this book consists of dialogue and, of course, those conversations were reconstructed rather than transcribed. And, in a few cases, the events have been condensed and told somewhat out of order.

To communicate a sense of the reactions of a nonscientist suddenly immersed in science, I've tried at points to explain something of the subject matter of the first year in medical school. In these explanations, I've striven to be clear and comprehensible rather than academically rigorous. Those familiar with the material will have readily identified where I made oversimplifications and ignored exceptions.

The book was written in a ten week period over the summer following my first year and was typed and revised during stolen moments of the second year. This method of composition accounts for some, though by no means all, of the crudities of the text. Accordingly, I'd like to extend my gratitude to a number of my friends who were kind enough to read a draft of the book and offer invaluable criticisms: Andrew Arthur, Randall and Mary Bassett, David Bloomberg, Thomas and Susan Crean, Marie Feltin, Joanna Kahn, Jane LeCompte, Wayne Pease, Julie Sullivan, David Winn, and John Zerzan. Thanks also to Jean Brown who typed the final draft, Copy Editor Ruth Weissberger who suggested numerous stylistic improvements, my literary agent Roslyn Targ and Editor-in-Chief Joyce Engelson who supplied the editorial and emotional support without which this book would never have seen the light of day.